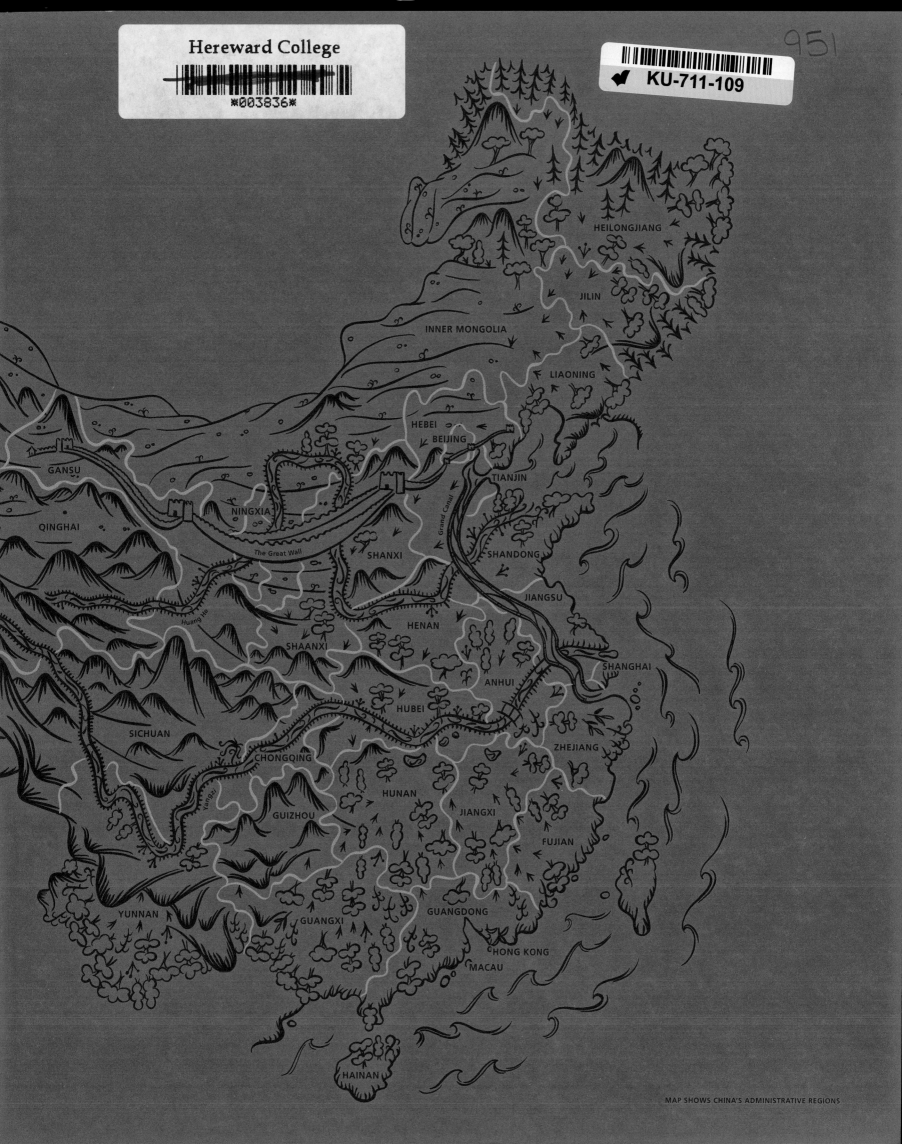

MAP SHOWS CHINA'S ADMINISTRATIVE REGIONS

CHINA

CHINA

ALISON BAILEY | RONALD G. KNAPP | PETER NEVILLE-HADLEY

J.A.G. ROBERTS | NANCY S. STEINHARDT

FOREWORD BY ANCHEE MIN

LONDON, NEW YORK, MELBOURNE,
MUNICH, AND DELHI

Senior editor Paula Regan
Project editors Corinne Asghar, Sam Atkinson,
Victoria Heyworth-Dunne

Senior art editor Gulizar Cepoglu
Project art editor Jenisa Patel
Designers Anna Hall, Isabel de Cordova,
Gadi Farfour, Philip Fitzgerald
DTP designer John Goldsmid

Managing editor Debra Wolter
Managing art editor Karen Self
Art director Bryn Walls
Publisher Jonathan Metcalf

Production controller Melanie Dowland

Picture researcher Sarah Smithies

Photography Christopher Pillitz
Additional photography Chester Ong
and Gary Ombler
Illustrations Phil Gamble

Researcher / interviewer Zhou XingPing

First published in Great Britain in 2008 by
Dorling Kindersley Limited
80 Strand, London WC2R 0RL

A Penguin company

Copyright © 2007 Dorling Kindersley Limited
Foreword © 2007 Anchee Min

2 4 6 8 10 9 7 5 3 1

A CIP catalogue record for this book
is available from the British Library

ISBN: 978-1-4053-1627-9

Colour reproduction by GRB, Italy
Printed and bound in Singapore by Star Standard

See our complete catalogue at
www.dk.com

CONTENTS

目录

FOREWORD   6

LANDSCAPE CHINA'S HORIZONS
Highest Step Mountains, Plateaus, and Grasslands   10
Middle Step Deserts, Steppes, and River Basins   36
Lowest Step Hills and Coastal Plains   64

HISTORY THE STORY OF CHINA
The Roots of China (to 1122 BCE)   80
The Age of Ideas (1122–206 BCE)   82
China Takes Shape (206 BCE–220 CE)   86
An Empire Divided (220–618)   90
A Golden Age (618–907)   94
Power Moves South (907–1279)   98
China Under Mongol Rule (1279–1368)   102
Early Modern China (1368–1644)   104
The Three Emperors (1644–1800)   110
China in Crisis (1800–80)   112
The End of Empire (1880–1928)   116
The Road to Revolution (1928–49)   118
The People's Republic (1949–76)   120
China After Mao (1976–2010)   124
The Future of China   128

PEOPLE A DAY IN THE LIFE

Loess Valley Farmer	132
Calligrapher	140
Tea Trade Workers	146
Craftsman	154
Mosuo Matriarch	162
Retired Teacher	170
School Child	174
Buddhist Monk	184
Chinese Herbalist	192
Cricket Seller	202
Festival Host	208
Entrepreneur	216
Sea Fisherman	220
Opera Performer	226

CULTURE THE SPIRIT OF CHINA

Ways of Thought	234
Philosophy and Religion	242
The Way of the Brush	252
Classical Literature	266
Traditional Opera	276

ARCHITECTURE BUILDING A NATION

Shengwu Lou	282
Wu Fang Ting	288
Courtyard House	292
Stilt House	296
Jin Mao Tower	300
Couple's Garden Retreat	308
Beijian Bridge	312
Juyongguan	314
The White Pagoda	318
Xuankong Si	324
Tin Hau Temple	328
Temple of Heaven	332
Longxing Si	336
Id Kah Mosque	342
Yongle Gong	346
Xumifushou Miao	350

INDEX	356
ACKNOWLEDGEMENTS	360

FOREWORD

前言

In gold-thread dress, with jade ornaments

Giggling, she melts into the throng with trails of scents

In the crowd once and again

I look for her in vain

Music vibrates from the flute

The moon is full and bright

Night's wind adorns plum tree with flowers

Blows down stars in showers

When I turn my head to leave disappointed and sad

She appears where lantern light is dimly shed

This 12th-century poem by Xin Qi-ji came to my mind when I opened this book. The images of my beloved motherland, its mountains, rivers, and people stirred my memory. I was born and raised in China and lived there for 27 years. China has been the subject of all my books, including *Red Azalea*, *Becoming Madam Mao*, *Empress Orchid*, and *The Last Empress*. For so many years I wanted to describe to my Western friends where I came from but was unable to. With this book, I can.

The creators are not Chinese, yet they have captured the essence of my country. Looking at the chapter "Landscapes: China's Horizons", I wondered how the photographers managed to reach each shooting spot on their human legs, and I wondered how early in the morning they had to get up (or how late they had to stay up) in order to catch the perfect light (or shadow) and how many times they tried.

I thought I knew China, but the perspective offered here amazed me. For example, I would never have thought of showing traditional Chinese candies set beside modern Western-style drinks (*see pages 182–83*). Another unexpected yet brilliant choice was "The Way of the Brush" (*see pages 252–65*). The calligraphy is mixed with images of bamboo, mountains, blossoming peach trees, and clouds, yet it represents what Chinese calligraphy is all about. When I was a child and was first taught to use the brush pen, my teacher said, "Hold up your brush as straight as bamboo; make your characters sit as still as a mountain; guide your strokes and let them 'blossom' like beautiful peach-flowers and be unpredictable like the clouds in the sky." And here you have them all.

"Classical Literature" (*see pages 266–75*) embodies the four-thousand-year-old history of China through wisdom, morality, and philosophy. I was glad that this book introduces *Romance of The Three Kingdoms*, *Journey to the West*, *Water Margin*, and *The Story of the Stone*. I especially appreciate the illustration showing the hero of *Romance of The Three Kingdoms* standing in his boat while crossing the river on a mission to rescue his emperor. This image gives a clear idea of how much one's loyalty towards the emperor is valued. It explains why the modern-day emperor, Mao Zedong, was able to manipulate the nation and create the Cultural Revolution disaster.

China's recent transformation is demonstrated through the "Architecture" and "People" chapters. The spectacular architectural "tour" includes the ancient Suspended in the Air Monastery and Shanghai's modern Jin Mao Tower. It is both symbolic and art at its best. In "People: A Day in the Life", the photo of a girl painting her face getting ready to perform a Chinese opera moved me (*see page 226*). I used to be her. I remember the time when my friends and I were obsessed with Madam Mao's propaganda operas,

which delivered communist messages to the masses during the Cultural Revolution. Although the lyrics were changed, the tunes were traditional. It was during this time that schools were turned into brainwashing camps, and Mao's *Little Red Book* was the only book we were supposed to read. My family ran out of food and I fought with neighbouring children for food scraps in rubbish dumps. I was afraid, and I gave myself to the operas, because only in the operas was I able to escape the life I was living. By painting my face into a beautiful mask, I lived the life of a heroine. I can tell from her facial expression and her apple cheeks that the girl in the photo is not painting her face to escape misery. Her stomach is full and she is having fun.

ANCHEE MIN

LANDSCAPE

风
景

CHINA'S HORIZONS

With an area similar in size to that of the United States, and twice that of Europe, it should not be surprising that China's landscapes are so varied and so vast. Few areas of the world have been as extensively altered by human actions as has China, where centuries of occupancy has shaped large regions into cultural landscapes, from impressive stepped rice paddies to towering cities. This transformation over time has created landscapes of utility as well as immense beauty. China's landmass can be viewed as a series of three "steps". Its major rivers have their origins in the western, "highest step" of the Tibet-Qinghai Plateau, before spreading eastwards through the gorges, valleys, and plains of the "middle step", and flowing into the sea at the coast of the flat, fertile "lowest step". A visual journey across all three steps reveals the incredible diversity and beauty of China's horizons – a beauty that photographers have been inspired to capture, and artists to paint.

Few places in China can rival the grandeur of the Tibet-Qinghai Plateau. Defined by

高级阶梯 its strikingly high mountains and sweeping plateaus at an average height of more than 4,000 metres (13,000 feet), this lofty region is known as the "Roof of the World". Mount Everest towers along the southern border with Nepal, with scores of other ragged peaks above 7,000 metres (23,000 feet). With its long winters and limited rainfall, the plateau remains an unexplored and largely uninhabited expanse. The warmer, wetter Lhasa-Shigatse area in Tibet is the only major centre of population.

HIGHEST STEP
MOUNTAINS, PLATEAUS, AND GRASSLANDS

YANGZI RIVER ON MOUNT TANGLHA, QINGHAI
Wreathed year-round in low-lying clouds and mist,
Mount Tanglha slowly accumulates snow and ice
across its undulating slopes. The meltwater feeds
the headwaters of the mighty Yangzi River.

诗 | The wind … is the breath of heaven and earth. Into every corner it unfolds and reaches;

without choosing between high or low, exalted or humble, it touches everywhere.

"The Wind", Song Yu (290–223 BCE)

KHAM REGION, SICHUAN
Deep valleys and abundant snowfall characterize the stark landscape of the eastern portion of the Tibetan plateau. Here, an isolated gravel highway provides access to the remote areas of Tibet from Sichuan.

诗

At the palace of rocks, spring clouds white –

white clouds are best for the green moss;

brush apart the clouds, tread the rocky path:

what ordinary man could come along?

"The Palace of Rocks", Yuan Jie (719–772)

MOUNT GANGGA, SICHUAN
The eastern fringe of the Tibetan plateau presents contrasting landscapes, some mantled with snow, others short grasses, and rocky surfaces. Mount Gangga is known for its alluring granite rock outcrops.

诗 | Half into the mountains – a mountain monastery.

A man in the country now, I climb to it on an autumn day.

It is right in their midst, with lovely rocks askew –

Solitary on the summit on its very highest layer.

"Climbing a Mountain Monastery", Dun Xunhe (846–904)

SAKYA MONASTERY, TIBET
The Buddhist Sakya Monastery is dramatically set on
the Tibetan foothills. The Sakya is known as the
colourful sect, and enclosures around its monasteries
are painted with grey, red, and white stripes.

诗 | Evening wind, morning frost: these things make solitude beautiful.

"Autumn Plants, Flowers, Bamboo, Rocks", Yun Shouping (1633–90)

SONGZANLIN MONASTERY, YUNNAN
Draped across the slopes of a hillside, Songzanlin Monastery is also known as "the little Potala Palace". Modelled on the Dalai Lama's Lhasa palace, the 17th-century Buddhist monastery is home to 1,200 monks.

祈
祷

Let your love flow outward through the universe,

To its height, its depth, its broad extent,

A limitless love, without hatred or enmity.

"Sutta Nipata", Buddha

MEILI SNOW MOUNTAINS, YUNNAN
The holy peaks of the Meili Snow Mountains are an important Buddhist pilgrimage site. Scattered across the mountains along the pilgrimage routes are clusters of white stupas or chortens.

诗 | No one knows this mountain I inhabit:

deep in white clouds, forever empty, silent.

"Cold Mountain", Han Shan (7th–9th century)

KHAMPA DZONG, TIBET
Built directly into the bedrock of an inclined outcrop, with a sweeping view to the south of the Himalayan snowfields, this imposing fortress was sited on an important trade route between India and Tibet.

诗 | I never tire in my search for solitude;   I wander aimlessly along out-of-the-way trails   Where I have never been before,

The more I change direction,   the wilder the road becomes.

"In Search of Solitude", Chao Yi (1727–1814)

TIBETAN PLATEAU, NEAR BURANG
Bound by the Gangdise Mountains, the western regions of the Tibetan plateau contain only vast rocky landscapes that cannot support crops, so the population lives by herding sheep, yaks, and goats.

诗 | When you look down into silence, you see no friend;

when you lift your gaze to space, you hear no echo.

It is like striking a single chord –

it rings out but there is no music.

"Literature: A Rhapsody", Lu Ji (261–303)

TIBETAN DESERT
Tibet is known for its white mountain glaciers
and blue lakes. However, areas of western Tibet
feature desolate, tawny deserts with "barchans"
(crescent-shaped sand dunes that move).

歌 A path strewn with a sprinkling of red;

A broad plain carpeted all over with verdure.

"Treading on Fragrant Grass", Yan Shu (991–1055)

ZHONGDIAN, YUNNAN
Zhongdian, or "Shangri-La", is skirted by snow-capped mountains, and dotted with alpine lakes and picturesque Tibetan villages. The leafy spurge plant carpeting the fields turns deep red in the autumn.

引
语

The wise find pleasure in water; the virtuous find pleasure in hills.

The wise are active; the virtuous are tranquil.

The wise are joyful; the virtuous are long-lived.

The Analects, Confucius (551–479 BCE)

JIUZHAIGOU, SICHUAN
"The valley of the nine villages", Jiuzhaigou is
celebrated for its rugged gullies, mixed forests, and
vivid turquoise-coloured lakes. The area is a UNESCO
World Heritage Site and World Biosphere Reserve.

The basic principles of farming are:

choose the right time, break up the soil,

see to its fertility and moisture,

hoe early, and harvest early.

Basic Principles of Farming, Fan Shenzhi (1st century CE)

VILLAGE NEAR GUI'DE, QINGHAI
This village of walled courtyard houses is situated
adjacent to the upper Huang He (Yellow River).
Farmers here grow dry-land crops such as wheat,
barley, broad beans, and potatoes.

诗 | Sea birds soaring in defiance of the wind,   And northern birds here fleeing the cold: When buds open, they'll flock back north,

But frost-fall always sends them south again.   Greetings echo across Star River distances,   as companions sleep along rivers and lakes.

"Dwellings in the Mountains", Xie Lingyun (385–433)

QINGHAI LAKE, QINGHAI

China's largest lake has water of pristine clarity. In a semiarid region, its shores provide substantial land for farming and grazing. Its rocky outcrops attract thousands of migrating birds, like these cormorants.

中
级
阶
梯

The middle step of China is a land of profound contrasts. In the north are the arid deserts and semiarid steppes of Xinjiang and Inner Mongolia, with their stiflingly hot summers and freezing winters. Extensive basins and narrow valleys are found in the well-watered and warmer Sichuan, Guizhou, and Yunnan provinces in the south, home to China's famous terraced rice paddies. The Red Basin in Sichuan is surrounded by ranges of high mountains, which shelter the area from the cold northern winds, and form a division with the lowest "step".

MIDDLE STEP
DESERTS, STEPPES, AND RIVER BASINS

ZHANGJIAJIE, HUNAN
Zhangjiajie, also called the Wulingyuan scenic area,
has some 3,000 narrow sandstone pillars and peaks.
Ravines, streams, pools, waterfalls, caves, and two
natural bridges can be found between the peaks.

歌

When ice on the pond is three feet thick

and white snow stretches a thousand miles,

my heart will still be like the pine and cypress,

but your heart – what will it be?

"Winter" from *Four Ziye Songs*, Ziye (c.265–420)

TIANCHI LAKE, MOUNT TIAN SHAN, XINJIANG
In a vast region better known for its deserts and
steppes, the crescent-shaped "Heavenly Lake" is an
unexpected expanse of crystal-clear water, fed by
melted snow on Mount Tian Shan's upper slopes.

散
文 | Our humble region is called the mountain of flames. It's covered with flames for over 800 miles,

and all around not even a single blade of grass can grow. If you walk on this mountain, you will turn to liquid even if you have a bronze skull and an iron body.

Journey to the West, Wu Cheng'en (c.1590)

FLAMING MOUNTAINS, BURQIN, XINJIANG
From a distance, the Flaming Mountains of Burqin appear to be on fire. Their bright, reddish colours flicker like burning embers when the sun's rays interact with the weathered stone surfaces.

诗 | The ancient palace is a heap of ruins.

The road has vanished.

The landscape is the same.

The works of men are being obliterated.

"Passing a Ruined Palace", Wen Tingyun (813–870)

GOACHANG, XINJIANG
A ruin since the 14th century, Goachang was once a
wealthy hub on the Silk Road. The town was spread
out along the foot of the Flaming Mountains, with
inner and outer cities, and a separate palace complex.

诗 | Through how many panels of mountains and seas

Do the high parapets of the long wall

Wind and wind?

Our eyes follow, slope after slope

And we understand

How it ate up the dragon hearts of our grandfathers

And in the end they built it for whom?

"The Great Wall", Nalan Xingde (1655–1685)

THE GREAT WALL, BEIJING
Simatai to Jinshanling is one of the most dramatic
sections of the Ming dynasty Great Wall and offers
spectacular views in relative isolation. The mountain
ranges it crosses rise and fall like a writhing dragon.

圣
歌

Just as the soft rains fill the streams, pour into the rivers, and join together in the oceans,

so may the power of every moment of your goodness flow forth to awaken and heal all beings –

those here now, those gone before, those yet to come.

Traditional Buddhist blessing and healing chant

LESHAN GIANT BUDDHA, SICHUAN
Carved out of the cliff face at the confluence of three rivers in southwestern Sichuan, this is the tallest stone Buddha statue in the world. Building began in 713 and was completed 90 years later.

引
语 | The master said, "With coarse rice to eat, with water to drink, and my bended arm for a pillow; I have still joy in the midst of these things.

RICE TERRACES, YUANYANG, YUNNAN
The Hani and Yi minorities have created remarkable step-like terraces for growing rice in the hilly areas of Yunnan. In spring, when the terraces are full of water, they resemble irregular silver ladders.

诗 How nice is the spring breeze at the pavilion on the lake,

My thought of departure was tied by willow wands and ivy vines.

The yellow orioles stop here often and seem to know me well:

Before they depart from the pavilion they call four or five times.

"Farewell at the Pavilion on the Lake", Long Li (7th–9th century)

BLACK DRAGON POOL, YUNNAN
Black Dragon Pool, with Yulong (Jade Dragon)
Mountain in the background, frames a magical
setting for structures like the Naxi minority's Moon-
Embracing Pavilion and white marble bridge.

诗 | From the vault of light at the going down of the sun,　　　the voices of the birds mingle with the voice of the torrent.

The path beneath the stream winds into the distance;   Joy of solitude, will you ever come to an end?

"The Magnolia Enclosure", Pei Di (b.716)

SWAN LAKE, BAYANBULAK, XINJIANG
China's only nature reserve for swans comprises
hundreds of interconnected ponds and interwoven
streams. It is part of a vast highland steppe known as
"Rich Fountains" in the Mongolian language.

You ask me why I dwell in the green mountain;

I smile and make no reply for my heart is free of care.

As the peach blossom flows downstream and is the unknown,

I have a world apart that is not among men.

Green Mountain, Li Bai (702–762)

RAPESEED FIELDS, LUOPING, YUNNAN
Set among the eroded karst landscapes in the east of
Yunnan are extensive fields of rapeseed plants.
In February and March, their golden blossoms
sustain an important beekeeping industry.

诗 | Red hills lie athwart us a menace in the west,

and fiery mountains glare terrible in the south.

"The Red Hills", Bao Zhao (d.466)

JUNGGAR BASIN, XINJIANG
Although the Junggar Basin is characterized by
grasslands, portions of it are studded with razor-like
ridges. The multicoloured rock formations have been
eroded into irregular shapes by the wind.

In the secrecy of the wood I see no one;

The bright moon reaches me with its light.

"The Hermitage of the Bamboos", Wang Wei (701–761)

WOLONG NATURE RESERVE, SICHUAN
The giant panda is an emblem of China. The Wolong Nature Reserve preserves a habitat in the wild for this endangered animal, and fosters scientific research to assist its breeding.

诗 Every plant and tree knows spring will soon be gone

A hundred pinks and purples compete with their bouquets

Willow fuzz and elm pods lack such clever means

They only know how to fill the sky with snow.

"Late Spring", Han Yu (768–824)

BIRCH FOREST, HEILONGJIANG
The tightly packed birch trees and woodland plant
life in the forests of Heilongjiang sustain the Oroqen
(literally "people using reindeer"), a small ethnic
minority group who live by herding and hunting.

诗 My new province is a land of bamboo groves: their shoots in spring fill the valleys and hills.

The mountain woodman cuts an armful of them and brings them down to sell at the early market.

"Eating Bamboo Shoots", Bo Juyi (772–846)

BAMBOO FOREST, CHANGNING, SICHUAN
A sea of bamboo of an extent unequalled elsewhere
in China spreads across the ridges and hills of
southern Sichuan. The rapidly growing plant is used
for many products, from scaffolding to baskets.

低
级
阶
梯

China's lowest step encompasses the rich fertile flood plains formed by the Songhua and Liao rivers in Manchuria as well as the Huang He (Yellow River) and Chang Jiang (Yangzi River). The latter serves as China's major transport artery and has created China's most productive agricultural area. In southern China, rugged mountain ranges are separated by valleys where rice and tea are grown. China's lowest step includes its principal industrial areas, the great imperial capitals, and the pulsating cities, including Beijing and Shanghai, that make up the modern nation.

LOWEST STEP
HILLS AND COASTAL PLAINS

HONG KONG SKYLINE FROM VICTORIA PEAK
Hong Kong's impressive modern architecture was
constructed on extensive areas of reclaimed land.
This view across Victoria Harbour shows Kowloon
Peninsula with the New Territories in the far distance.

诗 Hidden dragons entice with their mysterious forms,

Flying geese echo their distant cries,

Resting in the sky, I am shamed by the clouds' floating,

And lodged by the river, humbled by its fathomless depths.

"Climbing the Tower by the Pond", Xie Lingyun (385–433)

HUANGSHAN MOUNTAINS, ANHUI
The dramatic granite peaks, weather-shaped trees,
and lingering clouds of the Huangshan (Yellow)
Mountains in southern Anhui Province are a frequent
subject of traditional Chinese painting.

引
语

Cutting stalks at noontime,

Perspiration drips to the earth.

Know you that your bowl of rice,

Each grain from hardship comes?

Cutting Stalks at Noontime, Zheng Zhanbao

ZHONGHUA, GUILIN HILLS, GUANGXI
These recently harvested rice fields reveal only the
stubble of once-flourishing plants stuck in the muddy
bottom. The weathered limestone landscape
presents fantastic shapes in the distance.

歌 | Thunder roars past creeks and mountains,

Dark clouds bringing warm days;

From shady clusters, sprouts begin to rear their heads.

Wearing silver hairpins, girls respond to each other in songs –

Whose basket shows that she has picked the most?

As they come home, the fragrance still clings to their hands;

Their choicest crop is offered first to the magistrate.

"Picking Tea: A Ballad", Gao Qi (1336–74)

TEA PLANTATIONS, FUJIAN
Tea plants are draped across the hills of
Fujian and other neighbouring provinces,
where the subtropical climate and favourable
mountain soil are ideal for growing tea.

诗 | A rainhat of young bamboo skins, a coat of lotus leaves,

Nothing busying his mind, he keeps to the fishing jetty.

I suppose that single boat of his has no fixed resting place –

Where will he go this evening, his fishing pole in hand?

"The Song of the Fishermen", Gao Shi (c.716–c.765)

FISHERY, MEIZHOU ISLAND, FUJIAN
Fujian Province is famous for a fishing industry that draws on offshore ocean trawling. Fish are also bred in the bays along the coastline, with breeding areas demarcated by nets and poles.

歌 What a fine evening this is, that I've come to this islet midstream!

What a fine day this is, that I share a boat with you, my prince!

"Song of the Boatswain of Yue", Anon

GRAND CANAL, WUXI, JIANGSU
Threading its way along a 2,000-kilometre (1,245-mile) route from Beijing to Hangzhou, the Grand Canal is a lifeline for towns like Wuxi, which depend on long-distance barges and local boats for rice.

诗 | Pounded earth was raised to form a forest of parapets,

An awesome file of turrets and beacon towers,

Taller in measure than the Five Mountains,

Broader across than the Three Dikes,

Precipitous as a sheer escarpment,

Rising straight up like a bank of long clouds.

"The Desolate City: A Rhapsody", Bao Zhao (414–466)

SHANGHAI SKYLINE
Looking eastwards, this view captures the buildings
and neighbourhoods of "old" Shanghai in the near
distance. The futuristic part of the "new" city of
Pudong can be seen across the Huangpu River.

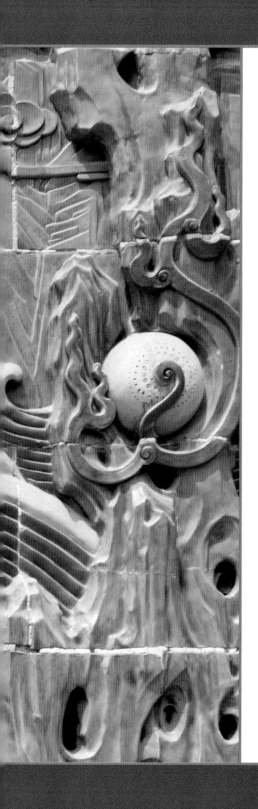

HISTORY

历
史

THE STORY OF CHINA

China's history, once thought to be a sequence of obscure dynasties, is now regarded in a very different light. The discovery of the First Emperor's terracotta army in the 1970s dramatized the remote past. We now know that the Han Empire rivalled the Roman Empire in its power and sophistication, and that the Tang and Song empires recorded the highest levels of technological and artistic achievement in the world at that time. Under the Ming dynasty, extraordinary sea voyages were undertaken. The last great dynasty, the Qing, extended China's frontiers to their greatest extent. The arrival of Westerners, first as missionaries and traders and then as imperialists, accelerated a process of change that swept away the imperial system. The Chinese Communist Party rose to power and attempted to transform China into a socialist state. After Mao Zedong's death in 1976, Deng Xiaoping, leader of the People's Republic of China, set a new course, one that has led China to the brink of becoming a world superpower.

Neolithic cultures, marked by the cultivation of crops, the

史
前
史

domestication of animals, and the use of pottery, appeared in China from around 8000 BCE, a development helped by a change to a warmer and moister climate in East Asia. This transition to settled agriculture occurred not just in one area of the North China plain, as once believed, but also independently in several regional cultures. According to Chinese tradition, there were three ancient Chinese dynasties: the Xia, followed by the Shang, and then the Zhou. China's Bronze Age, which began around 3000 BCE, and developed further under the Xia, reached its height under the Shang, who dominated the middle reaches of the Huang He (Yellow River) in the second millennium BCE.

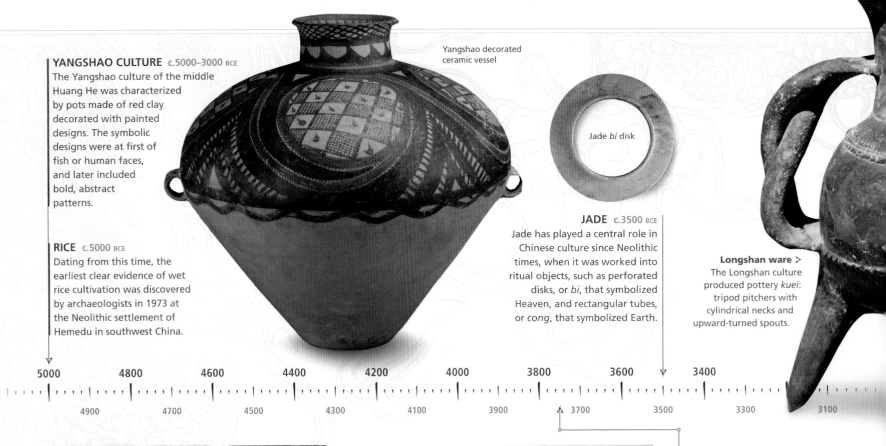

YANGSHAO CULTURE c.5000–3000 BCE
The Yangshao culture of the middle Huang He was characterized by pots made of red clay decorated with painted designs. The symbolic designs were at first of fish or human faces, and later included bold, abstract patterns.

Yangshao decorated ceramic vessel

RICE c.5000 BCE
Dating from this time, the earliest clear evidence of wet rice cultivation was discovered by archaeologists in 1973 at the Neolithic settlement of Hemedu in southwest China.

Jade *bi* disk

JADE c.3500 BCE
Jade has played a central role in Chinese culture since Neolithic times, when it was worked into ritual objects, such as perforated disks, or *bi*, that symbolized Heaven, and rectangular tubes, or *cong*, that symbolized Earth.

Longshan ware >
The Longshan culture produced pottery *kuei*: tripod pitchers with cylindrical necks and upward-turned spouts.

5000	4800	4600	4400	4200	4000	3800	3600	3400
4900	4700	4500	4300	4100	3900	3700	3500	3300	3100

a neolithic village

China's best-known Neolithic site, at Banpo near Xi'an, was occupied between 4500 BCE and 3750 BCE. Each house in the village, which comprised some 100 buildings, had a central pillar supporting a thatched roof and a fire pit. Some of the floors were dressed with white clay, and clay was also used to make ovens, cupboards, and benches. Six kilns and many pottery fragments have been found at Banpo. In the village cemetery, adults were buried in individual graves, often with a ceramic vessel beside the body. Infants were placed in pottery jars and buried near the houses. The inhabitants cultivated millet using polished stone tools. They kept pigs and dogs, sheep and cattle, and fished and hunted deer to supplement their diet.

< **A reconstructed village**
A modern reconstruction of Banpo forms part of a museum close to the original site.

SILK PRODUCTION c.3750 BCE
Silkworm cocoons found in the ruins of the Neolithic site of Banpo are the earliest evidence of the production of silk in China. Until the Han dynasty, the Chinese jealously guarded the secrets of silk production and authorities forbade the export of silkworms. However, by 300 CE knowledge of silk producing methods had spread to India and Korea.

THE ROOTS OF CHINA
NEOLITHIC AND BRONZE AGE CHINA, TO 1122 BCE

shang culture

The Shang dynasty emerged along the Huang He in northern China during the early second millennium BCE. Tradition states that the Shang moved their capital six times, and some of these centres have been identified at Zhengzhou in Henan Province and at Anyang, about 240 km (150 miles) to the east. Zhengzhou had a 6.5-km- (4-mile-) long city wall constructed using the "stamped earth" technique, within which lay large buildings and villages that specialized in making pottery, wine, bronze artefacts, and textiles. At Anyang, the ceremonial and administrative centre of the late Shang state were located.

The most significant discovery at both of these sites was of the shoulder bones of cattle, used for divining by interpreting the cracks that were formed when a heated bronze tool was applied. Many of them have inscriptions that illustrate the early development of the Chinese written language. The royal tombs at Anyang were looted long ago, but in 1976 an undamaged tomb was found: the grave of Princess Fu Hao, the consort of a Shang king. In it were the mummified remains of the princess, 16 human sacrifices, and an extraordinary collection of grave goods. These included bronze objects weighing 1.6 tons, an indication of Fu Hao's very high status.

∨ **Fu Hao's grave goods**
Among the elaborate contents of Fu Hao's tomb was this beaker inlaid with ivory and turquoise.

HUANG HE
c.2600 BCE
In the late Neolithic era, the Huang He shifted its course dramatically at least two times, causing widespread damage and long-lasting economic disruption.

XIA DYNASTY
c.1900–1350 BCE

SHANG DYNASTY
c.1766–1122 BCE

3000 · 2700 · 2600 · 2500 · 2400 · 2300 · 2200 · 2100 · 2000 · 1900 · 1800 · 1700 · 1600

LONGSHAN CULTURE c.3000–2000 BCE
Longshan culture spread along the middle and lower Yangzi valley. The culture produced black pottery using a potter's wheel, and also featured the use of oracle bones, ritual jade carvings, and rich burials in stepped pits.

WALLED SETTLEMENTS c.2500 BCE
The stamped earth technique was first used in the construction of walls around Longshan villages. Stamped earth walls were made by pounding thin layers of earth within a movable wooden frame. The earth then became as hard as cement.

BRONZE-WORKING c.1800 BCE
Under the Shang, bronze was worked into a series of ritual and domestic objects. Common shapes included the *jue* and *gu* in the form of wine vessels, and *ding* tripods. The bronzes were often adorned with animal designs.

THE XIA DYNASTY c.1900–1350 BCE
The Xia dynasty was long believed by historians to be a myth, but the recently discovered palace-like buildings and tombs at Erlitou in Henan are now thought to be the work of a real Xia dynasty that flourished between around 1900 and 1350 BCE. The genealogy of the Xia rulers was preserved in the *Historical Records* and later corroborated by evidence from oracle-bone inscriptions.

Shang rectangular bronze food vessel (*fang ding*)

< **Xia dynasty bronze**
This Xia bronze plate is intricately inlaid with a layer of turquoise mosaics that represent a dragon's scales.

In the late 12th century BCE, the Shang dynasty was defeated by the western state of Zhou at the battle of Muye. The Zhou then claimed that the mandate of heaven, and the right to rule, had been awarded to them. The Zhou period is divided into Western Zhou (1122–771 BCE), and Eastern Zhou, which is subdivided into the Spring and Autumn (771–481 BCE) and the Warring States (481–221 BCE) periods. The Zhou empire rapidly disintegrated into 170 independent states, a number that warfare later reduced to seven. The Zhou dynasty saw the birth of the major indigenous Chinese philosophies and the rise of the western state of Qin, which in 316 BCE began the campaigns that led to the establishment of the first unified Chinese state.

周
朝
至
秦
朝

WESTERN ZHOU
1122–771 BCE

The great philosopher
Kong Fuzi (Confucius)

THE MANDATE OF HEAVEN c.1105 BCE
According to Confucius, the mandate of heaven was a concept first articulated by the Duke of Zhou, brother of the first Zhou emperor, to justify their overthrow of the Shang dynasty. The Duke claimed that heaven would remove the legitimacy from an unjust ruler and pass the mandate of rule to someone else, and this was how the Zhou had acquired their right to the imperial throne. Later dynasties also used this idea to justify their seizure of power.

the hundred schools of thought

Kong Fuzi, or Confucius (551–479 BCE) – *see page 242* – was the most influential thinker in an era that gave rise to many competing schools. At the core of his message was filial piety, which required obedience to one's parents and care for them as they grew old. He advised rulers to treat their subjects with benevolence and employ good officials. His most vigorous opponent was Mozi (470–391 BCE), who argued for universal love in place of the conditional love Confucius promoted. Mencius (372–289 BCE) taught that if a ruler did not rule benevolently, then his people had the right to rebel. He believed human nature to be good, but Xunzi (298–238 BCE) asserted that "the nature of man is evil; his goodness is acquired." In Daoism (Taoism), whose oldest text, the *Daode jing*, was supposedly written by Laozi, the ideal ruler was the enlightened sage. The most important Daoist principle was *wuwei*: "Do that which consists in taking no action, and order will prevail."

1100   950   900   850   800   750   700

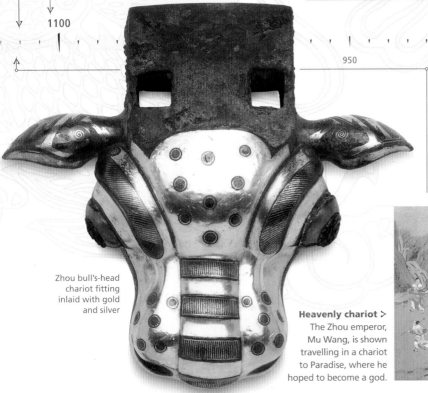

Zhou bull's-head chariot fitting inlaid with gold and silver

Heavenly chariot >
The Zhou emperor, Mu Wang, is shown travelling in a chariot to Paradise, where he hoped to become a god.

ZHOU CHARIOTS c.1122 BCE
Two-horse chariots, first brought to China during the Shang dynasty, were widespread throughout the Western Zhou period. They were finally supplanted by the previously uncommon four-horse chariot in the Spring and Autumn period.

SPRING AND AUTUMN PERIOD
771–481 BCE

FEUDAL SOCIETY c.800 BCE
Zhou rulers gave grants of land to their followers in return for promising military support. By the 8th century BCE, some 200 lords had semi-independent domains, creating a type of feudal system. Their appointment was formalized by the grant of a title, recorded on bronze vessels.

THE CALENDAR 841 BCE
King Li of Zhou was driven from the throne in 841 BCE, a date that Sima Qian, the Grand Historian writing under the Han dynasty, took as the first year for the consecutive annual dating of Chinese history.

THE AGE OF IDEAS
THE ZHOU AND QIN DYNASTIES, 1122–206 BCE

Zhou bell with dragon motif

< Funerary bells
The instruments found in the Marquis of Yi's tomb included a set of 65 bells, played by five musicians using mallets.

ZHOU MUSICAL INSTRUMENTS 433 BCE
Sophisticated musical instruments were already in use during the early Zhou period. Many of the instruments, such as large stone chimes, were not designed to be carried when played. The Marquis of Yi, a Zhou noble who died in the early 5th century BCE, was buried with a collection of more than 120 instruments.

HAN FEI c.280–233 BCE
The philosopher Han Fei was born a member of the aristocracy. His doctrine of Legalism, written down as the *Hanfeizi*, was centred on the powers and duties of rulers. Legalism became a popular philosophy at the court of the state of Qin.

THE RISE OF QIN
260 BCE
At Changping, the forces of Qin inflicted a catastrophic defeat on the army of Zhao, irrevocably establishing Qin as the strongest of the remaining Warring States.

QIN DYNASTY
221–206 BCE

600   500   400   300

650   550   450   350   250

IRON TECHNOLOGY
c.650 BCE
The Chinese had knowledge of how to produce iron from the 7th century BCE, possibly as an import from the Western world.

LAND REFORMS
594 BCE
Until reforms in the early 6th century BCE, peasant families were given a plot of land to feed themselves, but also had to farm a communal field that fed the aristocrat owners.

WARRING STATES PERIOD
481–221 BCE

THE FIRST COINS c.500 BCE
Under the Shang, cowrie shells and pieces of cloth were used as money. By the late Spring and Autumn period, a metallic currency had been introduced, with early coins being cast in the form of agricultural tools.

Knife- and spade-shaped Zhou coins

new weapons
Under the Shang dynasty, battles were fought by aristocrats using chariots, but during the Zhou period, changes took place in the conduct of war. In 685 BCE, Guan Zhong, chief minister of Qi, one of the Warring States, made civilians serve in the military, levying soldiers directly from villages. During the Warring States period, chariots were displaced by mounted cavalry supported by infantry. In *The Art of War* (c.500 BCE), the earliest known work on military strategy, Sunzi argued that a general might do anything to secure victory. He should block up the eyes and ears of his men to ensure that they would act solely according to his will. "All warfare," he wrote, "is based on deception." By the 5th century BCE, soldiers carried bronze halberds, swords with a bronze alloy cutting edge, and some iron swords. The key weapon was a crossbow with a bronze cocking mechanism that shot bolts with triangular bronze heads capable of piercing armour. Its first recorded use in war came at the battle of Mailing in 341 BCE.

Bronze dagger and sheath

<An autocratic ruler
After uniting China, Qin Shihuang was determined to bring all aspects of the state under his direct control, and to impose uniformity on the empire.

the first emperor

By 221 BCE, King Zheng of Qin had conquered the territories surrounding his own, creating the first unified Chinese state. King Zheng assumed the title Qin Shihuang, First Emperor of Qin. During his short but eventful 11-year reign, the First Emperor was responsible for a number of technological achievements that enhanced the infrastructure and defences of the new empire.

constructing an empire

To improve transportation, the emperor commissioned the construction of imperial highways and the 800-km- (500-mile-) long Straight Road from the capital of Xianyang to Inner Mongolia. Canals were dug, including the "magic canal", the earliest waterway to use land contours to avoid the construction of costly tunnels or locks. The canal joined the Yangzi River to the south and was first used to transport grain to the south to support military campaigns there. It is still in operation today.

To protect China from barbarian raiders to the north, the imperial general, Meng Tian, connected previously built walls into one giant barrier, which extended more than 4,800 km (3,000 miles) along the empire's northern borders. During the late 15th century CE, remnants of this barrier were used to form the foundations of the Great Wall.

infamy and immortality

Qin Shihuang was denounced by later historians as a cruel megalomaniac, a reputation earned in part from two notorious acts. In 213 BCE, after court scholars had criticized his rulership, he ordered that most of the books in the imperial archives be burned. Anyone who refused to cooperate with this policy was condemned to forced labour. The following year, 460 scholars were allegedly buried alive for daring to protest against the emperor's growing obsession with the search for immortality.

In 210 BCE, while on a pilgrimage to Penglai – rumoured to be the island of the immortals – the First Emperor died. He was laid to rest in the lavish tomb complex that he had commissioned two years earlier, guarded by an army of terracotta warriors. First excavated in 1976, this army, an extraordinary monument to the First Emperor's wealth and power, has ensured him the immortality that he so craved in his lifetime.

<Imperial coinage
Qin currency was standardized to a circular copper coin stamped through with a square hole, a design that became uniform in Chinese currency until the early 20th century.

引
语
In the state of an intelligent ruler there are no books, but the laws serve as teachers. There are no sayings of the former kings; the officials act as the teachers.

Philosopher Han Fei (d.233 BCE) on the absolute law of kings

The terracotta army ∧ ⟩
Standing guard over the as yet unexcavated tomb of Qin Shihuang are the ranks of the terracotta army, a legion of more than 8,000 life-size figures of soldiers and horses. Each soldier is unique and once held real weapons.

汉
朝

The Qin Empire was destroyed by a rebellion headed by Liu Bang, by origin a peasant. Known as the Gaozu emperor, he established the Han dynasty and consolidated central authority. Under Wendi (180–157 BCE), the empire achieved new heights of stability and prosperity, while Wudi (141–87 BCE) further extended Chinese influence into Central Asia and Korea and reformed the administrative bureaucracy by recruiting on the basis of ability. After a brief usurpation by Wang Mang, a descendant of the Han restored the dynasty. Under the Later Han, territorial expansion continued. However, by the 2nd century CE, internal disputes and attacks by the Xianbei people to the north caused the dynasty's collapse.

LACQUERWARE 206 BCE
Although used under the Shang, lacquering became a major industry at the start of the Han period. Han lacquer is generally a soft, dark brown on which schematic bird and animal forms have been painted in red.

HAN DYNASTY
206 BCE–220 CE

Lacquer bowl with dedicatory inscription

CONFUCIAN VALUES
196 BCE
Although Gaozu was at first contemptuous of Confucian scholars, in 196 BCE he issued an edict promoting recruitment to the administration on the basis of merit.

A NEW CAPITAL 194 BCE
The Han capital of Chang'an (now Xi'an) was constructed on a north–south axis. The city was divided into 108 wards, each with a wall and gates that were locked at night.

death and the afterlife

The Han period saw a refinement of beliefs and practices concerning the dead, which is reflected in the type of goods found in burials. A vivid illustration of this was found in the tomb of the Countess of Dai at Mawangdui in Hunan province, dating from about 168 BCE. The mummified body of the princess was interred with various talismans that would have enabled her to make the journey to Paradise. These included a painting on silk that depicted the route her soul would take, first to the magical island of Penglai and from there to the gates of Paradise. The increased complexity of the belief in an afterlife is illustrated by the appearance, in tombs of this period, of bronze "TLV" mirrors. These mirrors, which have markings resembling the Roman letters T, L, and V, may have been used for divination. They are ornamented with a design incorporating the 12 symbols that were believed to represent the divisions of time, as well as the Five Phases (see page 241). They were intended to reassure the bearer that he or she stood in the correct relationship with the cosmos.

200	180	160	140
190	170	150	130

GAOZU EMPEROR 206 BCE
Liu Bang showed that a peasant might become emperor. He initially accepted the existence of ten independent kingdoms, but these were later redistributed to his relatives. Gaozu formalized the system of bureaucratic government, with the emperor being assisted by three officials who were supported by nine subordinate ministers.

Liu Bang, the Gaozu emperor

AN AGRICULTURAL ECONOMY 180 BCE
Many of the characteristic features of Chinese agriculture developed under Wendi: sophisticated irrigation techniques allowing intensive cultivation; a free peasantry that produced a surplus of primary goods; and vulnerability to natural disasters and excessive demands from the state.

Han brick depicting an agricultural scene

WUDI 141–87 BCE
Wudi's long reign saw aggressive expansion in Central Asia, Vietnam, and Korea, and reforms, both institutional and economic, including a drive against corruption. His rule ended in senility and a paranoid search for immortality.

ALCHEMY 133 BCE
Drawing on Daoist texts, Chinese alchemists sought to reverse the transmutations that created the universe's elements and so make an elixir of life. Wudi hoped to find this elixir and so become immortal.

CHINA TAKES SHAPE
THE HAN DYNASTY, 206 BCE–220 CE

Silk banner depicting Heaven and Earth from the tomb of the Countess of Dai

STATE MONOPOLIES
119 BCE

Emperor Wudi set up government monopolies on the manufacture and sale of iron and salt, creating an important source of revenue, but giving rise to a flourishing black market.

110

KOREA **108** BCE

Wudi's armies defeated the Korean Gosojeon kingdom, and established four military districts, one of which remained in Chinese hands until 313 CE.

THE IMPERIAL ACADEMY **124** BCE

Founded by the Han outside Chang'an, the academy initially had 50 students who studied Confucian classics and, if they passed an examination, became eligible for official appointments. Qualification for office through birth vanished only slowly, but academy students came to dominate the lower bureaucratic ranks.

the silk road

The Silk Road, a 8,000-km- (5,000-mile-) long trade route that linked Chang'an (present-day Xi'an) and West Asia saw commercial contacts along its route as far back as around 200 BCE. Its importance required military efforts on the part of the Chinese to secure control of the route. In 138 BCE, Wudi, the Han emperor, sent General Zhang Qian to subdue the Central Asian Yuezhi tribes and extend Chinese influence to the Pamir Mountains. In 91 CE, Ban Chao led an army to the shores of the Caspian Sea and sent an envoy to the Roman Empire.

trade and culture

Silk, in great demand in the Roman Empire, was the most valuable of the trade items carried along the route, and the Senate in Rome even tried to prohibit the manufacture of clothes

∨ Five-coloured silk
This 6th-century silk from Turfan shows that high-value goods were still traded even after the Han's fall.

from the material, because its import caused a huge outflow of gold from the empire. The Silk Road also became an important route for the transmission of technology and religious ideas. Dunhuang, where the Silk Road forked north and south of the Takla Makan Desert, became a major centre of Buddhism, as well as a repository of Buddhist art and literature.

The Silk Road was at its most important under the Tang (618–907), when Chang'an was the world's greatest city. To the Chinese capital came caravans of exotic goods from Central Asia, as well as followers of Zoroastrianism and Nestorian Christianity. The Silk Road declined with the rise of Islam from the 7th century, but was revived in the 13th century when the Mongol conquests brought relative political stability. Once again it became a major commercial route for travellers, such as the Venetian merchant Marco Polo.

∧ Silk Road city
The ruins of Jiaohe on the northern branch of the Silk Road. Under the Han, the city was the capital of an independent kingdom.

∨ Heavenly horse
A Later Han bronze depiction of the highly prized Ferghana breed.

Sima Qian, the
Grand Historian

The scholar
Ban Zhao

TOMB STATUES

c.100 BCE

The Han began to erect
statues over important
sites in the 1st century
BCE. These sculptures
later developed into
"spirit roads", avenues
of stone monuments
that led to the sites
of imperial tombs.

THE FIRST CENSUS 2 CE

China's first-ever census
gave the country's taxable
population as 57,671,400.

BAN ZHAO c.45–115 CE

China's first female historian,
Ban Zhao, wrote *Admonitions
for Women* urging women
to practice humility and
obey their husbands. She
advised that if a woman's
husband died she
should not remarry.
Ban Zhao was praised
by Confucianists as
China's greatest
female scholar.

THE GRAND HISTORIAN 85 BCE

Sima Qian, the Grand Historian, compiled
the *Shiji*, known as the *Historical Records*,
a comprehensive survey of the history of
China, using surviving archival material.

IMPERIAL KITCHENS 7 BCE

The importance of food to
the early Chinese is shown by
records of imperial staffing
dating from Han times: the
palace kitchens were worked
by more than 3,000 slaves.

100		80		60		40		20		BCE–CE		20		40	
	90		70		50		30		10		10		30		50

concubines and eunuchs

As early as the 8th century BCE, Chinese emperors
had kept castrated males as palace servants.
Some were given menial jobs such as cleaning or
working in the kitchens, whilst others filled the
role of court entertainers. The most senior
eunuchs were given the task of guarding the
harems in which lived the imperial concubines –
women who, though not wives of the emperor,
could bear legitimate heirs to the imperial throne.
The number of concubines (and by extension of
eunuchs) grew under the Han dynasty, and by the
1st century CE there were around 3,000 eunuchs
living in the palace. These formed a formidable
power base, and a source of factionalism that
weakened the imperial government's capacity to
implement reforms. Later, Confucian historians
(perhaps unfairly) laid the blame for the Han's
decline squarely at the door of eunuch ministers.

◁ **A beautiful concubine departs**
Wang Zhao Jun, concubine of Emperor
Yuan, and one of China's "Four Beauties",
sets off to be the bride of a Xiongnu king.

WANG MANG 9–23 CE

Previously acting as regent to
the infant emperor Ruzi, Wang
Mang usurped the Han throne
at the beginning of the 1st
century CE. Wang abolished
private land ownership and
reintroduced monopolies in
salt and iron. He conducted an
experiment to test the claims of
a man who asserted that when
coated in feathers he could fly
great distances and spy out
the movements of China's
enemies, the Xiongnu nomads
of Central Asia. In 23 CE, Wang
was driven from the throne
and killed by rebels.

**MULTISTOREY
BUILDINGS** 25 CE

The wooden buildings of the
Han era were often made up
of multiple storeys, with an
enclosed courtyard for livestock
at ground level, living quarters at
midlevels, and a watchtower at the
top. This architectural style was
later adapted for Buddhist pagodas.

Ceramic tower ▷
This Han dynasty pottery
model of a three-storey
building is 1m (3ft) tall.
It was buried in a tomb.

the invention of paper

Cai Lun, a court eunuch who lived c.50–121 CE, is said to have been the first person to make paper. He mixed the inner bark of a mulberry tree and bamboo fibres with water and pounded them with a wooden tool. Draining the mixture through woven cloth, leaving only the fibres, made a type of paper that was light, cheap, and easy to make. His invention was adopted rapidly for documents and books. Chinese papermakers developed coated and dyed paper, as well as paper that was protected against insects. Around 600 CE, woodblock printing on paper was invented, and by 740 CE the first newspaper appeared in China. Papermaking arrived in Korea and Vietnam in the 3rd century CE and Japan in 610 CE. Knowledge of the process spread to the West around the 8th century CE.

∧ **Papermaker**
Boiling bamboo in chalk and water was part of the papermaking process.

Model of Zhang Heng's seismograph

THE SEISMOGRAPH 132 CE
The invention of a seismograph, an urn-like instrument with a central pendulum, is credited to the astronomer Zhang Heng. An earthquake caused the pendulum to swing and activate a set of levers. One of eight dragons placed around the rim released a bronze ball, which fell into the mouth of a toad, so indicating in which direction an earthquake had occurred.

100   120   140   160   180   200   220
90   110   130   150   170   190   210

BAN CHAO 91 CE
Ban Chao was a Chinese general who campaigned against the Xiongnu people and restored Chinese control over the Tarim Basin. In 91 CE, he was made Protector General of the Western Regions, and in 98 CE he led an army across the Pamirs to the shores of the Caspian Sea.

THE OX-DRAWN PLOUGH 72 CE
Engineer Wang Jin, famous for his hydraulic projects on the Yellow River, promoted an improved version of the ox-drawn plough. The cast-iron ploughshare had first appeared in China in the 3rd century BCE. Its shape reduced friction and made it possible to plough using only one or two oxen.

THE WHEELBARROW c.100 CE
Though carrying devices resembling the wheelbarrow are described as early as the 1st century BCE, the oldest image of a wheelbarrow in China comes from a frieze relief made on a tomb wall in Sichuan in the early 2nd century CE.

THE FIRST DICTIONARY c.100 CE
The *Shuowen Jiezi* (*Explaining Simple and Analyzing Compound Characters*), compiled by Xu Shen and presented to the emperor in 121 CE, is the first dictionary of the Chinese language and among the earliest dictionaries in the world. The work indicated both the pronunciation of characters and their meaning, and established a method for the organization of successive Chinese dictionaries.

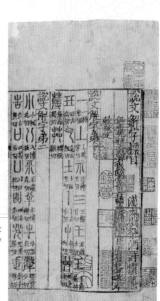

A page from the first Chinese dictionary

From 220 to 589, no single central government ruled China.

三国至隋朝

The Western Jin briefly reunited the country after 280, but from 316 the north and the south were again divided. In the north, a period of fragmentation, known as the Sixteen Kingdoms, lasted until 384, when the Toba established the Northern Wei dynasty with its capital at Luoyang. In 534, that dynasty split and a further period of political division ensued until, in 589, Wendi reunified north and south China under the Sui dynasty. Although this was a period of political weakness, it also saw developments such as Daoist experiments with alchemy, and the beginnings of landscape painting.

⋀ A cave of Buddhas
The complex of caves and grottoes at Longmen, near Luoyang, contains over 100,000 Buddhist statues and images and some 40 pagodas.

early buddhism in china

Buddhism originally reached China from the Indian subcontinent. By the end of the 2nd century CE, Buddhist communities had been formed at Luoyang and elsewhere, and the translation of Buddhist scriptures into Chinese had begun. Buddhism gained its first adherents in the south among Chinese who had been attracted to neo-Daoism, whose concentration on ideas of being and non-being had similarities with Buddhist thought. In the north, the religion obtained official sponsors. Fotudeng, a monk from Central Asia, reached Luoyang in 310 and obtained the patronage of the Later Zhao dynasty. Daowu, the first Northern Wei ruler, appointed an administrator, Faguo, for the Buddhist communities. Emperor Wu of the Northern Wei (424–51) was persuaded by his Confucian advisers to carry out a pogrom against Buddhist monks, but the persecution did not last long. In 460, work began on the Buddhist cave temples at Yungang, and in the 490s construction commenced at cave temples at Longmen.

Seated Buddha from Northern Wei period

220	240	260	280	300	320	340
230	250	270	290	310	330	350

THE THREE KINGDOMS 220–265
The Three Kingdoms – Wei, Shu Han, and Wu – fought exceptionally bloody struggles for dominance in the mid-3rd century. The period has been romanticized in Chinese tradition, and is the source of many folk tales and popular heroes.

< Court scene
A scene from *Romance of the Three Kingdoms* (see page 268), a novel set during this period.

GU KAIZHI 344–406
The founder of traditional Chinese painting, Gu Kaizhi was also a poet and calligrapher. No originals of his paintings survive, though some copies remain. His best-known work, *Admonitions of the Instructress to the Palace Ladies*, outlines how ladies of noble birth should behave.

WANG XIZHI 353
A famous calligrapher, Wang Xizhi's style is known from tracings and rubbings of his work. His best-known piece of calligraphy is *Record of the Orchard Pavilion Gathering*.

Copy of Gu Kaizhi's *Goddess Luo Rhapsody*

AN EMPIRE DIVIDED
THE FIRST PERIOD OF DISUNITY AND THE SUI DYNASTY, 220–618

Official seals >
Bronze seals, sometimes in the form of animals, were used for stamping official documents.

INK SEALS c.600
Chinese seals were originally used by the emperor or by his appointees to authenticate official documents. By the 6th century, seals came to be used more widely by artists and calligraphers to establish ownership of their work. The frequent use of seals contributed to the development of woodblock printing and, ultimately, to the production of books.

∧ Sacred fight
Monks from the Shaolin monastery participate in a session of martial arts practice.

THE SHAOLIN MONASTERY 495
The Buddhist monk Batuo, who had been preaching in China for over 30 years, founded the Shaolin monastery in Henan Province at the end of the 5th century. Over the next hundred years, it became associated with an eponymous style of martial arts boxing. Active to this day, the monastery has separate abbots to care for martial arts and for more contemplative disciplines.

THE KAIHUANG CODE 583
Before he established Sui rule over the whole of China, Wendi promoted the Kaihuang Code, which defined laws in plain terms and became the model for later Chinese legal codes.

| 440 | 460 | 480 | ↓ 500 | 520 | 540 | 560 | 580↓ | 600 | 620 |

| 430 | 450 | 470 | ↑ 490 ↑ | 510 | 530 | 550 | 570 | 590↑ | 610 |

THE EQUAL FIELD SYSTEM 485
Under the Northern Wei dynasty, each able-bodied man was given a holding of 7.5 ha (19 acres), part granted in perpetuity, the rest to revert to the state at his death.

THE NORTHERN WEI DYNASTY 493
The Northern Wei gradually established an ascendancy over northern China from the late 4th century, when they defeated the Xiongnu. Although they retained many non-Chinese customs, such as not paying salaries to government officials, the Wei became increasingly sinicized after the move of their capital to Luoyang in 493.

SUI DYNASTY
589–618

TIBET c.600
Early in the 7th century, Tibet became a unified state. King Song-tsen Gampo (620–49) initiated a program of sinicization and expanded Tibetan influence as far as modern-day Sichuan.

Northern Wei cavalry

< **Imperial journey**
Emperor Yangdi
toured his empire
on the Grand
Canal, travelling
on luxurious ships
that were in effect
floating palaces.

the grand canal

In 605, Yangdi, second emperor of the Sui dynasty, ordered the construction of a "Grand Canal". The ambitious project, an unparalleled feat of engineering that linked together several earlier canals and connected five river systems, took over six years to complete. Once in operation, the canal greatly enhanced the speed of communications and the transportation of goods across the empire, providing the basis for China's prosperity during the succeeding Tang dynasty.

The total length of the new canal was about 2,400 km (1,500 miles). Roads and postal stations were constructed by the water, and huge granaries, one of which could hold more than 33 million bushels (1.2 million cubic meters) of grain, were built at key points. Various sections of the canal were employed for the transportation of rice to the north, and to allow the rapid movement of troops for military expeditions, including Yangdi's invasion of Korea in 612.

The canal's construction – which included the building of flash locks to permit barges to traverse shallow stretches – involved many complicated engineering techniques. The build could only be achieved by large-scale state funding and by drafting thousands

of male and female labourers to work on the project – many of whom died. The whole project thus served to destabilize the short-lived Sui dynasty.

later development

Major cities developed along the banks of the canal, such as Kaifeng, the Song capital from 960, whose population of 600,000 to 700,000 made it probably the largest city in the world at the time. In the 13th century, a fresh section of canal was built from Hangzhou to Beijing, the new Yuan dynasty capital. Marco Polo wrote that it was "a huge canal of great width and depth" affording passage for very large ships.

By the 15th century, large sections of the canal were unusable due to silting, and grain had to be transported by sea and by land instead. The waterway was renovated by the Ming emperor Yongle from 1411; 300,000 labourers toiled for 100 days to clear 210 km (130 miles) of canal and construct 38 locks. When the work was completed, 3,000 flat-bottomed barges were used to transport up to 300,000 tons of grain a year to Beijing.

< **Canal boatman**
As well as large grain-carrying
vessels, the Grand Canal
opened up navigation for a
host of smaller, local boats.

It then becomes the most noble canal improved and adorned with sluices and bridges of singular workmanship and beauty, and after a long course ... gently falls into the Yellow River.

An Embassy to China, Lord Macartney (1737–1806)

∧ **Working canal**
This section of the Grand Canal in Jiangsu Province is one of several still-navigable stretches of the waterway in south China.

In 618, the Sui dynasty was replaced by the Tang, inaugurating

唐朝 an era of political, cultural, and economic success. Under Taizong (626–49), the government was reformed and the boundaries of the empire extended to Central Asia. Under Xuanzong (712–56), literature and the visual arts flourished, while Chang'an, the capital, became the centre of a cosmopolitan

world. From 755 to 763, the empire was shaken by the rebellion of An Lushan. Although the uprising was suppressed, the Tang never fully recovered, and in 874 a new revolt broke out, led by Huang Chao, who captured Chang'an. The rebels were eventually defeated, but Tang power was broken, and in 907 a former follower of Huang Chao established the Liang dynasty.

Tang silver parrot-pattern pot

THE FIRST CHRISTIANS 635 CE
Nestorians, Syrian Christians who believed that Jesus had two separate identities, human and divine, reached China and presented their scriptures to the Taizong emperor. Their first church was built at Chang'an in 638. An account of Nestorian teachings was inscribed on a monument in 781. This stone was buried after 845, when Nestorianism and other foreign religions were suppressed.

SILVERWORKING 618 CE
Under the early Tang, many silversmiths reached China from Persia. Their craftsmanship and Chinese traditions of metalworking combined to produce gold and silverwork of the highest quality.

THE ARRIVAL OF ISLAM 651 CE
The first official Muslim envoy to China reached Chang'an and was received by Emperor Gaozong. Although the envoy failed to persuade him to embrace Islam, Gaozong allowed the Muslims to proselytize in China and to build a mosque.

620   640   660   680

630   650   670

TANG DYNASTY
618–907 CE

TAIZONG 626–49 CE
The Taizong emperor's reign is seen as a brilliant one. His relationship with his ministers was regarded as exemplary. He instituted a system of state schools, whose graduates gained a place through a formal examination system. In 657, his general, Su Dingfang, defeated the Western Turks at Issyk Kul and advanced China's influence as far as the borders of Persia.

the empress wu

The consort of Gaozong, Empress Wu, was the only woman to rule as emperor of China. After Gaozong's death in 683, she dominated his weak successors. In 690, she usurped the throne and established her own dynasty, finding support principally outside the traditional aristocracy. She encouraged Buddhism and approved the construction of a Buddhist Hall of Light, which was allegedly used for wild religious rites supervised by the abbot, who was also the empress's lover. Her extravagant building programme and expensive frontier campaigns against the Qidan and Tibetans emptied the treasury. From 697, she became enamoured of the Zhang brothers, who caused scandal by parading around in fancy costumes and overriding the authority of senior ministers. In 705, the ministers had the Zhang brothers killed and forced the Empress to abdicate. She died later that year.

Portrait of the Empress Wu

BUDDHISM REACHES TIBET 650 CE
Song Tsen Gampo, who ruled Tibet between 618 and 650, is traditionally credited with bringing Buddhism to Tibet. He is said to have received Buddhist teachers and to have commissioned the translation of Buddhist scriptures. He also married two Buddhist princesses, one from Nepal, the other Chinese, and built the Jokhang temple in Lhasa.

Sculpture of the Buddha, near Lhasa

A GOLDEN AGE
THE TANG DYNASTY, 618–907

Foreign fashions >
These Tang ceramic figures
reveal foreign influences, such
as the floral designs on the
robe of the princess (centre).

< Nestorian stele
Erected by a monk in Chang'an,
this tablet records the early
history of Chinese Nestorianism.

MANICHAEISM 694 CE
Followers of the 3rd-
century Iranian prophet
Mani reached China in the
7th century. Their faith,
which drew elements from
Christianity, Zoroastrianism,
and Buddhism, flourished
under the Tang, but after
intermittent persecutions,
was banned by the Ming.

600

690

the cosmopolitan tang

During Xuanzong's reign, China's relations with the outside
world flourished. Chinese influence in Central Asia was at
its zenith, and Chang'an, with its population of over one
million making it the world's largest city, became the centre
of a cosmopolitan civilization. Along the Silk Road came
the caravans of Persian and Sogdian merchants. Horses
were imported from the Tarim Basin, glass goblets from
Byzantium, jade from Xinjiang, crystals from Samarkand,
and cotton from Turfan. In exchange,
the Chinese sent silk, tea, paper, and
ceramics. Korean and Japanese
students came to Chang'an to study
Confucianism and Buddhism. Some of these competed in
the state examinations, others adopted Chinese names
and served at court. Religions practised at the Tang capital
included Buddhism, Daoism, Zoroastrianism, Nestorianism,
and Islam. Central Asian harpists and dancers gave
performances at court, while Turkish folk songs influenced
Chinese poets. Figurines found in Tang tombs provide vivid
images of the Tang's contacts outside China, with
many of them showing foreigners with large
noses and hairy faces, or depicting horses – the
most prized varieties of which were found in
Central Asia – and their grooms.

decline of tang authority

The Tang's sophisticated culture depended
largely on their control of Central Asia.
China conquered the Eastern Turks in
630, and dominated the Western Turks
after a victory at Issyk Kul in 657, but
struggled to contain Tibetan expansion in
the 7th and early 8th centuries. More
serious were the advances made into
Central Asia by Muslim armies
following the conquest of Persia in the
630s and 640s. By the early 8th
century, the Muslims had reached
Tashkent. An uneasy state of truce
that lasted four decades prevented
outright confrontation with the
Chinese until 751, when a revolt
against Muslim rule in Samarkand
led to Tang intervention and a
disastrous Chinese defeat at the
Talas River. The Tang lost control over
the Central Asian Silk Road, revenues
declined, and China's cultural focus
turned inwards again.

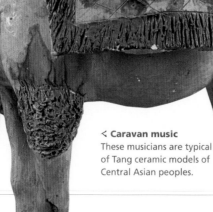

< Caravan music
These musicians are typical
of Tang ceramic models of
Central Asian peoples.

< Tang bowl
This Tang porcelain bowl with matching foot was found in a tomb near Xi'an that dates from 667.

the rebellion of an lushan

In the 740s, Emperor Xuanzong became infatuated with his concubine, Yang Guifei, and her cousin, Yang Guozhong, became a powerful figure at court. Yang Guozhong's rival, An Lushan, was a military governor of the northern borders whose success had ingratiated him with the emperor and who had become the favourite, perhaps the lover, of Yang Guifei. In 755, An Lushan, fearing attack from Yang Guozhong, rebelled and forced the emperor to flee from Chang'an. During the flight, the commander of Xuanzong's escort demanded the death of Yang Guifei, and the emperor was forced to order her execution. An Lushan was assassinated in 757, but it was not until 763 that his rebellion was finally suppressed.

< Court in exile
The emperor's flight from Chang'an was the end of a golden age for the Tang.

PORCELAIN c. 700
Several types of ceramic produced during the Tang period may be described as porcelain. One early example is Xing ware, developed in Hebei. By the late Tang period, Dingzhou ware was also being produced in Hebei. This latter form of porcelain was the forerunner of the famous Ding ware of the Song dynasty.

700 710 720 730 740 750 760 770 780 790 800

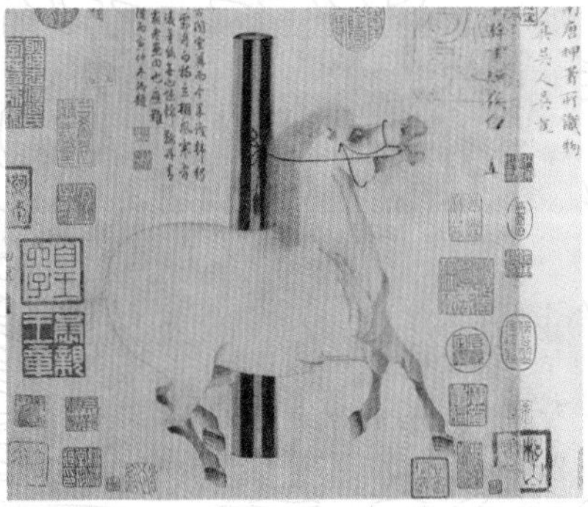

Shining White of the Night by Han Gan

TANG ART UNDER XUANZONG 740–60
Xuanzong's reign saw important advances in the visual arts. Wu Daozi (c.700–60) created a Chinese style of Buddhist sculpture, and landscape painting evolved under the poet-artist Wang Wei (701–61). Han Gan (c.715–81) painted *Shining White of the Night*, a depiction of the emperor's favourite horse.

CLASSIC OF TEA 780
Lu Yu wrote the *Classic of Tea*, the earliest account of the methods of growing and drinking tea. First, tea leaves were baked into a cake. The tea was prepared by dropping a shaving from the cake into a bowl or cup and pouring boiling water, to which salt had been added, over the tea.

TANG POETRY 700–800
Tang poetry became the model that Chinese poets tried to emulate, but could never surpass. Its two most famous practitioners were Li Bai (702–62), China's best-loved poet, and Du Fu (712–70), whose failure in the state examinations left him with a lasting disappointment.

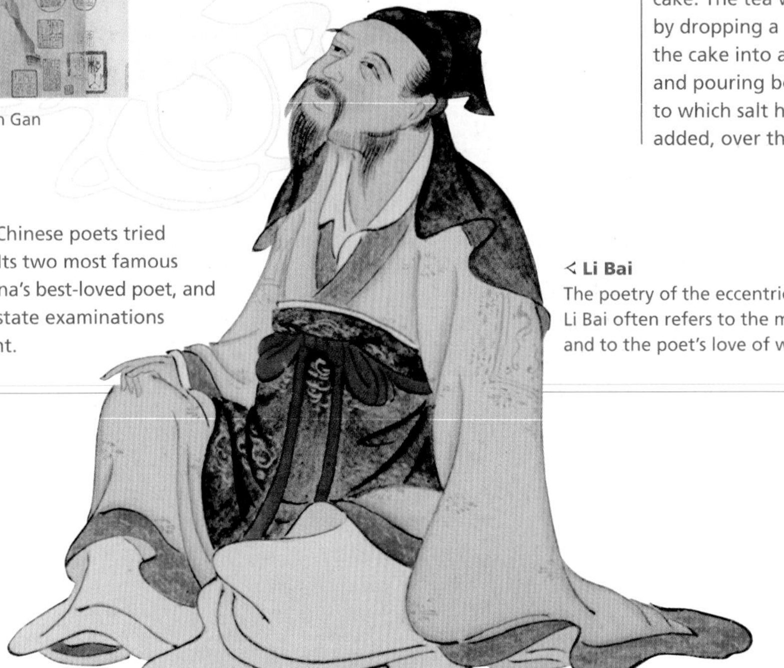

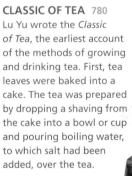

< Li Bai
The poetry of the eccentric Li Bai often refers to the moon and to the poet's love of wine.

Sharp as a diamond >
The *Diamond Sutra* is so named because it was held that "its teaching will cut like a diamond blade through worldly illusion."

The Forest of Stelae, Xi'an

THE NINE CLASSICS 837
The Nine Classics, the Confucian texts that included the *Book of Changes*, the *Book of History*, and the *Book of Odes*, were inscribed on a series of 114 stone tablets. These inscriptions can still be seen in the Forest of Stelae in Xi'an.

DUAN CHENGSHI 853
The earliest known version of the fairy tale *Cinderella* was written down by Duan Chengshi, most likely from a folk tale told by peasants.

DIAMOND SUTRA 868
The *Diamond Sutra*, the oldest example of a printed book, was found at Dunhuang at the end of the Silk Road. Printed in 868, it comprises seven strips of yellow-stained paper printed from carved wooden blocks and pasted together to form a scroll over 5m (16ft) long.

820   840   860   880   900
810   830   850   870   890

HAN YU 819
The Confucian scholar Han Yu, an opponent of Buddhism, protested against the emperor worshipping the supposed finger bone of Buddha. Han Yu's attack was typical of a growing campaign against Buddhism in China.

< Tea box
This gilded tea container illustrates how ritualized the drinking of tea had become during the Tang.

THE DISSOLUTION OF BUDDHIST MONASTERIES 845
Criticism of the wealth and influence of Buddhism reached its height when Emperor Wuzong ordered the surrender of monastic land. Statues were melted down for their copper, more than 4,600 monasteries and 40,000 temples and shrines were destroyed, and 250,000 monks and nuns were secularized.

DECLINE OF THE TANG 874
The Tang did little to assuage widespread famine and a new revolt broke out that lead to their fall. The Tang followed a typical dynastic cycle, where at first capable emperors led efficient governments and the economy prospered, but later weak emperors were dominated by self-serving courtiers and the economy collapsed. Rebels would finally overthrow the old order and create a new dynasty, and the cycle would begin again.

< Sacred mountain
Wutai Shan in Shanxi Province once boasted more than 350 Buddhist temples; only 47 remain.

宋朝

After the fall of the Tang, China experienced another period of disunity. The Qidan Liao dynasty ruled the northeast, while the south fragmented into ten kingdoms. The north experienced a succession of five dynasties until 960, when Zhao Kuangyin established the Song dynasty, which, at its height in the mid-11th century, ruled over much of China. In 1125, the Jurchen from eastern Manchuria defeated the Qidan Liao, who still held part of the northeast, and they then founded the Jin dynasty. The Jin expanded into northern China, and by 1127 had confined the Song to the south, where they survived as the Southern Song until 1279. Although a period of military weakness, the Song dynasty is also remembered as one of great artistic achievement.

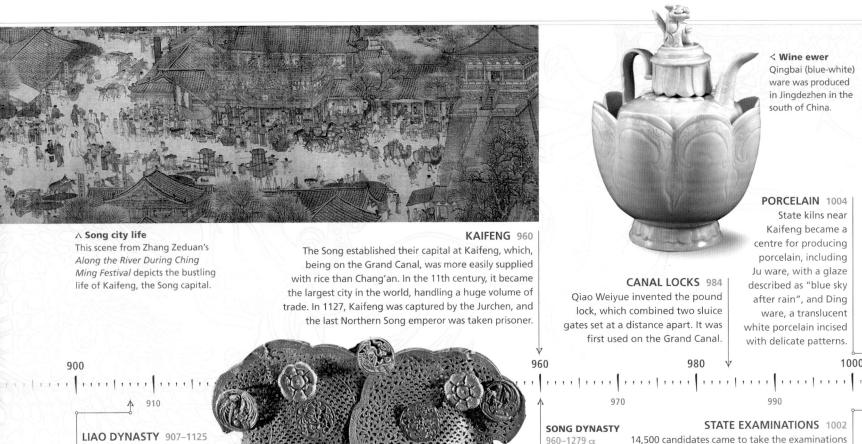

∧ Song city life
This scene from Zhang Zeduan's *Along the River During Ching Ming Festival* depicts the bustling life of Kaifeng, the Song capital.

< Wine ewer
Qingbai (blue-white) ware was produced in Jingdezhen in the south of China.

KAIFENG 960
The Song established their capital at Kaifeng, which, being on the Grand Canal, was more easily supplied with rice than Chang'an. In the 11th century, it became the largest city in the world, handling a huge volume of trade. In 1127, Kaifeng was captured by the Jurchen, and the last Northern Song emperor was taken prisoner.

CANAL LOCKS 984
Qiao Weiyue invented the pound lock, which combined two sluice gates set at a distance apart. It was first used on the Grand Canal.

PORCELAIN 1004
State kilns near Kaifeng became a centre for producing porcelain, including Ju ware, with a glaze described as "blue sky after rain", and Ding ware, a translucent white porcelain incised with delicate patterns.

900   910   960   970   980   990   1000

LIAO DYNASTY 907–1125
The Liao dynasty was established in 907 by Abaoji, an ambitious leader of the Qidan tribes of Mongolia, who established a Chinese-style capital at Liaoning. The Qidan Liao dynasty ruled part of north China until 1125, retaining their own customs in the north, but employing Chinese officials in the south.

SONG DYNASTY
960–1279 CE

STATE EXAMINATIONS 1002
14,500 candidates came to take the examinations in Kaifeng in this year; under the Song, the exam system first instituted by the Han became the most important method of choosing officials.

Gilded crown from the Liao dynasty

Scholar officials >
The number of officials selected for their success in the state examinations increased under the Song.

POWER MOVES SOUTH
THE SECOND PERIOD OF DIVISION AND THE SONG DYNASTY, 907–1279

< Divine flyers
A Northern Wei fresco
from Cave 327 at Dunhuang
depicts flying *apsaras* or
celestial nymphs.

< Divine flyers
A Northern Wei fresco
from Cave 327 at Dunhuang
depicts flying *apsaras* or
celestial nymphs.

Firecrackers >
Gunpowder was put
to civilian as well as
military use, such as
firecrackers to set off
on festive occasions.

GUNPOWDER 1044
A formula for gunpowder was first published
under the Song, 200 years before any such recipe
appeared in Europe. A 9th-century Daoist text
had referred to the ingredients of gunpowder,
but without specifying the exact formula.

POPULATION GROWTH 1020
China's population
reached an estimated
100 million, two-thirds
of whom lived in the
south of the country.

THE DUNHUANG CAVES c.1035
Between the 4th and 11th centuries BCE, Buddhist
monks excavated and painted the temple complex at
Dunhuang. Some time after 1002, the monks decided
to store surplus document scrolls and silk paintings in
a cave, formerly used as a chapel. The collection was
so large it filled the cave from floor to ceiling. In
1035, the entrance was sealed, and cave and contents
were forgotten until they were rediscovered in 1907.

WANG ANSHI 1068
Emperor Shenzong authorized
the scholar Wang Anshi to institute
reforms. He raised money for the
army by imposing a monopoly on tea,
challenged wealthy families who were
evading taxes, and provided interest-
free loans to debt-burdened peasants.

1020 **1040** **1060** **1080**

1010 1030 1050 1070 1090

PAPER MONEY 1024
Having noticed the
success of notes issued
by Sichuan merchants,
the government issued
its own paper currency,
which was subject to a
three percent service
charge and was valid
for three years.

Song merchant's
bill of exchange

MOVABLE TYPE 1045–58
The first printing system using movable type was
invented by Bi Sheng. Although printing with carved
wooden blocks was developed as early as the late
9th century, Bi Sheng's system allowed for repeated
use of the type models to make different books.

THE COMPASS 1044
The earliest floating compass
in the world comprised a dish
of water in which a magnetized
iron "fish" floated, which
indicated the direction of south.

WATER CLOCK 1090
Engineer Su Song's
astronomical clock was
a 12-m- (40-ft-) high
wooden tower topped
by a bronze sphere
that reproduced the
movements of the
sun, moon, and
stars. It was driven
by a 3.3m (11ft)
water wheel.

AGRICULTURAL GROWTH 1012
During the Southern Song period, agricultural
output was increased by the adoption of
new seed types, such as fast-ripening Champa
rice from Vietnam. Irrigation was extended
and labour-saving devices developed.

Model of Su Song's
astronomical clock

Deck of traditional
Chinese playing cards

song painting

The poet, artist, and statesman Su Dongpo (1036–1101) said that a scholar painting a landscape borrows the forms of mountains and trees to express his feelings. During the Song dynasty, painting, in particular landscape painting, reached new heights. Outstanding landscape painters from the period include Fan Kuan (active c.990–1020), Mi Fu (1051–1107), and Xia Gui (1195–1224).

Other styles of painting also flowered under the Song. Huizong, the last emperor of the Northern Song (reigning 1100–26), was proficient in the bird-and-flower style of painting. Under the Southern Song, Chan Buddhist painting flourished. Its most famous exponent was the artist Mu Qi (c.1200–70), who painted the famous *Six Persimmons*.

Detail of Xia Gui's *Streams and Mountains with a Clear Distant View*

PLAYING CARDS c.1120
The earliest reference to playing cards in the world appeared in China, though how the cards were marked and what games were played is not known.

THE END OF THE NORTHERN SONG 1126
From 1125, the Jurchen Jin, after conquering the Liao dynasty, turned their attention to the Song empire. The capital, Kaifeng, fell to the Jin in 1126, forcing the Song court to flee south, and bringing an end to the retrospectively named Northern Song.

1120   1140   1160   1180

1110   1130   1150   1170   1190

THE JURCHEN JIN DYNASTY 1115–1234
The Jurchen were a semi-nomadic people who had been subjugated by the Qidan Liao in the 10th century. In 1115, their leader, Aguda, rebelled and established the Jin dynasty. The Jin empire at its height encompassed north China, Manchuria, and Inner Mongolia. In Chinese areas, the Jin employed Chinese officials and adopted Chinese customs.

HANGZHOU 1135
In 1135, the Gaozong emperor abandoned northern China and fixed his capital at Hangzhou, at the end of the Grand Canal. Under the Southern Song, Hangzhou succeeded Kaifeng as the world's largest city. The hub of China's most important silk-producing region, its lively commerce encouraged the use of sophisticated commercial methods, including the adoption of paper money.

SEABORNE TRADE 1162
Under the Xiaozong emperor, maritime trade became an important part of the economy and tariffs contributed significantly to the imperial revenue. The earlier invention of the compass, and the development of large junks with four or six masts, made trade with distant countries possible.

View of West Lake in Hangzhou

∨ **Warrior king**
Genghis Khan's campaigns in
China led to the defeat of
the Jurchen Jin Empire.

genghis khan

The Mongols were pastoral nomads living in present-day
Mongolia. Temujin, the son of a Mongol tribal leader, was
born in about 1167. According to the Mongolian text *The
Secret History of the Mongols*, he claimed the leadership of
his tribe after his father had been poisoned. Temujin raised a
disciplined army, which he divided into groups of 1,000 men,
and devised new military tactics using accomplished warriors
on horseback. In 1206, he was given the title Genghis Khan,
universal sovereign of the steppe peoples. In 1210, he invaded
the Xi Xia kingdom (in modern-day Gansu), cutting China's trade
routes to the northwest, and in 1215 he captured the Jurchen
Jin capital. For the next decade Genghis turned his attention
westwards, fixing his attention on Central Asia. He returned in
1226 to destroy the Xi Xia kingdom, but died the following year.

THE SIEGE OF KAIFENG 1232–33
The Mongols, under the command of Genghis's son,
Ogedai, laid siege to Kaifeng in their campaign to
destroy the Jurchen Jin empire. The Jin employed the
latest technology – gunpowder rockets and proto-
flamethrowers known as "firelances" – in defense of
the city, but to no avail; Kaifeng fell the following year.

Chinese firelance

GUO SHOUJING 1276
Guo Shoujing (1231–1316), an outstanding
scientist, persuaded Khubilai Khan that the
calendar should be revised. He went on to
design astronomical instruments and set up
observation stations for that purpose. His
final figure for the length of a year was only
26 seconds away from the modern calculation.

Guo Shoujing's observatory at Dengfeng

| 1200 | 1210 | 1220 | 1230 | 1240 | 1250 | 1260 | 1270 | 1280 |

NEO-CONFUCIANISM 1200
The various strands of Confucian thought
were synthesized by the philosopher Zhu Xi
(1130–1200), who also emphasized the Dao,
the "Way" that individuals
should follow through self-
cultivation and by studying
the Confucian classics. Zhu
Xi's philosophy evolved into
an obligation of obedience
of subject to ruler, child to
parent, wife to husband, and
younger to elder brother.

The Neo-Confucian
philosopher Zhu Xi

song women

Some historians have suggested that under the Song, women's freedom in society deteriorated,
and point to the spread of foot-binding, the condemnation of the remarriage of widows, and
the curtailment of women's property rights to illustrate their position. However, foot-binding
was originally associated with dancers and concubines, and this practice may have been
adopted by women to promote their attractiveness. Also, Song law permitted the remarriage
of widows, but by so doing the woman renounced her loyalty to the family into which she had
been incorporated, so there was a strong prejudice against it. Song law gave daughters a share
of property half the size of a son's share. However, this contradicted the
Neo-Confucian ideal of succession by a son for ritual and property
purposes, and was also against Mongol law. This led to a
curtailment in women's rights after the Southern Song
dynasty fell to the Mongols in 1279.

Song ladies preparing silk >
Though Song women had more rights
than in some later dynasties, they still
had very little power outside of the
traditional roles laid out for them.

In 1260, Möngke, the Great Khan of the Mongols, appointed
元
朝
his brother, Khubilai, to govern north China. In 1268, Khubilai attacked the Southern Song, finally defeating them in 1279 and establishing the rule of the Mongol (or Yuan) dynasty over all China. An invasion of Japan in 1281 was frustrated by a typhoon (or *kamikaze*) and thereafter, until his death in 1294, Khubilai concentrated on ruling China. His grandson, Temür, who reigned until 1307, continued many of the benign aspects of Khubilai's rule, but his successor, Khaishan, ruled in a more arbitrary manner. Tugh Temür, who reigned from 1329, was a patron of Buddhism. Yuan rule was weakened by the early reign of Toghon Temür, and in 1368 the court fled to Manchuria.

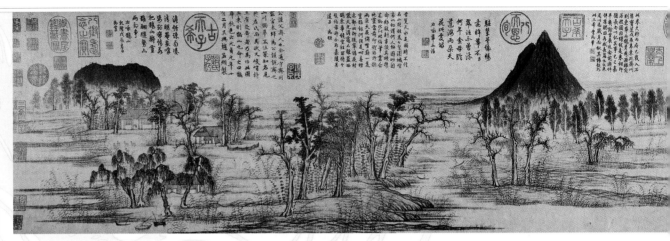

MONGOL LAW 1279
Khubilai divided the population into four groups: on top were the Mongols, below them came the *semu ren*, or other Central Asians, then the inhabitants of north China, and finally Chinese from the newly conquered south. Mongols and foreigners were tried according to the *jasagh*, a set of legal rules promulgated by Genghis Khan, while the Chinese were tried according to their own law.

Handscroll *The Autumn Colours on the Qiao and Hua Mountains* by Zhao Mengfu

ZHAO MENGFU 1322
The scholar and painter Zhao Mengfu became court artist to the Yuan dynasty. He was renowned for his skill in painting horses, but his fame rests on his revitalization of landscape painting.

CHINESE EXCLUSION 1328–40
Bayan, Toghon Temür's chief minister, forbade Chinese to hold government office, one of a series of anti-Chinese measures intended to defend Mongol cultural identity.

YUAN DYNASTY
1279–94 CE

1280   1300   1320   1340

1290   1310   1330

MISSIONARIES 1295
The stability that the Mongols brought allowed European missionaries to travel to China, including the Italian Franciscan monk John of Montecorvino.

< **A mission leaves**
A 14th-century miniature shows the Pope blessing a group of missionaries on their way to China.

< **Pottery player**
The importance of drama under the Yuan is shown by the number of figurines of actors that survive.

THE PLAGUE 1337
A severe outbreak of bubonic plague occurred in several Chinese districts, killing millions. It took ten years for the disease – known as the Black Death – to spread to Western Europe.

Deadly symptom >
A Chinese medical document displays the tell-tale black tongue of plague sufferers.

YUAN DRAMA 1279
Drama as a literary form appeared in the late 13th century. Plays known as "Yuan northern dramas" were written for performance in Beijing. Many playwrights of the Yuan dynasty were educated southern Chinese who had been excluded from a role in government service.

IBN BATTUTA 1340
A North African Arab, the scholar Ibn Battuta travelled the length of the known Islamic world, from West Africa through India to China. He noted that fine porcelain cost less in China than common pottery in Arabia.

CHINA UNDER MONGOL RULE
THE YUAN DYNASTY, 1279–1368

Matters of state >
Khubilai Khan consults with his advisers and scribes in a Persian artist's rendering of the Mongol court.

MONGOLS IN DECLINE 1356

Explanations of the fall of the Yuan dynasty emphasize Chinese hatred of the Mongols, their failure to temper their rule to meet Chinese expectations, and the decline of their military power. The dynasty might have survived for longer but for a series of disasters, beginning in the 1350s with the flooding of the Huang He (Yellow River) and the conscription of thousands of labourers needed to reopen the Grand Canal. Rebellion broke out, and in 1368 the court was forced to flee to Manchuria.

khubilai khan

In 1260, Khubilai, Genghis Khan's grandson, was elected Great Khan. He laid out a Chinese-style capital at Kaiping in Inner Mongolia. Later renamed Shangdu, or "upper capital", it would become known to the West as Xanadu. In 1268, Khubilai invaded southern China, and after a five-year siege he captured the strategically important city of Xiangyang. In 1275, a large Southern Song army was defeated and further Song resistance to the Mongols collapsed.

Khubilai adopted Da Yuan, or "Great Origin", as the name of his dynasty. He retained many features of Song government, but did not restore the imperial examination system, so that native Chinese were unable to advance in the administration. The Chinese and Mongols were subject to separate legal systems, the punishments for the latter being particularly severe. A Mongol convicted of a crime was tattooed as well as receiving any other punishment prescribed by the *jasagh*, the Mongol legal code.

foreign influences and later years

To counterbalance Chinese influence, Khubilai employed foreigners in key positions. The Venetian merchant Marco Polo, who originally travelled with his father to China, spent 17 years with the Yuan court. He was sent by Khubilai on a variety of diplomatic missions, including to Burma, and

1350

Yuan dynasty porcelain vases

BLUE AND WHITE PORCELAIN 1350

In the early 14th century, the painting of porcelain using cobalt under the glaze, giving a striking blue colour, was developed at Jingdezhen in south China. The temple vase (*above right*) decorated with a four-clawed dragon is an outstanding example of the type.

Venetian Tatar >
Marco Polo in the traditional dress of the Tatars, a sub-group within the Mongol empire.

was employed for three years as a tax inspector for the city of Hangzhou. His *Travels*, composed after his return, gave a detailed account of Khubilai's court, of Cathay (north China), and of Hangzhou, which he called Quinsai. Khubilai also employed Muslims to carry out specialized tasks in the fields of finance, medicine, astronomy, and architecture. The most notorious of these Central Asians was Ahmad, who imposed a much-resented salt monopoly on southern China and for two decades directed the Great Khan's financial administration.

After successful expeditions to Yunnan and Korea, in 1281 Khubilai tried to invade Japan, but a *kamikaze*, or "divine wind", destroyed his fleet. The failure of his later military ventures – including an attempt to conquer Korea – caused great financial difficulties and led to severe inflation. The deaths of his favourite wife and his son, Zhenjin, cast a shadow over his final years. When Khubilai died in 1294, a succession dispute broke out, which was ended with the accession of Khubilai's grandson Temür.

Zhu Yuanzhang ascended the throne in January 1368, shortly before the Mongol court fled China. He named his new dynasty Ming – brightness – and took the title Hongwu. He ruled until 1398, by which time he had firmly established what became the most durable dynasty in Chinese history. His fourth son, the Yongle emperor, became famous for dispatching a series of overseas naval expeditions. After Yongle's death in 1424, the dynasty began a slow decline, which culminated in its collapse in 1644 in the face of peasant rebellion and Manchu invasion. The Ming period was one of the finest epochs in Chinese cultural history, in which great scholarly works were compiled, new literary genres flourished, and innovative styles of calligraphy and painting emerged.

明
朝

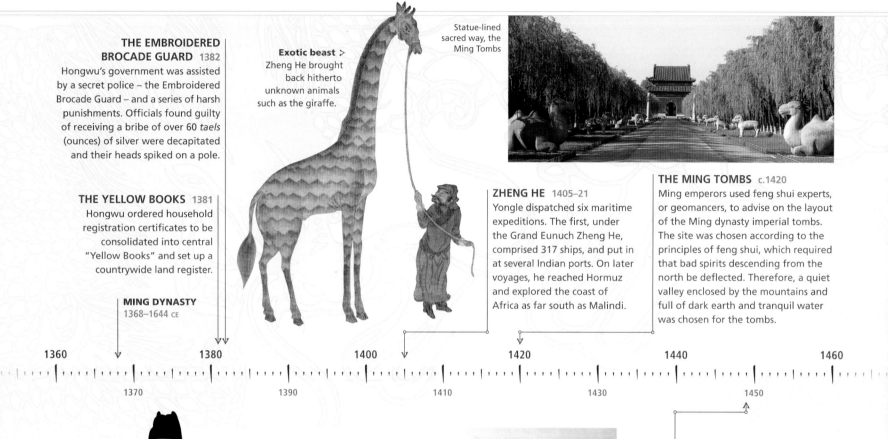

THE EMBROIDERED BROCADE GUARD 1382
Hongwu's government was assisted by a secret police – the Embroidered Brocade Guard – and a series of harsh punishments. Officials found guilty of receiving a bribe of over 60 *taels* (ounces) of silver were decapitated and their heads spiked on a pole.

Exotic beast ▷
Zheng He brought back hitherto unknown animals such as the giraffe.

Statue-lined sacred way, the Ming Tombs

THE YELLOW BOOKS 1381
Hongwu ordered household registration certificates to be consolidated into central "Yellow Books" and set up a countrywide land register.

MING DYNASTY
1368–1644 CE

ZHENG HE 1405–21
Yongle dispatched six maritime expeditions. The first, under the Grand Eunuch Zheng He, comprised 317 ships, and put in at several Indian ports. On later voyages, he reached Hormuz and explored the coast of Africa as far south as Malindi.

THE MING TOMBS c.1420
Ming emperors used feng shui experts, or geomancers, to advise on the layout of the Ming dynasty imperial tombs. The site was chosen according to the principles of feng shui, which required that bad spirits descending from the north be deflected. Therefore, a quiet valley enclosed by the mountains and full of dark earth and tranquil water was chosen for the tombs.

1360   1380   1400   1420   1440   1460
1370   1390   1410   1430   1450

hongwu, the peasant emperor

Zhu Yuanzhang was born in 1328, during the Mongol dynasty's decline. After his parents died in a famine, Zhu joined the Red Turban rebels. He built up a personal army, captured Nanjing, and in 1368 founded the Ming dynasty as Hongwu. His central government, which retained many Mongol features, consisted of a Secretariat headed by two chancellors, a Bureau of Military Affairs, and a Censorate (which supervised the work of imperial officials). Branch secretariats administered the provinces. The system worked well until 1380, when Hongwu accused his chancellor, Hu Weiyong, of conspiracy and had him and 30,000 of his supporters put to death. Hongwu then became his own chancellor.

Under Hongwu, the examination system was revived and a quota system that reserved a proportion of passes to particular groups was introduced. Only 871 *jinshi*, or "presented scholars", were appointed in his reign to a bureaucracy numbering 15,000 officials.

The emperor Hongwu

THE TUMU INCIDENT 1449
Esen, the leader of the Oirat Mongols, launched a massive invasion of China in this year and defeated a Ming force near Datong. Zhengtong, the 22-year-old emperor, led a counterattack, encouraged by the influential eunuch Wang Zhen. The emperor's forces were ambushed at Tumu and Zhengtong was captured. Although the Oirat failed to go on to capture Beijing, the incident brought to an end the expansionist tendencies of the Ming dynasty.

EARLY MODERN CHINA
THE MING DYNASTY, 1368–1644

< **Bulwark against nomads**
The 11km (6¾ mile) section of
the Great Wall at Jinlanshing
has 100 defensive towers.

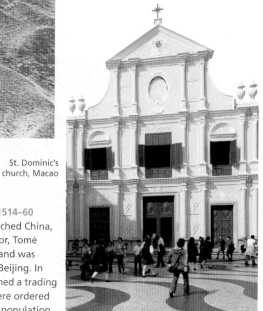

St. Dominic's
church, Macao

THE GREAT WALL 1474

After the Tumu incident, the Ming, lacking the resources
to control the steppe edges where nomadic incursions
originated, adopted a defensive strategy. They began the
construction of a Great Wall to contain the Mongol threat,
starting in the Ordos region, where the danger was gravest.

WANG YANGMING 1506

The Neo-Confucian philosopher who held that the mind
shapes the world, rather than vice versa, was influential
at court until banished for offending a eunuch.

THE PORTUGUESE IN CHINA 1514–60

In 1517, three years after they reached China,
the Portuguese sent an ambassador, Tomé
Pires, who arrived at Guangzhou and was
eventually permitted to travel to Beijing. In
the 1550s, the Portuguese established a trading
station at Aomen (Macao), but were ordered
to remain apart from the Chinese population.

1480   1490   1500   1510   1520   1530   1540   1550   1560

THE LITERATI 1487

The "Eight-Legged Essay", an extremely
restrictive form of writing, was made
a mandatory part of the civil service
examinations. The literati, or gentry,
who achieved success in this system
were a remarkable example of
upward social mobility. However,
their rise also came from the
careful acquisition of land, and
this, and the selection process,
favoured conservative thinking.

THE SUZHOU GARDEN 1513

The Humble Administrator's Garden in Suzhou
was originally a monastery garden, which Wang
Xianchen, an administrator under Zhengde, took
over. Working with the artist Wen Zhengming,
he had elaborate gardens constructed, creating
artificial islands and ornate bridges and pavilions.
The Suzhou Garden – much remodelled – is
viewed as one of the four great Chinese gardens.

JAPANESE PIRATES
1550s

In the 16th century,
restrictions on foreign
trade helped promote
the appearance of
Japanese *wokou*
(pirates), who in the
1550s established
bases on the coast of
Zhejiang. The Chinese
tried to drive off the
raiders, but peace was
only restored when
the ban on foreign
trade was lifted.

< **Bureaucrats**
A military and a
civil official, twin
aspects of the Ming
administration.

View of the
Suzhou Garden

< **A timeless city**
The Forbidden City has changed
little in the 400 years since this
painting on silk was made.

beijing and the forbidden city

In 1406, the Ming emperor, Yongle, decided to transfer his capital from Nanjing to Beijing, near the former Yuan capital of Dadu, from where he could exercise tighter military control over the north of the country. The need to secure adequate food supplies for Beijing's population meant restoring and extending the Grand Canal, a project that took until 1415. In addition, vast quantities of lumber and bricks and the deployment of thousands of labourers and artisans were needed for the new city's construction. By 1417, the major buildings of the palace complex had been completed and Yongle took up residence in the new capital city.

a city within a city

The layout of Beijing, like that of previous Chinese capitals, was designed to reflect the pattern of the cosmos. The outside walls – which were 12m (40ft) high and 22.5km (14 miles) long – faced the four cardinal positions of the compass. Within the walls' nine gates stood the imperial city, and within the city lay the imperial palace, the Forbidden City – so named because nobody could enter or leave without the emperor's permission. This, the largest palace complex in the world,

was said to have 9,999 rooms. The glazed tiles of its roofs were yellow, the imperial colour. At the very centre of the palace, the enthroned emperor played the role of intermediary between Heaven and earth.

inside the forbidden city

Beyond the southern Meridian gate, the Outer Court includes the Hall of Supreme Harmony, where the emperor sat on the Dragon Throne on formal occasions, and the Hall of Preserving Harmony, used for banquets. In the Inner Court lay the residence of the imperial family, the concubines, and the eunuchs. Among its buildings are the Palace of Heavenly Purity, which served as an audience hall, and the Hall of Mental Cultivation, the primary place for the emperor to transact official business. Behind the Inner Court lay the Western Palaces and Imperial Gardens.

In 1949, almost 40 years after the fall of the last Chinese dynasty, the fleeing Nationalist government removed most of the city's treasures to Taiwan. The Forbidden City, once the most private dwelling in China, is now open to the public as a museum.

Dragon Throne >
The Dragon Throne was the
seat of imperial power in
China for more than 500 years.

Passing without proper authorization through the gates of the Forbidden City incurs a hundred blows of the bamboo … Death by strangulation is the punishment due to any stranger found in any of the emperor's apartments.

R. K. Douglas, *Society in China* (1901)

∧ **Roofs of the Forbidden City**
Only imperial buildings were allowed to use yellow tiles for their roofs; lesser buildings had to use tiles of green or red.

government by eunuchs

Eunuchs – castrated servants – were the only adult males apart from the emperor who were allowed to enter the imperial harem, and as such they had exceptional access to the throne. During the Ming dynasty, the palace eunuchs were put in charge of imperial finances, and also had the power to dismiss officials or to draft imperial decrees. As under previous dynasties, many eunuchs frequently conspired with the imperial concubines to govern corruptly or embezzle government revenues. The Hongwu emperor sought to curb their power, and in 1384 decreed that any eunuch interfering in government affairs would be executed. The policy, however, was short-lived, and in 1420 Yongle appointed eunuchs to head the Eastern Depot, the headquarters of the secret police. Liu Jin, a eunuch in the reign of Zhengde, was so unpopular that, after his execution, his body was dismembered and eaten raw by his enemies. The later Ming emperors also failed to temper the influence of eunuchs such as Wei Zhongxian, who claimed to be second in rank only to the emperor.

< Mighty eunuch
Wei Zhongxian colluded with Emperor Tianqi's wet-nurse to seize power, but the plan failed.

MANCHU SINICIZATION 1631
Nurhaci's son, Abahai, introduced Chinese-style institutions among the Jurchen tribes, and in 1635 he changed the name of his people to Manchu, adopting the dynastic name Qing, which means "clear".

THE MANCHU STATE 1589
The Ming emperor granted a title to Nurhaci (1559–1626), the unifier of the Jurchen tribes (from whom the Manchu descended). Nurhaci organized his people into banners (named for the patterned flag borne by each group), which formed the destructive cavalry forces of the Manchus. Nurhaci employed Chinese officials, and in 1616 founded the Latter Jin dynasty in Manchuria.

URBANIZATION AND INDUSTRY 1621
In the Ming period, towns and industries flourished. Jingdezhen, the porcelain centre in Jiangxi, had a population of over a million, as did the silk-producing city of Hangzhou. The Jesuit Alvaro Semedo estimated that 200,000 looms were in operation in and around Shanghai.

FALL OF THE MING 1644
Rebel forces under Li Zicheng entered Beijing after a long campaign, and the Ming emperor hanged himself. Li was in turn ousted by invading Manchus, who inaugurated the Qing dynasty in China.

1570   ↓1590   1610   1630↓   1650

MATTEO RICCI 1598
After arriving in Beijing, Jesuit Matteo Ricci used his knowledge of the Chinese classics to obtain acceptance at court, but only after three years was he allowed to enter the Forbidden City. Ricci produced a map of the world and compiled a catechism in Chinese.

The Jesuit missionary Matteo Ricci

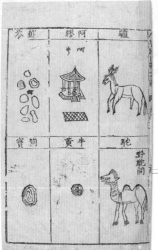

COURTESAN CULTURE 1643
Although Confucianism praised the virtue of female chastity, courtesans – high-class prostitutes or mistresses – thrived in the late Ming period. Plays depicted romances between talented scholars and devoted courtesans. The most famous courtesan, Liu Rushi, became the concubine of the artist Qian Qianyi. Together, the pair composed poems and compiled books.

BOOK PUBLISHING c.1600
Three famous novels appeared under the Ming: *Romance of the Three Kingdoms*, *Journey to the West*, and *Water Margin*. Major compilations also appeared, including the *Bencao Gangmu*, a medical encyclopedia.

< Medical compendium
Pages from the *Bencao Gangmu* illustrate the medical qualities of snakes, camels, and donkeys.

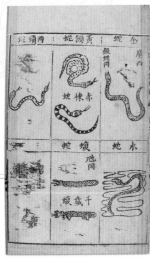

Terracotta courtesans >
Dressed in fine robes, these courtesans are shown delicately poised, bearing a plate and box.

∨ **Silk workers**
The international silk trade, which had
been in operation since the Han dynasty,
reached new heights under the Ming.

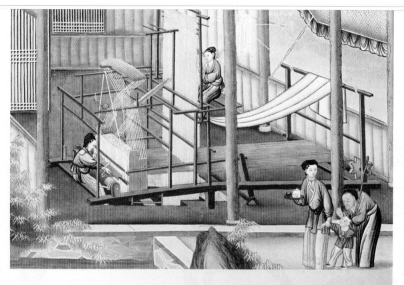

trade in silk and porcelain

The discovery by Portuguese explorers in the 15th century of sea routes around the Cape of Good Hope in South Africa initiated an era of direct European involvement in the East Asian maritime trade. The Ming court had, by the late 15th century, pulled back from its earlier policy of sending out naval expeditions to South Asia and Africa and instead turned inwards, mistrustful of foreign merchants, who were regarded at best as a nuisance, and at worst as pirates. From 1525, maritime trade was actually banned by imperial decree. But this did little to stifle demand for Chinese products, such as silk and ceramics, and the decrees were ignored by foreign merchants who continued a thriving black-market trade.

european traders

Trade in East Asia was given a further boost by the Spanish conquest of the Philippines in 1565, and the galleon trade that began soon after between Manila and Acapulco in Mexico. Spanish ships transported high-value Chinese commodities, such as silk, lacquer, and porcelain, in exchange for Spanish silver. There was also an insatiable demand in Europe for Ming blue and white porcelain, which came to be known as Kraak ware (from a corruption of "carrack", the type of Portuguese vessel used for the carrying trade). The demand for goods from China – and for the spices that could be sourced in the Indonesian archipelago – led to the foundation of trading companies such as the Dutch East India Company, which in 1624 established a base at Zeelandia on Taiwan. The Dutch began largely to supplant the Portuguese, who came to be confined largely to their outpost at Macao, which they had held since 1557. Their capture in 1602 and 1604 of two Portuguese carracks carrying more than 200,000 pieces of porcelain helped fuel the craze in Europe for Chinese ware, which in the English language came to be known simply as "china".

Much of the Kraak ware was produced at the potteries of Jingdezhen. In the late Ming period, factories there began to produce ceramics made for the export market, such as bowls carrying Latin inscriptions and flasks with European crests, which anticipated the porcelain ware bearing European family coats of arms that would be made in large quantities under the Qing.

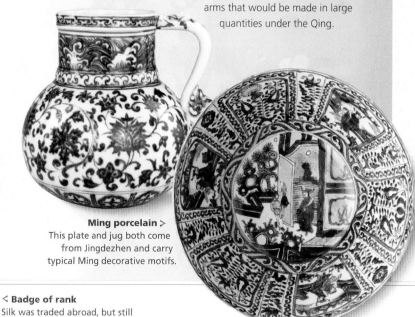

Ming porcelain ⊳
This plate and jug both come
from Jingdezhen and carry
typical Ming decorative motifs.

⊲ **Badge of rank**
Silk was traded abroad, but still
had uses at home; this "mandarin
square" would have been sewn
onto an official's clothing.

The Qing created a successful form of Sino-Manchu rule in

清
朝
which former Ming officials retained their posts alongside Manchu appointees. Yet Manchus held the top jobs, and their military posts were established across the country. Manchu women wore their hair in a distinctive style, did not bind their feet, and were not permitted to marry Han Chinese. Under a

sequence of three able emperors, Kangxi (1662–1722), Yongzheng (1723–35), and Qianlong (1736–95), the Chinese Empire reached its greatest extent, incorporating Taiwan and Xinjiang. Under the Qianlong emperor, who wrote poetry and commissioned scholarly enterprises, literature reached new levels of sophistication.

The Kangxi emperor enthroned

THE REVOLT OF THE THREE FEUDATORIES
1673

The Three Feudatories were lands held by three Chinese collaborators who had helped the Manchus gain power. These generals were rewarded with semi-independent fiefdoms in south China. In 1673, under threat of dismissal, they rebelled. After the leading rebel, Wu Sangui of Yunnan, died in 1678, the insurrection collapsed.

QING DYNASTY
1644–1911

the kangxi emperor

Kangxi was a minor when he came to the throne in 1660, and for seven years power was exercised in his name by a regency. As an adult, Kangxi ruled in the manner of a Chinese emperor, and this led to the acceptance during his reign of the Manchu as a legitimate Chinese dynasty. He worked conscientiously, reading up to 50 official documents a day. He visited Confucius's birthplace and made the appropriate sacrifices there, and he went on extended tours of the country, listening to people's complaints. In general, his government followed the practices of the Ming, but he reformed the imperial household and established a system of confidential communication with provincial informants.

A Manchu emperor was expected to acquire military skills and to wage war. Kangxi defeated a major rebellion in the 1670s, and in the 1690s led several campaigns against the Mongol Zunghars, which broke their dominance in Central Asia. Kangxi's last years were marred by worries over the succession. His heir was judged insane, and Kangxi refused to name a replacement. As a consequence, Yongzheng, the next emperor, is believed to have usurped the throne.

| 1640 | 1660 | 1680 | 1700 | 1720 |

1650 · 1670 · 1690 · 1710

the queue

In 1645, a decree ordered all male Chinese to show that they had submitted to the Manchus by adopting the Manchu hairstyle, which involved shaving the forehead and braiding the remaining hair into a long braid, or queue. The consequence of failing to comply was summed up in the saying "lose your hair or lose your head."

As the Manchus advanced south, most provincial towns complied with their demands, such as handing over the tax registers. However, the imposition of the Manchu hairstyle caused immediate resentment. When news of the decree reached Jiangyin, about 160km (100 miles) upriver from Shanghai, a resistance movement formed in which elite and popular elements came together in a transitory alliance. The Manchus besieged the city, which held out for 87 days. Using cannons, they breached the walls and then massacred the inhabitants.

19th-century barber trimming a queue

THE JESUITS 1692
Encouraged by the willingness of the Jesuits to compromise with the Chinese practice of ancestor worship and other local rites, Kangxi issued an edict permitting the teaching of Christianity.

TAIWAN 1683
Ming loyalists, originally led by Koxinga, captured the Dutch fort of Zeelandia on Taiwan in 1661, and used it as a base to oppose the Qing until a Manchu force occupied the island 22 years later.

CASTIGLIONE 1715
The Milanese missionary and artist Giuseppe Castiglione became a popular painter at the Qing court. He combined Chinese techniques with Western naturalism and perspective, and was also architect of the emperor's first Summer Palace.

The Summer Palace, outside Beijing

THE THREE EMPERORS
THE EARLY QING DYNASTY, 1644–1800

< Tibetan palace
The main residence of the Dalai Lama until the flight to India in 1959 of the 14th Dalai Lama, the Potala palace was first begun in the 1650s.

tibet becomes a chinese protectorate

Tibet had suffered political fragmentation after the 9th century, and was conquered by the Mongol empire, thereafter falling into the Ming sphere of influence. In 1642, when the Ming dynasty was on the point of collapse, the Dalai Lama (the spiritual leader of Tibetan Buddhism) obtained Chinese recognition of Tibetan independence. In 1717, the Zunghar, a confederation of Mongol tribes, occupied Tibet, and favoured the Dalai Lama's rivals for power. In 1720, the Qing court sent a military force to escort the Dalai Lama back to Lhasa, and it appointed a Chinese Resident as his adviser. In 1750, Zunghar opposition to Chinese influence led to a civil war. Qianlong used the opportunity to install the Dalai Lama as the temporal ruler of a state enjoying internal autonomy, while at the same time declaring Tibet to be a protectorate of China.

Qing teapot with coat-of-arms and peony pattern

SUPPRESSION OF ETHNIC MINORITIES 1726
The Miao (Hmong) and other minorities in southwest China were ruled by their own hereditary leaders, who held official ranks. Finding this system incompatible with the principle of universal and absolute rule, Yongzheng abolished the Miao leadership and began a process of enforced sinicization.

QIANLONG'S GOLDEN AGE
1736–95
Under Qianlong, China's boundaries reached their farthest extent, the economy expanded, the population increased, and, for much of his reign, the country was at peace.

BRITISH EAST INDIA COMPANY 1784
In Britain, the government cut duties on tea, leading to a huge rise in demand. Private British merchants began to export Indian cotton and opium to China. Their activities undermined the commercial dominance of the East India Company, which controlled English trade with India, and which held a post in Canton. In 1834, the British East India Company's monopoly ended and the British government assumed responsibility for trade with China.

1740   **1760**   **1780**   **1800**

1730   1750   1770   1790

The Hongs (International Factories) at Guangzhou

POPULATION GROWTH 1762
Government estimates put the population of China at more than 300 million.

WOMEN POETS 1775
In the 18th century, women's writing developed new styles, notably the poetry known as "plucking rhymes", and narrative forms in which women expressed their frustrations and aspirations. Among the poets was the talented writer and artist Liu Qilan.

BEIJING OPERA 1790
To celebrate his 80th birthday, the Qianlong emperor summoned opera troupes from all parts of the country to perform before him. The singing styles of those who attended in time blended to form the new genre known as Beijing opera.

THE GUANGZHOU SYSTEM 1760
The Qing court, suspicious of foreign contacts, confined maritime trade to Guangzhou. The only Chinese permitted to take part were a group known as the Cohong, who were held responsible for the debts of foreign traders, who in turn were allowed to stay in the port only during the trading season.

< Opera scene
Tsao, the main villain in Beijing operas set during the Three Kingdoms, escapes his enemies.

111

By the late 18th century, the Qing empire was in decline,

清
朝
undermined by the corrupt rule of the Qianglong emperor's favourite official, Heshen, and by an epidemic of opium addiction. The attempt to suppress the illegal opium trade triggered the First Opium War (1839–42) against the British, a conflict that the Qing lost, further undermining their prestige. The Taiping rebellion from 1850 sparked a new cycle of popular disturbances that further destabilized the power base of the Manchu regime. Increased cooperation with the Western powers staved off the collapse of the Qing dynasty for a period, but its slow decline continued with China's defeat by the French in Vietnam.

Widow arch,
Anhui Province

POPULATION GROWTH c.1800
By the end of the 18th century, China's population had doubled to approximately 300 million.

TEA EXPORTS c.1800
The demand for Chinese tea in Europe exploded during the 18th century – by the beginning of the 19th century, the British were importing 13.5 million kg (30 million lb) of tea a year.

THE TREATY OF NANJING 1842
The agreement that finally ended the First Opium War became the first of the "unequal treaties" that conferred benefits on Western powers without any advantages for China. It provided for the opening of five ports to British trade, the cession of Xianggang (Hong Kong) to Britain, the abolition of the Cohong (the Chinese merchant monopoly), and consent to a fixed trading tariff.

WIDOW ARCHES 1827
Traditionally, Chinese widows who did not remarry could have their chastity honoured by the building of an arch. The fashion for constructing these arches became so widespread during the Qing dynasty that in 1827 the government restricted the practice.

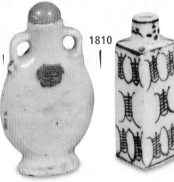

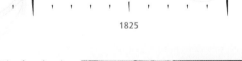

1800   1810   1820   1830   1840

1815   1825   1835

Opium bottles
sealed with wax

Trio of smokers in a
late-19th-century
opium den

the opium trade and the first opium war

In the 18th century, the practice of smoking opium, a highly addictive narcotic derived from the poppy, became widespread in China. The drug was grown by the British in India, and the British East India Company licensed private merchants to ship it to China, where it was sold in exchange for tea. Alarmed by rising levels of addiction, the Chinese government attempted to stem the flow. In 1838, Lin Zexu was sent to Guangzhou to suppress the opium trade. Foreign traders were forced to surrender their opium and cease trading in it on pain of death. The British dispatched an expeditionary force with instructions to force the Chinese to compensate British traders for their opium, thus beginning the First Opium War (1839–42). Having blockaded Guangzhou, the British moved north. Only after the British capture of Shanghai in mid-1842 did the emperor authorize the negotiation of the Treaty of Nanjing, in effect a humiliating capitulation.

CHINA IN CRISIS
THE MID QING DYNASTY, 1800–80

the empress dowager

In 1861, the Xianfeng emperor died, and the six-year-old Tongzhi emperor ascended the throne. His mother, the concubine Yehonola, assumed the title of Empress Dowager Cixi and took charge as regent. Cixi's dominance over the Qing court was so strong that she retained control even after Tongzhi's death in 1874, and in all she held on to power for nearly five decades until her death in 1908.

The empress dowager has been portrayed as an unprincipled person; she stands accused of having murdered her daughter-in-law, and misappropriating naval funds to reconstruct the Summer Palace. Cixi's policies focused on retaining her personal power and on keeping China closed to the outside world. Finally forced to acknowledge the precariousness of the Qing's rule, in the early 19th century she endorsed a reform program, hoping thereby to save the dynasty, but by then it was already too late.

The Empress Dowager Cixi

Manufacturing >
Porcelain-making was one of China's longest-established native industries.

INDUSTRIAL GROWTH 1872
The leading statesman Li Hongzheng proposed that China's programme of "self-strengthening" should include industrial ventures, and in the late 19th century, both new and old industries were modernized.

THE ARROW WAR 1856–60
The boarding of the British-flagged ship *Arrow* by Qing customs officials sparked the Second Opium War, in which the French fought alongside the British. The Treaty of Tianjin, which ended the war, opened up the Yangzi to foreign trade.

THE TIANJIN MASSACRE 1870
Chinese gentry fearful of the spread of Christianity supported accusations of abuse by foreign missionaries of Chinese children in their care. A French Catholic orphanage in Tianjin was attacked and 19 foreigners killed.

RUSSIAN ADVANCES 1871–81
Under cover of a Muslim uprising, Russia moved in to occupy the Ili Valley in Chinese Turkestan for a period of ten years. The region occupied was later to become the autonomous region of Xinjiang.

1850   1860   1870   1880

1845   1855   1865   1875

THE TAIPING REBELLION 1850
Hong Xiuquan, the child of a Hakka farmer, believed he was God's Chinese son. In 1850, Hong declared the establishment of the Taiping Tianguo, the Heavenly Kingdom of Great Peace, and raised a rebellion. In March 1853, the Taipings captured Nanjing. They prohibited the use of opium and relations between the sexes. In 1862, the Taipings nearly captured Shanghai, putting the Qing regime in mortal danger, but they were driven back by forces raised by gentry leaders. In July 1864, Nanjing was retaken and Hong Xiuquan committed suicide.

Coastal battle >
French forces seize a strategic fort at Hué during the conflict with China over Vietnam.

WESTERNIZATION 1860
In 1842, the scholar Wei Yuan recommended "building ships, making weapons, and learning the superior techniques of the barbarians." In 1860, Feng Guifen called for the adoption of Western knowledge and the manufacture of Western weapons. The program was called "self-strengthening".

THE SINO–FRENCH WAR 1882–85
From 1862, France began to encroach on Vietnam, challenging Chinese influence in the area. In 1882, the French seized Hanoi, leading to a direct confrontation with China, and during the conflict France destroyed the Fuzhou shipyard. The Treaty of Tianjin of 1885 recognized a French protectorate over Vietnam.

< Defeat of the Taipings
Imperial forces were assisted by a foreign-raised "Ever Victorious Army" in their campaigns against the rebels.

‹ San Francisco fashion
In the early years of the 20th century, the men of San Francisco's Chinatown wore clothes that were a mixture of Eastern and Western styles.

Chinatown, New York ›
The Chinese quarter of New York sits amid the towering skyscrapers of Manhattan.

the chinese diaspora

China has a long history of migration, with Chinese communities forming at trading posts throughout East Asia wherever Chinese merchants settled. However, the great Chinese Diaspora began in the 19th century. The two Opium Wars with Britain (1839–42 and 1856–60) severely weakened the Qing dynasty, and in their wake a combination of overpopulation, famines, and social and economic strife forced many Chinese to seek a better life abroad.

migrant workers

With the abolition of slavery in the West, Chinese migrants found that their labour and skills were in high demand. Some settled in the colonial territories of the Western powers, but many moved to the US, Canada, Australia, New Zealand, and Western Europe. The discovery of gold in California and Australia in the mid-19th century, and the construction of the Canadian-Pacific Railroad in the 1880s, created a huge need for labour, much of which was met by Chinese migrants. Typically, the wages and conditions were poor, and the treatment of workers harsh.

Some migrant Chinese remained in the ports where they landed, leading to the formation of the "Chinatowns"

that are today such a familiar and integral part of many of the world's great cities. San Francisco's Chinatown, for example, grew up in the 1850s as a gateway for immigrants arriving from China.

world war II to the present

In 1943, the United States repealed its Exclusion Act, which had banned Chinese immigration since 1882, and many Chinese served in the US armed forces in World War II. When Mao's Communist Party came to power in China in 1949, thousands of educated Chinese moved to the United States, and during the 1970s Chinese refugees arrived from Vietnam, fleeing the conflict there. A new wave of migration, chiefly to the UK, occurred after the British Government agreed in 1984 to hand Hong Kong back to China.

There are now more than 40 million "Overseas Chinese", half of whom live in Southeast Asia. The United States is home to some 3.3 million Chinese, and Europe's Chinese population numbers around 1.7 million. In today's multicultural societies, the contribution of Chinese communities is greatly valued. Unfortunately, the illegal smuggling by criminal gangs of Chinese migrants into countries such as the UK has led to a new round of exploitation.

> Remove [the Chinese] tomorrow and the residents of Palmerston would be left without fish, vegetables, or fruit, to a large extent without meat, without laundries for their washing, neither would there be any tailors, cooks, or domestic servants.
>
> The Governor of South Australia, 1899

Building a Russian railroad >
From the mid 1800s, Chinese migrant labourers were often the workers who created modern transportation systems for other nations.

Following defeat by Japan in the war of 1894–95 and the disastrous Boxer Uprising of 1900, the Qing dynasty sought to transform itself into a constitutional monarchy. From 1901, a "New China" began to emerge, but rapid social change weakened the dynasty's control and in 1911 a military revolt ushered in the Republican era. At first a semblance of central authority survived, but after the death of the president of the republic, Yuan Shikai, in 1916, China fragmented into a series of fiefdoms ruled by warlords. The Nationalists and the Communist Party formed an alliance to reunify the country, but their differing ideologies proved irreconcilable, and in 1928 the Nationalists established a new regime based at their capital, Nanjing.

二
十
世
紀

< Prisoners
This group of Boxers was captured by US troops in Beijing.

Landfall >
Japan attempted a landing on the Manchurian coast in February 1904.

the boxer uprising

"Spirit Boxers" first appeared in Shandong in 1896. The sect, which sprang from a peasant movement enraged at foreign influence in China, practiced a form of ritual boxing said to protect them from Christians. By 1899, violent clashes between Boxers and Christians were increasingly common, and by May 1900, Boxers were arriving in Beijing. In June, the Empress Dowager threw in her lot with the Boxers, blaming the disorder on foreign aggression. The foreign diplomatic missions of Beijing were besieged for 55 days, until the arrival of a multinational relief force. The signing of the Boxer Protocol in September 1901 marked the end of the uprising, which had claimed the lives of tens of thousands of Chinese Christians and more than 200 foreigners.

THE SCRAMBLE FOR CHINA 1895
Following China's defeat by Japan, Western powers rushed to obtain new concessions. Russia was allowed to extend the Trans-Siberian railroad across Manchuria, Germany used the murder of two missionaries as an excuse to seize the city of Qingdao, and Britain acquired a 99-year lease on the "New Territories" in Hong Kong.

THE RUSSO–JAPANESE WAR 1904–05
War broke out between Russia and Japan, two empires that were seeking to expand their territory to include Manchuria. Though China was not involved in the conflict, most of the fighting took place within its borders.

The revolutionary Sun Zhongshan

1880

1890

1895

1900

1905

CONTROL OF KOREA 1894
Japan sent troops into Korea, provoking war with China. The Chinese army and navy were both defeated, and by the Treaty of Shimonoseki of 1895 China had to renounce all its claims to Korea.

LATE QING REFORMS 1901–05
In the wake of the Boxer Uprising, the Empress Dowager grudgingly accepted proposals for reform, including a ban on footbinding and the creation of a parliament.

SUN ZHONGSHAN 1905
Sun Zhongshan (Sun Yat-sen) was a Western-educated doctor who, in 1905, formed the Revolutionary Alliance with a manifesto to drive out the Manchus and establish a republic. After the 1911 revolution he became president, but resigned the post to Yuan Shikai. Having reorganized the Nationalist Party, he died in 1925.

< Japanese in Manchuria
The war with China over Korea spread to Manchuria, Taiwan, and the Yellow Sea.

THE END OF EMPIRE
THE LATE QING DYNASTY AND THE EARLY REPUBLIC, 1880–1928

< Bombers
Revolutionary bomb squads were supplied with a white bag holding eight hand grenades.

the may fourth movement

Following the end of World War I, the Paris Peace Conference of May 4, 1919 decided that the former German interests in Shandong should not be returned to China but be retained by Japan, which led to dramatic protests in Chinese cities. This upsurge of nationalism gave birth to a radical movement that reevaluated Chinese cultural institutions. The May Fourth Movement encouraged the diffusion of a wide range of ideas from the West and was associated with the magazine *New Youth*, edited by Chen Duxiu, future cofounder of the Chinese Communist Party. *New Youth* contained articles on topics including attacks on Confucian teachings of filial piety, discussions of the relevance of Bolshevism to China, and calls for a "literary revolution" to replace the classical style with the vernacular.

Covers of *New Youth* magazine

THE 1911 REVOLUTION 1911

In October 1911, Nationalist soldiers in Wuchang rebelled against the empire, and called upon forces throughout the rest of the country to revolt. The Qing emperor was forced to abdicate, and the Republic of China was formed in 1912.

CCP FOUNDED 1921

The First Congress of the Chinese Communist Party was held in July 1921. It was attended by Mao Zedong, a student activist from Hunan, but not by the Party's cofounders, Chen Duxiu and Li Dazhao. The Party committed itself to supporting industrial disputes, and in 1923 it formed an alliance with the Guomindang.

THE TRIADS 1927

Criminal gangs known as the triads operated out of the city of Shanghai. The Nationalists used the triads to destroy the labour movement in the city in the "white terror" of 1927.

YUAN SHIKAI 1915

President of the republic, Yuan Shikai, declared himself the first emperor of a new dynasty. He was forced to step down, and died the following year.

President Yuan Shikai

1910

1920

1915

1925

1930

GUOMINDANG FOUNDED 1912

Founded by Sun Zhongshan, the Guomindang, or Nationalist Party, united various revolutionary parties. It won the first national election in 1913, but was expelled from parliament later that year.

THE WARLORD ERA 1916–28

After the death of Yuan Shikai, control of China was exercised by several regional warlords. These included Zhang Xun, who in 1917 tried to restore the Qing dynasty.

FACTORY LIFE 1920s

Women and children supplied much of the labour in Shanghai's cotton mills and other factories. Young girls' pay supplemented the earnings of their families, who remained in their villages. They hoped to save enough for a dowry and to return home to marry.

MAO ZEDONG AND THE PEASANTS 1927

In January 1927, the young communist Mao Zedong made an investigation into the peasant movement in Hunan. He predicted that "in a very short time, several hundred million peasants ... will rise like a tornado or a tempest." His prediction proved premature, as later that year the Nationalists began to suppress the movement.

Nanjing Road, the busy commercial street of Shanghai, in 1936

shanghai

Until 1842, Shanghai was a minor river port. However, in that year the Chinese government capitulated to Western demands for trade concessions, resulting in a number of ports along the eastern seaboard, including Shanghai, becoming essentially European outposts. Shanghai grew into China's first truly modern industrial city, and by the 1920s it was the fifth-largest city in the world and the centre of the country's domestic and foreign commerce. Foreign residents were answerable only to the laws of their own country, which made the city an attractive base for entrepreneurs, criminals, and revolutionaries. Shanghai was also a centre for political intrigue, where the Communist Party first took shape. This mix was a potent one, and Shanghai's reputation for glamour and excess derives from the politically combustible period between the two world wars. It all came to an end in the 1940s when foreigners gave up their rights in the face of growing Chinese opposition.

Between 1928 and 1937 the Nationalist government initiated

二十世纪 a series of economic and industrial reforms. However, these reforms barely touched China's impoverished rural hinterland. The Japanese, as part of an empire-building strategy, occupied Manchuria in 1931, but the Nationalist leader Jiang Jieshi (Chiang Kai-Shek) concentrated on defeating the Communists, and in 1934 forced them to set out on the Long March. In 1937, Japan invaded and the country became divided between areas of Japanese, Nationalist, and Communist influence. After the war, the Nationalists attempted to reestablish control. However, in 1946, civil war with the Communists broke out, and within three years the Nationalists had been swept from mainland China.

A 1934 ten-yuan note from the Bank of China

NATIONAL CURRENCY 1933
Until the early 19th century, Chinese trade was conducted either in foreign currencies or in ounces of silver (known as *tael*). In 1933, the yuan became the first true national currency of China.

THE SOVIET REPUBLIC 1931
The Central Committee of the Communist Party relocated its headquarters to a base in Jiangxi province, where it created the Jiangxi Soviet Republic.

COMMUNISM AT YAN'AN 1936
At Yan'an, Mao Zedong reshaped the Communist Party. In his essay "On the New Democracy", he promised the bourgeoisie a place under a Communist government. Women were told that a revolution would transform their position, though the story "When I was in Xia Village" by the popular female author, Ding Ling (1904–86), questioned the Party's commitment to equality. Peasants organized mutual aid teams and established "run by the people" schools.

the long march
In October 1934, the Communists abandoned their Jiangxi base and broke through the Nationalist blockade. To shake off their enemies they marched far to the west, fighting all the way. The Long March, as the trek came to be known, extended over 8,000km (5,000 miles), and less than 20,000 of the 86,000 people who left Jiangxi completed the journey. In October 1935, Mao Zedong and the First Front Army reached the north Shaanxi rural base and established their headquarters at Yan'an.

Propaganda poster depicting the Long March

1930

1935

1940

1945

1950

JIANG JIESHI 1930
In 1928, Jiang Jieshi became leader of the Guomindang after a power struggle, consolidating his influence over the Nationalist alliance in 1930. He was Chairman of the government until the Communist victory of 1949, when he was forced to flee the mainland. Jiang went on to set up the rival Republic of China in Taiwan.

The Nationalist leader Jiang Jieshi

the red army
On August 1, 1928, the Communists staged an uprising at Nanchang, Jiangxi Province, and the military arm of the Communists in China, the Red Army, was born. The army adopted Mao's principles of guerrilla warfare: "the enemy advances, we retreat; the enemy camps, we harass; the enemy tires, we attack; the enemy retreats, we pursue." Its soldiers observed the Three Rules: obey orders, take nothing from peasants, pool all captured goods. One in three soldiers had to be a Party member. They wore no badges of rank and received the same pay. The Red Army was renamed the People's Liberation Army in 1946.

People's Liberation Army uniform

The Soviet Mosin-Nagant Model 1944, standard rifle of the Communist troops

ESTABLISHMENT OF THE PEOPLE'S REPUBLIC 1949
In July 1946, war broke out between the Nationalists and the Communists. The Nationalist forces were driven out of Manchuria and suffered a disastrous defeat at the battle of Huai-Hai. In January 1949, the Communists entered Beijing, and the People's Republic of China was established in October of that year. The Nationalist government fled to Taiwan.

THE ROAD TO REVOLUTION
THE NATIONALIST ERA, 1928–49

the sino-japanese war

Since the late 19th century, Japan had been following a policy of expansionism, and in 1931 it set its sights on China. In September, Japanese soldiers sabotaged a part of the Japanese-owned South Manchurian railroad, south of Mukden. Japan then blamed Chinese dissidents for the incident, which became the pretext for an ensuing occupation of Manchuria. March 1932 witnessed the inauguration of the Japanese-controlled state of "Manchukuo" in Manchuria under the puppet-ruler Henry Puyi. Jiang Jieshi was convinced that it was in China's interests to avoid confrontation, but by December 1936 he finally agreed to resist Japanese encroachment. Under the terms of a second alliance, the Communists and the Nationalists joined forces against the common enemy.

the real war begins

The battle at Marco Polo Bridge near Beijing on July 7, 1937, marked the beginning of a full-scale war with Japan. In December, Japanese troops captured the Nationalist capital of Nanjing, and perpetrated the catalogue of atrocities that have come to be known as the "Rape of Nanjing", which led to an estimated death toll of 300,000. The Nationalist capital was thereafter moved to Chongqing. Jiang Jieshi also moved more than 600 factories and several universities to areas outside Japanese control. Despite these precautions, during the occupation inflation rose in China by 230 per cent per year, the salaries of officials declined, and levels of corruption soared.

wane of the nationalists

By 1940, Nationalist armies were on the defensive, leaving the Communists to continue the offensive. The Japanese response was the "three all" policy – kill all, burn all, destroy all – in villages suspected of harbouring Communists. After the Japanese attack on the US air base at Pearl Harbor, the United States and China became allies, and US forces fought in China. Japan's ambitions in China were ended after the bombing of the Japanese cities, Hiroshima and Nagasaki, and the consequent Japanese surrender in August 1945.

∧ The puppet-ruler Puyi
After the fall of Manchukuo and the Japanese surrender, Puyi was incarcerated. When he left prison, he was a firm supporter of communism.

< Japanese troops
Japanese forces overran mainland China during the Sino-Japanese War, occupying a large area of the country by 1944.

The Communist Party under Mao Zedong's leadership faced
二 serious challenges in securing its territory and remodelling its
十 political structures. Mao embarked on wholesale educational
世 and economic reforms, transforming Soviet-style agricultural
纪 cooperatives into communes, a policy that led to a disastrous
famine. With his political position weakened, in 1966 Mao launched the Cultural Revolution, a movement to roll back a perceived return to capitalism, which lasted for three years. During Mao's latter years in power, his policies were modified, but he failed to establish a political successor before his death in 1976.

Chinese troops on the march in the Tibetan highlands in 1950

President Nixon (right) visits the Great Wall

NIXON IN CHINA 1972
US president Richard Nixon visited China in February. From the Chinese point of view, the visit was a great success, as it resulted in an agreement on peaceful coexistence between the two countries without China having to make concessions regarding the claim to the Republic of China in Taiwan.

THE "LIBERATION" OF TIBET 1950–51
China's army invaded eastern Tibet to "liberate" the country from supposed imperialist forces. Chinese troops and officials occupied key positions and Tibet became the Xizang Autonomous Region.

A propaganda poster of Mao visiting farmers

COLLECTIVIZATION OF AGRICULTURE 1954
Farmers were encouraged to form cooperatives, where crops were divided according to the land and labour supplied by each family. In 1955, cooperatives merged into collective farms, in which private land-ownership was abolished and crops were divided by labour alone.

AFTER MAO 1976
After Mao Zedong's death in 1976, Deng Xiaoping, a man of diminutive stature but enormous charisma, became *de facto* leader of the Republic until 1997. He instituted a wide range of economic reforms.

1950   1960   1980

1955   1975

NEW MARRIAGE LAW 1950
A new marriage law was introduced in which women could choose their partners freely and were given equal rights relating to divorce, custody of children, and property. However, its effects were limited and in rural areas it was widely ignored.

THE KOREAN WAR 1950
The United Nations sent forces to assist South Korea in their fight against Communists in North Korea, and came close to the Chinese border. They were driven back by China and an armistice was agreed in June 1953. The war cost China more than 700,000 casualties.

Propaganda poster promoting collectivization

the great leap forward
In 1958, Mao's economic strategy turned to rapid collectivization and industrialization in the Great Leap Forward. Cooperatives were organized into 24,000 People's Communes, each with around 5,000 families. These communes were instructed to prospect for iron ore and to produce steel in "backyard furnaces", but they were given unrealistic industrial targets. The communes also had very little labour to spare for agricultural production, resulting in a famine that cost the lives of between 16 and 27 million people; Anhui Province alone suffered about two million deaths. The experiment was abandoned in 1961, and Mao came close to being overthrown in the chaos that followed.

THE GANG OF FOUR 1976
The "Gang of Four" – which comprised Mao's wife Jiang Qing, Shanghai Party chief Zhang Chunqiao, literary critic Yao Wenyuan, and Wang Hongwen, a factory worker – had a leading role in the Cultural Revolution. When Mao Zedong died in September 1976, the Gang were arrested for plotting to usurp power; all were found guilty at a show trial. Jiang Qing and Zhang Chunqiao received the death sentence, which was later commuted to life imprisonment. The others, Yao Wenyuan and Wang Hongwen, were also given prison sentences.

THE PEOPLE'S REPUBLIC
CHINA UNDER MAO, 1949–76

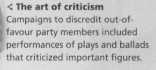

Tiananmen Square parade ▷
Rallies and marches by the Red Guards were a common sight during the Cultural Revolution.

the cultural revolution

The origins of China's Great Proletarian Cultural Revolution lay in personality clashes and policy disagreements within the Communist Party itself. After Mao's failure in the Great Leap Forward, other prominent Party members began to come to the political fore, such as Liu Shaoqi, Zhou Enlai, and Deng Xiaoping. Possibly fearing that he was being marginalized, Mao called for a revolution "to struggle against and overthrow those persons in authority who are taking the capitalist road."

the red guard movement

Teachers were blamed for the faults of the "old" education. With Mao's encouragement, radical students in universities formed "Red Guard" organizations that set out to destroy the "four olds": old ideas, old culture, old customs, and old habits. The Red Guards took this as an invitation to destroy anything, object or concept, which might be described as bourgeois. Intellectuals, artists, writers, and teachers were all persecuted, and with the covert support of Mao, the Party leadership was also challenged. The revolutionary movement was not restricted to the cities; Red Guard groups in rural areas were also incited to criticize local party officials. In all, the Red Guards were responsible for thousands of people being publicly humiliated or hounded to death.

By 1967, mass organizations were fighting pitched battles in the streets, Jiang Qing, Mao Zedong's wife was criticizing the People's Liberation Army, the foreign ministry had been seized by radicals, and the British diplomatic mission in Beijing had been burned down. China was on the verge of civil war, and to control the situation Mao empowered the army to suppress disorder. After a further upsurge of student violence the following spring, all of the Red Guard organizations were disbanded. Many members were sent down to the countryside as part of a policy of "reeducation".

aftermath of the revolution

Revolutionary committees were instituted with representatives from mass organizations, the Party, and the army. By April 1969, a new Party leadership, with Lin Biao identified as Mao's successor, was agreed, and the Cultural Revolution itself was over. However, the influence of the movement was felt throughout China in the early 1970s until the death of Mao Zedong and the arrest of the Gang of Four, who were blamed for many of the excesses carried out during the Revolution.

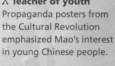

∧ **Teacher of youth**
Propaganda posters from the Cultural Revolution emphasized Mao's interest in young Chinese people.

◁ **The art of criticism**
Campaigns to discredit out-of-favour party members included performances of plays and ballads that criticized important figures.

121

< The Little Red Book
Quotations from Chairman Mao Zedong, first published in 1964, was required reading in China during the Cultural Revolution.

The cult of Mao >
Mao Zedong created a cult of personality around his image through propaganda. Though the years immediately after his death saw a diminution of his status, since the early 1990s Mao's popularity has revived.

mao zedong

Five years after Chairman Mao's death in 1976, the Party declared that Mao Zedong Thought would remain "a guide to action for a long time to come." It conceded that Mao had made "gross mistakes" at the time of the Cultural Revolution, although his contribution to the Party's success far outweighed those errors.

early career

Mao Zedong, the son of a rich peasant, was born in Hunan in 1893. He arrived in Beijing at the time of the May Fourth Movement, and it was here that he first became aware of communist ideology. He joined the Chinese Communist Party at its inception in 1921, and rose quickly up its ranks; he was elected to the Central Committee just two years later. Living at the Communist's Jiangxi base from 1931, Mao developed a three-pronged revolutionary strategy based on the Red Army, land reform, and women's emancipation.

Mao's leadership on the Long March was a vital element in the Party's survival. At Yan'an he developed policies that transformed the lives of peasants in the area. Four years after China's victory

Mao Zedong badge dating from 1969

in the Sino-Japanese War, Mao had defeated the Nationalists and established the People's Republic of China in 1949.

chairman of china

Mao's more radical ideas were set aside during the early period of collectivization of agriculture. But then, aspiring to set China on a new revolutionary path, he initiated the Great Leap Forward, an industrial and agricultural disaster which caused the worst famine of the 20th century. Mao attempted to recover his position through the Cultural Revolution, but his willingness to overturn the leadership of the Party and to encourage the violence of the Red Guards demonstrated that he had lost touch with the needs of the people.

Some recent commentators on Mao's career have concluded that he was driven by a personal lust for power. That is perhaps a harsh judgment on a man who believed China might be transformed from semi-colonialism and warlordism to become a great nation. As a revolutionary leader he played an extraordinary role, but time demonstrated that he lacked the necessary skills to rule a country.

Poverty gives rise to the desire for change, the desire for action, and the desire for revolution. On a blank sheet of paper free from any mark, the freshest and most beautiful characters can be written.

Mao Zedong, "Introducing a Cooperative" (15 April, 1958)

Mao's army ▷
The Red Army, the military arm of the Communist Party in China, took for its tenets the ideologies espoused by Mao Zedong.

二
十
世
紀

In the four years after Mao's death, Deng Xiaoping campaigned for the rehabilitation of the victims of the Cultural Revolution. Through the next decade he presided over an extraordinary shift in China's economic policies, but his final years were clouded by the mishandling of the Tiananmen Square demonstrations in June 1989. Nevertheless, he continued to dominate the political scene until his retirement from official positions in 1990, and his influence was still felt afterwards. Deng Xiaoping died in 1997, but the trend towards reform continued under his successors. The growing acceptance of China as a player on the international scene was demonstrated when the city of Beijing was selected to host the 2008 Olympic Games.

< Art after Mao
This sculpture of the headless bust of Mao by Fui Jianguo stands in the streets of the famous Dashanzi Art District (also known as 798) in Beijing.

The demonstrations in Tiananmen Square

TIANANMEN SQUARE PROTESTS 1989
When Hu Yaobang, an important political reformer, died in April 1989, demonstrations were held in his memory. Students camping on Beijing's Tiananmen Square began a hunger strike to force the government to give broader political freedoms. The army moved in, but the protesters remained resolute. On the night of 3–4 June, troops opened fire on the demonstrators and between 400 and 800 people died.

MODERN ART 1985
The creation of the Beijing Young Artists' Association marked the beginning of a "New Wave" in the Chinese art world that advocated artistic freedom and independence from official ideology.

ECONOMIC GROWTH 1992
In 1992, a new initiative begun by Deng Xiaoping led to a revival of the flagging economy, a massive increase in foreign trade and foreign investment, and a wave of government investment in Shanghai.

JIANG ZEMIN 1993
Following Deng Xiaoping's retirement in 1990, Jiang Zemin became the most powerful figure in China when he took up the presidency in 1993.

THE HANDOVER OF HONG KONG 1997
After 155 years of British colonial rule, Hong Kong was finally returned to Chinese rule as a Special Administrative Region.

1980

1985

1990

1995

2000

one-child families

A 1953 census showed that China's population was growing at an alarming rate. Plans were initiated over the next 25 years to control the rate of childbirth, but with little success. In 1979 the government adopted the draconian one-child policy. Couples who agreed to restrict their families to one child received a package of benefits, whereas couples who had a second child lost part of their income. Exceptions were made for children born with congenital defects and for ethnic minorities. The policy challenged the deeply held belief that a family needed a son to preserve the ancestral line. Its enforcement involved the widespread practice of abortion and encouraged female infanticide. A wider range of exemptions was introduced in 1984. Since then the policy has been fully enforced in urban areas, but has been less effective in the countryside.

A propaganda poster for the one-child policy campaign

THE THREE GORGES DAM 1995
Construction began on the world's largest hydroelectric generating plant, the Three Gorges Dam. The social costs included the relocation of over a million people and the destruction of six historic walled cities. Critics warned of the risk of earthquake damage and suggested that smaller dams would have achieved comparable benefits.

THE ASIAN GAMES 1994
Following the creation of a professional soccer league in 1993, China played host to the Asian Games the following year. The national team were runners-up in the tournament.

Zou Jie, striker for Dalian Shide FC

CHINA AFTER MAO
MODERN CHINA, 1976–2010

Femme fatale >
Maggie Cheung played
the assassin Flying Snow
in director Zhang Yimou's
colourful epic, *Hero* (2002).

HU JINTAO 2003
Hu Jintao replaces Jiang Zemin
as President of the Republic.

TOURISM IN CHINA 2003
In the early 1970s, travel restrictions were
gradually lifted on tourism to China. Eager
to see attractions like the Great Wall, the
Forbidden City, and the terracotta army,
foreigners flooded into the country. In 2005,
China surpassed Italy as the world's fourth
most popular tourist destination, and it is
estimated that by 2020 China will become
the most popular tourist destination.

2010

2005

THE TIBET RAILWAY 2006
The world's highest railway, between
Xining and Lhasa, opened on July 1, 2006.
It was claimed that the line will encourage
investment, but critics say its purpose is to
strengthen China's control over Tibet.

Train crossing the Lhasa Bridge in Tibet

modern chinese cinema

Until the 1980s, China produced few internationally
known movies; the handful of films produced during
the Cultural Revolution had been crude exercises in
propaganda. In the mid-1980s a new generation of
graduates emerged from the Beijing Film Academy.
Calling themselves the "Fifth Generation", they
discarded traditional methods of storytelling and
opted for a more unorthodox approach.

chen kaige and zhang yimou

The most famous of the Fifth Generation directors
were Chen Kaige and Zhang Yimou. The former was
the director and the latter the cinematographer on
Yellow Earth (1984), a film that told the story of a
communist soldier sent to the countryside to collect
cheerful folk songs for the Communist Revolution.
Staying with a peasant family, he learned that the
songs local people sang were about hardship and
suffering. The film presented an ambiguous view
of peasant society under Communism.

Chen Kaige later directed the critically acclaimed
Farewell My Concubine (1993), which followed the
fortunes of two Beijing opera singers through five
decades of turbulent Chinese history, from the

Warlord Era to the Cultural Revolution. Zhang Yimou
also turned his hand to directing; his early films *Red
Sorghum* (1987), *Ju Dou* (1990), and *Raise the
Red Lantern* (1991), all of which examined the role
of women in Chinese society, were acclaimed in
China and received accolades in the West. The
three films also made an international movie star
of Zhang Yimou's then lover, the actress Gong Li.

the revival of wuxia

In 1999, the Taiwanese director Ang Lee's *Crouching
Tiger, Hidden Dragon* achieved remarkable success in
the West. Though the film was coproduced by Hong
Kong, China, Taiwan, and the US, the plot came from
the Chinese tradition of *wuxia* storytelling, combining
swordplay, martial arts, and Dao Buddhist philosophy.
Zhang Yimou capitalized on
this taste for *wuxia* in visually
stunning and commercially
successful movies such
as *Hero* (2002), *House
of Flying Daggers* (2004),
and *Curse of the Golden
Flower* (2006).

Favoured concubine >
Zhang Yimou's *Raise the Red
Lantern* (1991), which starred
Gong Li, told a tragic tale of
rivalry among concubines.

∧ **Communist dreams**
Qiang Liu portrayed the
disillusioned soldier Hanhan
in Chen Kaige's landmark
film *Yellow Earth* (1984).

< **Winner's smile**
Gymnast Teng Haibin
brought home one of
the 32 gold medals
won by China at the
Athens 2004 Olympics.

the beijing 2008 olympics

In August 2008, the Beijing Olympics
and Paralympics will take place under
the slogan "One World One Dream".
The Olympics will stage 28 summer
sports with about 10,500 athletes
competing, and the Paralympics will
comprise 20 sports. It is estimated that
half a million foreign tourists and over
2.5 million domestic visitors will flock to
the Chinese capital to watch the Games.

political and environmental concerns
When the Beijing Olympic bid was being
considered, questions were raised about
China's civil rights record and treatment
of Tibet. Concerns about freedom of
reporting, security measures, political
demonstrations, and the risk of terrorist
activity were also considered. Despite
these issues, however, the Olympic
Committee chose Beijing to host the
Games by an overwhelming majority.

Air pollution continues to be a
worry – China has the highest sulfur
dioxide emissions in the world, and
Beijing is prone to smog. Traffic is a
major contributor to the city's pollution
problem. New bus and rail passes have
been introduced to encourage the use
of public transportation, and restrictions
will be placed on car use during the

Olympics. To further improve air quality,
many factories have been relocated
outside the city, and coal-fired homes
have been converted to gas.

an olympic setting
The project to stage the Olympics, costed
at $45 billion, is extraordinarily ambitious.
About one third of the capital has been
regenerated. A new freeway and two
new bypasses have been built, and
320km (200 miles) of city streets have
been widened or constructed. The length
of the Beijing subway is being doubled,
and the world's biggest airport terminal,
designed by British architect Norman
Foster, will receive Olympic visitors.

Spectacular buildings to house the
events have been designed, including
the "Bird's Nest" national stadium, so
called because of its intricate fabric of
interwoven steel. A lavish swimming
centre, the National Aquatics Center
(or "Water Cube"), has also been built.

Some events will take place away
from the capital. Tianjin, Shanghai,
Shenyang, and Qinhuangdao
will host football matches,
sailing races will be held at
Qingdao, and Hong Kong is
hosting the equestrian events.

New stadia >
The 18,400-seat National Indoor Stadium,
shown in a computer simulation flanked by
the "Bird's Nest" and "Water Cube", will
host the 2008 gymnastics competition.

There's a lot of hard work to do, but I am confident
we can hold an excellent Games. I think the world
will come to understand us a lot better.

Wang Wei, secretary-general of the Olympic bid committee

∧ **China celebrates**
Tiananmen Square in Beijing
filled with revellers on the night
it was announced that the city
would host the Olympics in 2008.

Does the future belong to China? As the world's most

中
国
的
未
来

populous nation, and as an emerging economic and military superpower that dominates Asia and is extending its interests globally, the answer would appear to be "yes". The economic achievements that the country has made in recent years point toward a world in which China will be the dominant power.

However, a moment of reflection leads one to consider the tensions that still exist in China today between tradition and modernity, and the gravity of the environmental challenges and social issues that must be tackled. How will these problems be resolved – and when and how will the pressure for political change force the Chinese government to transform?

SOCIETY

TOWN AND COUNTRY

Millions of Chinese in rural areas subsist on less than a dollar a day. Many people migrate to the cities to find better-paid work, taking the arduous and dirty jobs that urban dwellers are no longer willing to do, or providing cheap labour in factories manufacturing China's surging exports.

Migrant labourers on a construction site

YOUNG URBAN CHINESE

According to recent surveys, young people who live in cities aspire to a high level of education and a well-paid career. A third of those questioned condone premarital sex, though most look forward to being married.

COMMUNICATIONS REVOLUTION

The internet and cell phones have made it increasingly difficult for the Chinese government to control the expression of opinion. China has created an "Internet police force" to prevent the spread of politically suspect material.

∧ **Youth culture**
In the cities, affluent young people spend their earnings on food, clothing, and entertainment.

ECONOMY

ECONOMIC SUPERPOWER

Between 1978 and 2003, China's exports rose from $8.8 billion to $438 billion. Despite fears of overheating, the Chinese economy continues to expand rapidly. In 2006, China overtook Britain as the world's fourth-largest economy – by 2025 it could well be the largest.

Shanghai's bustling stock exchange

< **Shanghai skyline**
The boom in China's economy is reflected in its ultramodern architecture.

ENTREPRENEURS

Rapid changes in the economic and legal environments are enabling private entrepreneurs, many of whom have foreign connections or have studied abroad, to make their fortunes.

THE FUTURE OF CHINA
THE PEOPLE'S REPUBLIC BEYOND 2010

Yang Liwei ➤
China's first crewed space-flight took place in 2003; Yang Liwei was the pilot on board the *Shenzhou 5*.

POLITICS

REGIONAL ALLIANCES
Recently China has sought to strengthen its international position by entering into regional alliances. Since 1995 China has settled territorial disputes, notably with India, and developed relations with the European Union and with regimes in Africa and South America.

SPACE PROGRAMME
A desire for international prestige lies behind China's commitment to its space programme. China plans an uncrewed mission to Mars by 2033, followed by a crewed mission in the late 21st century.

CHINA AND TAIWAN
In 1981, Deng Xiaoping asserted that China no longer planned to recover Taiwan by force. China's policy is that Taiwan should become a special region of China with its own system of government, but the leadership of Taiwan still insists that the Republic of China is an independent sovereign state.

ENVIRONMENT

DESERTIFICATION
Climate change and industrialization have accelerated the encroachment of the Gobi and Takla Makan deserts. A project to plant trees in a "Great Green Wall" to hold back the sands aims to stop desertification by 2010 and begin reclaiming desert by 2030.

Desertification encroaching on Langtou Gou Village in Hebei Province

POLLUTION
Much of China's energy is supplied by burning unwashed coal, which leads to severe atmospheric pollution. The government has taken some steps to protect the environment, but its priority remains economic growth.

INFECTIOUS DISEASES
After the avian flu virus H5N1 was reported in 1997, 1.2 million chickens were culled. In 2002, 6,700 cases of SARS occurred in China and Hong Kong, leading to more than 600 deaths. The health authorities' slow response caused a severe loss of confidence.

Man wearing a mask during the SARS epidemic

PEOPLE

人们 A DAY IN THE LIFE

China's vast population has grown from 400 million to an estimated 1.3 billion in less than a century. Around 93 per cent of the population are "Han" Chinese, with 55 ethnic groups making up the remainder. In the first decades of the People's Republic, the Communist Party organized every detail of individuals' lives but today, a new unspoken social contract between people and government has relaxed controls so long as the resulting partial freedom is not exploited to push for political change. The explosion in business and job opportunities that has followed economic reforms in recent years has led to a replay of Europe's 19th-century Industrial Revolution, with hundreds of millions moving from farming to factory work and to service industries in the cities. Nonetheless, around 70 per cent of Chinese still live a rural existence, creating huge disparities in lifestyle and wealth between country and city, and between generations. This chapter profiles 14 people from disparate areas and backgrounds to give a "snapshot" of life in China today.

Like millions of other Chinese, 52-year-old Chang Hanlin

农
民

and his wife live in a cave, carved by hand into the soft loess hillside of their village, living not only off the land, but in it. "This area is mountainous, and the earth is dry and hard – good for cave-making," says Chang. "And cave dwellings are economic to live in; cool in summer and warm in winter."

For many centuries, southerly winds have deposited light, sandy sediment from the uplands of Mongolia to depths of up to 200m (650ft) on the area within the great northern loop of the Huang He (Yellow River), the region the Chinese regard as the cradle of their civilization. The rich and fertile loess soil that results is dense yet yielding, and when it is dried has concrete-like qualities that the 200 cave-dwelling families in Chang's Shaanxi Province village of Changqu put to good use for constructing their homes.

The rhythm of Chang Hanlin's life matches that of the land, with daylight hours for much of the year given over to planting and tending to his various crops of corn, potatoes, millet, dates, sunflowers, and apples, and to the raising of chickens, pigs, and sheep. Chang and the other villagers grow almost all their own food – the nearest market is a two-hour walk away – and in the early winter, when Chang has little to do, his wife busies herself with preserving and storing rations to see them through to the spring.

Chang's simple farming tools and utensils are of types that have been in use for centuries, and the main source of motive power is a mule. The caves are a natural trap for the heat from cooking, and the stove – fired with wood or coal – is connected to the *kang*, a brick bed, heating it from underneath. The village does have electricity, but water must be brought back from a deep well, about a 30-minute walk away.

Chang's cave was cut 70 years ago, and the oldest in the village is about 300 years old. However, no new ones are being built. "As people get richer, they think living in a cave is backward, and they want to move to a modern apartment in the town," says Chang. "If a young man here wants to get himself a wife, he must at least line the cave with brick or tiles, to make it a bit more modern."

However, most of the young people have left to work in factories or on construction sites in the cities, adding to the vast migration now draining the Chinese countryside of life. Chang's two sons have also left. "They are away at postgraduate studies in Xi'an," says Chang proudly, although it has cost him all his savings as well as obtaining large loans from relatives to fund their education this far.

When his sons find well-paid city jobs, Chang plans to take the opportunity to leave behind his cave and join them.

∨ ⊳ THE CAVE HOUSE
Chang leads his donkey through the courtyard in front of the entrance to his house. Although some people in China still live in natural caves, the majority of cave dwellings are made by digging a large sunken courtyard and then cutting caves inward or, as with Chang's home, remodelling south-facing cliffs or hillsides to create comfortable living spaces.

⊳ EARLY MORNING CHORES
Chang sweeps up sand with a shovel and a home-made broom of a type used for centuries to keep cave-house entrances free of blown dust and leaf litter.

LOESS VALLEY FARMER
CULTIVATING THE "YELLOW EARTH" IN RURAL SHAANXI

< **SMOKING IN THE COURTYARD**
As the morning sun warms the hillside,
Chang stops to enjoy an early cigarette
in the courtyard before breakfast.

∨ **WELL-EQUIPPED KITCHEN**
Chang's underground kitchen has all
the utensils needed for stir-frying and
steaming, fast-cooking techniques
designed to use a minimum of fuel.

∨ **MAKING THE PORRIDGE**
Steam fills up the interior of the cave dwelling,
as Chang's wife cooks up a pot of millet porridge,
which will provide a nutritious and warming start
to a day of hard physical labour.

∧ **PREPARING INGREDIENTS**
Chang's wife carefully measures out
the spices, herbs, condiments, and other
ingredients that will be required for
the cooking of the day's meals.

> **FAMILY BREAKFAST**
Perching on the edge of his bed, Chang
eats breakfast with his wife and young
daughter in the large main room that acts
as bedroom, living room, and kitchen.

常 | We have electricity now, but no running water. I have to get the water we need from a well in the village.

∧ **TEA BREAK**
Chang enjoys a cup of tea before work begins. Behind him, the original earth of the cave walls is decorated with a colourful collection of pictures and hangings.

< THE MULE CART

Chang's mule cart can be adapted to carry everything from dry goods to liquid fertilizer and even, in emergencies, family members.

ᐯ MILLING CORN

Chang's wife uses the now-blindfolded mule as a milling machine, pulling the mill stone so that it grinds the corn.

ᐯ COLLECTING BAGS OF MILLET

Chang walks alongside his mule cart, loaded with millet bought from the local town. Although a two-hour journey, it is the only way to obtain extra grain needed to supplement his own crops.

ᐱ TENDING TO HIS MULE

Back home, Chang makes sure his mule has enough to eat. Motorized vehicles have yet to make much impact in Changqu village, so it is especially important to care for the animals.

< ᐱ COLLECTING THE CORN FLOUR

After multiple revolutions of the milling stone, the corn is reduced to a fine flour that is carefully swept up and sifted to remove any remaining solids and grit.

< GATHERING SUNFLOWER PLANTS
Chang gathers up sunflower stems from his hillside plot. The plants' seeds are crushed to produce oil, or eaten as snacks. The stems of the plants are used for animal fodder or fuel.

< CARRYING THE BUNDLE HOME
Chang walks steadily beneath a mountain of sunflower stems as he carries them down the mountain. Long years of labour have accustomed him to such heavy burdens.

∨ A FARMER'S HANDS
A lifetime of physical toil and constant exposure to the sun have sculpted Chang's lean frame and weathered his dry, roughened hands.

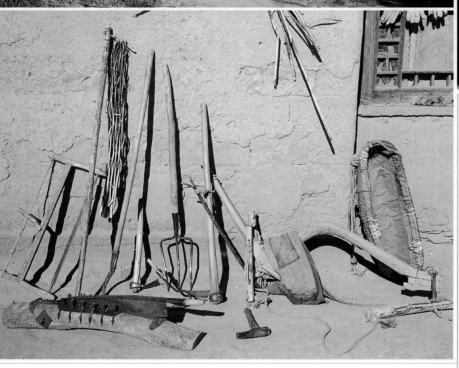

∧ TRADITIONAL TOOLS
Chang still uses types of tools that have long been abandoned in the West. Lack of mechanization means he must use tools that he can make and maintain himself.

migration to the cities

China is in the middle of one of the greatest mass movements of human beings the world has ever seen. Already there are around 100–150 million migrants from rural areas at work in the cities, and a further 200 million are expected to arrive over the next two decades.

Among the 800-million-strong rural population, up to 80 per cent of the men are underemployed. Those who find work in the cities send wages home to support their children and parents, whom they rarely see. This influx of money often visibly raises the standard of living in a village, even as the fields are left untended, but working-age men and women have become an increasingly rare sight in rural settlements.

Although blamed for the rise in crime, migrants in fact take ill-paid and dangerous jobs that the urban residents won't touch. Most jobs are in construction but the migrants also run food stalls, work in restaurants, recycle the cities' rubbish, and work as nannies and housekeepers.

常 On a hill near the village we have a temple for the Dragon King who controls the weather. In April, we sacrifice a pig to him, praying for good rains.

> FEEDING THE CHICKENS
Chang's wife cares for the family's chickens, whose eggs provide an important supplement to an otherwise basic diet during the winter months.

∨ STORAGE CAVE
The Chang family uses adjacent caves for storage, taking advantage of the space made available by families who have moved to the city.

∧ ANIMAL FEED STOCKS
Chang's wife gathers the feed for the animals from large sacks and storage buckets. This feed is vital sustenance for the mule and the family's two pigs, one of which will be killed at Spring Festival (Chinese New Year).

< SWEEPING THE YARD
Chang gathers dry fodder for future use. He weighs it down with old tyres from the mule cart in an effort to prevent it being blown around the courtyard by the strong autumn winds.

> PRESERVED FOOD
Chang's wife has worked hard throughout the autumn to preserve fruits. She stores them in neat jars that will later help keep the family going through the long, cold winter.

<< TAKING A BREAK

Chang takes a well-earned rest. After a lifetime of hard physical labour and bringing up three sons, he is now contemplating retirement in the city.

∨ INTERIOR CAVE DECORATION

Wallpaper is impractical in caves, so old calendars, propaganda posters, and pictures of scenic views serve instead to brighten up the interior.

∨ A VILLAGE WEDDING

In the evening, Chang attends the wedding of a young couple who have chosen to stay in the village rather than leave for the city. The bride wears a red dress; it is a symbol of good fortune.

∧ HOMEWORK TIME

Chang's daughter concentrates on her homework, oblivious to the communist heroes behind her. Like many youngsters, she is under pressure to study hard and be admitted to a university.

∧ WEDDING ORCHESTRA

These musicians, with their mix of traditional and Western instruments, are doing their best to entertain guests and bystanders and give the wedding a real sense of occasion.

刘 | I practise calligraphy and painting as a
way to express my feelings and my spirit.

Liu Mu, owner of a studio and private gallery, and a senior

书
法
家

official with the China National Academy of Painting, began practising calligraphy at the age of 14. "My grandfather saw it as the start of one's education, so I began training when I was a child. It was regarded as a basic skill of a person who knows how to read and write, and it has influenced my whole life."

As well as taking his grandfather's advice, as a young boy Liu was also impressed by a comic book about the life of the late-13th-century painter Wang Mian, an unschooled herder of water buffalo. Wang rose from an impoverished background to become famous for his paintings of plum blossoms and a vigorous and individual style of calligraphy.

Coming from a rural farming family himself, although one with some tradition of studying, Liu became determined to follow in Wang Mian's footsteps. Liu's teacher agreed with his grandfather that good painting could only follow a mastery of calligraphy. "So I practised hard," he says, "and learned styles from the most rigid and formal to the flamboyant *cao* (grass) script, in which characters are dashed off with a single stroke of the brush."

In 13th-century China, when Wang Mian was a practising artist, calligraphy was taught at school as one of the "three perfections" along with poetry and painting. Nowadays, though, calligraphy is regarded as a traditional art and is no longer part of the standard curriculum. "Primary and middle school textbooks have very little about calligraphy, and some schools

don't even offer painting due to a lack of art teachers," laments Liu. "In the past few years more retired people have started to take up calligraphy, but that's just for entertainment."

Few artists can make a living from calligraphy these days, and like Liu they have other jobs. "Most famous calligraphers are working as teachers in art schools or universities," he says. "I take immense pleasure in teaching a younger generation to master one of China's oldest art forms for themselves."

Opinion is unanimous that the greatest calligrapher in Chinese history was Wang Xizhi, born 17 centuries ago, whose semi-cursive, free-flowing *xing* or "walking" style has remained a model for generations of student scribes. His 28-line, 324-character preface to the *Orchid Pavilion* poems, the original of which was buried with a Tang dynasty emperor, is considered to be the greatest masterpiece of calligraphy.

"There's now a lively market for modern calligraphy, as well as antique material, with prices for contemporary pieces starting to catch up with those for older works," Liu notes with satisfaction. Fewer people may practise calligraphy these days, but fortunately the appreciation of it has not died out.

∨ EARLY MORNING TAI CHI
Like many older Chinese, Liu begins his day with the traditional shadow-boxing exercises designed to keep him supple and healthy. Legend has it the exercises were created by a Daoist monk in the 14th century.

∧ THE ARTIST'S STUDIO
Liu's studio is in a busy Beijing secondary school, about an hour from where he lives, and the sound of the playground fills his workspace.

∨ PREPARING TO WRITE
Liu grinds a stick of ink with a little water on an ink stone that acts as both a grinding surface and a reservoir for the liquid. A good ink stone is solid and smooth, and made of stone or pottery.

∧ THE FOUR TREASURES
Liu holds a brush, one of the "four treasures of the studio" along with ink, paper, and ink stone. Mastery of them was traditionally the basis of a good education.

CALLIGRAPHER
A TRADITIONAL BRUSH AND INK ARTIST, BEIJING

∨ CHOOSING THE RIGHT BRUSH

Liu selects a medium brush suitable for calligraphy, making sure its natural bristles collect to a flexible point, enabling him to produce strokes of varying widths.

<∨ A PROFESSIONAL'S TOOLS

Although he works in traditional black ink for his calligraphy pieces, Liu also uses a range of different paints and pigments when painting on a larger scale.

<∨ THE FINAL STROKE

After completing a piece of calligraphy, Liu adds his personalized seal in red ink. Older pieces may also carry the seals of their previous owners, which if illustrious may add to its value.

∨ **OFFERING ADVICE TO A STUDENT**
A student visits Liu in his studio to discuss his landscape painting and obtain advice. One of Liu's large-scale paintings is displayed on the wall behind them.

> **ENJOYING A QUIET MOMENT**
Liu takes time to think about the composition of future works, plan lectures on calligraphy and painting, and consider the content of his next exhibition.

∨ **PAINTING A LANDSCAPE**
Liu adds the finishing touches to his painting. His works reflect the influence of a famous teacher with whom he studied between the ages of 16 and 19.

∧ **TAKING A TEA BREAK**
Liu, who appreciates fine tea, drinks a potent brew from a connoisseur's thimble-sized cup during an afternoon break with his two assistants.

> **CALLIGRAPHY BRUSHES**
Various sizes and textures of brush suit different styles of calligraphy. Bigger brushes are occasionally used to produce giant characters on large sheets.

∨ TASTING AT THE TEA SHOP

On his way home, Liu stops at Beijing's wholesale tea market to sample various brews in one of the 600 tea shops there. Tea is one of Liu's biggest passions.

∧ MAKING FUTURE PLANS

At the gallery attached to his studio, Liu and his assistants discuss business, prices, the state of the market, and future exhibition plans.

▷ A MEETING AT THE ACADEMY

Leaving his studio, Liu walks to the National Academy of Painting where he works as Vice-Director of Education.

∧ DINNER AT HOME

After making the hour-long bus trip back to his comfortable modern apartment in the Beijing suburbs, Liu sits down to a simple meal prepared by his wife.

< SEALED IN RED
Once finished, a piece of calligraphy is "signed" using the artist's seal. A red ink, or paste, is typically used, as it stands out against the black ink of the calligraphy.

More than 3,300 years ago, the Chinese would try to predict the future by heating bones and tortoise shells, and reading the resulting cracks. They carved their conclusions into the same shells, leaving us the earliest Chinese characters yet discovered. While few modern characters resemble these rigid and angular markings, the lineage of many can be traced through subsequent styles that were adapted to make them easier to write with a brush. The "modern" styles in use today have been around since at least the 5th century CE.

书
法

Calligraphy is considered a branch of painting, and scrolls of well-executed characters are as much in demand as traditional portraits or landscapes. Historically, famous artists, writers, and poets were also great calligraphers, and it is said that an artist's style reveals his personality; there is a famous saying in China that "Chinese characters reflect the man". In imperial times, the civil service examinations – the route to power and influence – required not only knowledge of the classics and a persuasive style of argument, but flawless calligraphy as well.

AN ARTIST'S TOOLS

< SOFT-HAIRED BRUSHES
Large characters require large brushes. The biggest of all have broom-length handles and are often used in parks to write calligraphy in water on paving stones.

∧ **A BRUSH FOR EVERY PURPOSE**
Calligraphy brushes are traditionally made
from natural hairs such as horse, rabbit,
and deer, and are judged according to
their pointedness, evenness, and resilience.

∧ THE FAMILY HOME
A Hua's home is built off the ground to help with ventilation in the steamy climate. It is similar in style to houses in neighbouring Laos and Myanmar.

∨ WORKING SHOES
The pair of state-factory-made canvas shoes that A Hua wears have good grip to cope with the damp, muddy slopes on which the tea bushes grow.

茶
工

In Zhalu village in the mountains of Xishuang Banna, bordering Laos and Myanmar, A Hua, her husband, and parents-in-law grow rubber and tea on 40 *mu* (2.3 acres) of land. Up here, the steamy subtropical climate of the region becomes cool and moist, and tea is picked year-round except for December and January, making the family an income of around 10,000 yuan (US$1,300) a year.

Helped by her mother-in-law, twenty-three-year-old A Hua does most of the work: picking the tea, collecting the milky sap from the rubber trees, and feeding the pigs and chickens. She's busiest in the spring, when she cuts the rubber at 4 a.m., returns four hours later to cook for the family, and then goes to pick tea until nightfall – a total of 14 hours' work a day.

Zhalu village is in one of the six best areas in the region for growing Pu'er tea, a variety unique to Yunnan Province and one that's increasingly in demand, providing a welcome boost to the family's income. "In the last eight years village life has gradually been getting better. Commercial buyers are coming more frequently to buy the tea, and competition is pushing up the market price," says A Hua. As a result, the family now has a television, a motorcycle, and a tractor.

A Hua's husband works as a negotiator for a tea factory, agreeing prices with the other villagers and making sure they don't pad their own high-quality product with cheaper leaves bought elsewhere. His employer is Luo Mingwei, one of three brothers who own a factory in the nearby town of Yiwu. Luo's parents worked for a state-

owned tea factory when he was a child, and his father took him on trips to the villages, teaching him how to tell good tea from bad. However, Luo chose a more profitable career as a veterinarian.

In the 1990s, buyers started to come from Taiwan, Hong Kong, Japan, and Korea, looking to obtain Pu'er directly from its source. Luo's two older brothers each had 20 years' experience at the state-owned factory, and in 2000 Luo gave up his veterinary career to join them in starting their own business. "Now the factory is worth over two million yuan," says Luo enthusiastically. "More and more people love Pu'er tea, the local government is now promoting the tea industry, and the price is still low with plenty of room to go up." He sees a bright future. "Most of our sales are to overseas Chinese, but drinking good-quality tea is becoming fashionable again here, too. If just ten per cent of Chinese at home start to drink Pu'er, it's going to be a huge market."

A Hua already has plans. To date, the furthest she's been from home is to the provincial capital of Kunming. "When I have more money I want to take the whole family to see Beijing, especially Tiananmen Square," she says. If Luo is right, she'll soon get her wish.

∧ OFF TO THE TEA FIELDS
A Hua sets off to pick tea with her mother-in-law and a neighbour. Their scarves and hats will protect them from the sun as the day progresses.

TEA TRADE WORKERS
TEA PICKER AND TEA FACTORY OWNER, YUNNAN

阿花 The tea we are picking now is called "winter tea". It has a delicate taste and it is rare, as few places have the climate to grow tea so late in the year.

< ∨ PICKING TEA

In the early morning mist, A Hua carefully selects leaves of just the right maturity in size, colour, and tenderness to make the best Pu'er tea.

∨ GREEN TEA LEAVES

A Hua returns home once she has filled her basket. Most of the tea leaves are heated and fermented, but some Pu'er is sold as green tea, just as it is picked.

∨ SCORCHING THE LEAVES

A Hua heats the newly picked tea leaves in a large iron wok over an open fire. This process, which blackens the leaves, is called *sha qing* ("kill the green").

< ∧ LEAVES LEFT OUT TO DRY

After scorching in the wok, the tea leaves are spread out and left in the sun to dry, ready for the buyer to come and inspect them.

∨ **DOING THE WASHING**
The women wash clothes and the feed
buckets in the yard with water obtained
from a public standpipe shared with
several other neighbouring houses.

∨ **PREPARING THE ANIMAL FEED**
A Hua's work does not end after picking
tea, and she spends the rest of her day
doing chores around the home, starting
with mixing feed and water for the pigs.

∧ > **FEEDING THE PIGS**
A Hua feeds the pigs, which are kept
in the cool basement area under the
house. Pigs and chickens are kept
largely for the family's own
consumption on special occasions.

> **LUNCH WITH THE TEA BUYER**
Luo Mingwei arrives for lunch. With
the family's livelihood dependent on
his custom, lunch is an opportunity to
come to an agreement on price.

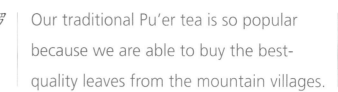

罗 | Our traditional Pu'er tea is so popular because we are able to buy the best-quality leaves from the mountain villages.

< ∨ CHECKING THE TEA
Luo Mingwei checks the leaves for fragrance, moisture, and consistency in quality, making sure that the Pu'er has not been mixed with lower-quality leaves.

< ∨ STRIKING A DEAL
China remains largely a cash economy, and once Luo is happy with the quality of the tea leaves and the crop has been weighed, he hands over the purchase price directly.

∧ TRANSPORTING THE TEA
A multipurpose tractor-trailor, perfect for the muddy mountain paths, is used to haul the purchased bags of tea back to Luo's nearby factory, where they will be processed, packaged, and eventually shipped.

> DOUBLE-CHECKING THE QUALITY
Once at the factory, the quality of the tea is checked again. This will affect how it is stored and processed.

∨ WEIGHING THE TEA
The new crop is carefully separated into batches of equal weight that will be steamed to soften the leaves, before being pressed into discs.

∧ QUALITY CONTROL
Frequent samples are taken during the preparation to ensure that the tea is consistent in quality, and of the right fragrance and maturity.

> PRESSING THE TEA
Although machines are used in modern factories, here the tea is pressed into cakes by placing each batch in a bag and compressing it with a stone.

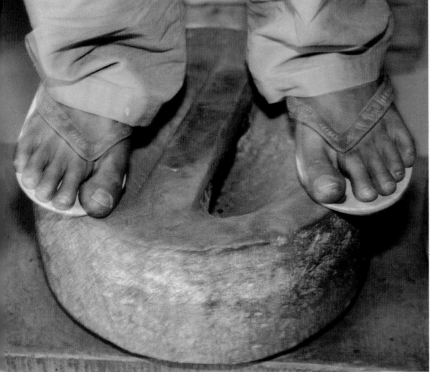

∧ SAMPLING THE PU'ER TEA

Mingwei and his brothers sample a batch of tea, over which much care is taken. They wash the leaves in boiling water and then infuse the tea in fresh water for a few minutes.

< ASCERTAINING THE STRENGTH

Traditionally, tea jugs and cups for tasting were made from porcelain. Modern examples, like Luo's set, are made from glass so that the colour and clarity of the tea can be assessed.

< TEA PARAPHERNALIA
Tea is most commonly brewed in tea pots or lidded cups (*gaibei*), before being poured into thimble-sized, handleless cups for tasting.

Only among limited numbers of urban sophisticates has coffee made any progress in China. For the majority, green, white, or black tea (known as red tea) remains the drink of choice, and is regarded as one of life's necessities. As an ancient Chinese saying goes, "firewood, rice, oil, salt, soy sauce, vinegar, and tea are the seven necessities to begin a day".

In China, green tea, using fresh leaves, is more popular than black tea, which has been carefully oxidized, lasts longer on the shelf, and has a higher caffeine content. Tea is such an important part of the Chinese diet that many carry some with them in a thermos or in a simple screw-top jar, which they refresh with boiling water throughout the day.

Tea tasting is different from drinking tea for refreshment. This hobby uses specific pots and cups and a step-by-step brewing process to ensure that each type of tea is sampled at its optimum strength. Tea connoisseurs can choose from hundreds of different kinds of Chinese tea, priced according to the type of leaf and its "vintage" (the year it was made).

品
茶

THE ART OF TEA TASTING

> TEA-TASTING SET
Yixing ware is one of the most popular for tea connoisseurs. All the cups are filled with one continuous movement; excess tea is caught by the tray below.

∧ **PACKAGED TEAS**
Tea can be bought in bricks, discs, or loose in bags and presentation pots. It was first used in China c.600 BCE as a medicine, and later it was even used as currency.

∨ THE INSTRUMENT SHOP
Selay's shop is in a modern building,
set in the heart of Kashgar's old town,
a sprawling Uighur bazaar area.

The small market town of Kashgar in the far west of Xinjiang

乐
师

Autonomous Region is far closer to Islamabad, Bishkek, and the other Central Asian capitals than it is to Beijing. The majority of its residents are Uighur, devout Muslims of Turkic descent. Ababakri Selay's family has been making traditional Uighur musical instruments here for five generations, living through Chinese imperial rule, independence, Russian influence, civil war, and Chinese rule again.

Yet through all the changes, and the recent arrival of Chinese pop music, the instrument-maker continues to find many buyers for his mulberry-wood *duttar*, snakeskin-faced *rawap*, and bowed *gijek*. Selay's shop sells nearly 40 different types of instruments, many of which he has invented and designed himself, fusing ideas from China and surrounding Central Asian countries. "In Kashgar people still enjoy the traditional songs more than pop music. Pop tunes catch on for a short time, but people soon come back to the traditional music and instruments," says Selay. "It has always been like this."

Selay sells not only to local players but to customers in distant Turkey as well as in neighbouring Tajikistan, Pakistan, and Kyrgyzstan, countries with which the Uighur share much of their culture. Occasionally, Western tourists in Kashgar buy an instrument simply for the fine craftsmanship of its sensuous curves and intricate inlays.

Now 80 years old, Selay leaves much of the running of his shop to his two sons, but still rises at 6 a.m. to wash and pray, before breakfasting on *nan* bread and tea with friends; he sometimes plays music with them,

too. He visits the shop each day to supervise his sons' instrument-making, ensuring that he passes down the same high level of craftsmanship as his own father passed to him. Selay's father, grandfather, and great-grandfather lived to the ages of 99, 102, and 104, respectively, and Selay expects an equally long retirement, basking in the respect he's earned for having completed the pilgrimage to Mecca, a journey that every Muslim strives to achieve at least once in their lifetime.

Kashgar, where Selay has lived his entire life, is going through a big change. The recent arrival of a long-distance railway line and Beijing's "Go West" modernization plans mean that the warren of Central Asian-style narrow streets in the heart of the town are now surrounded by modern buildings identical to those found across much of China. In addition, Uighurs may become the minority population as increasing numbers of Han Chinese settle in Kashgar. However, Selay is pragmatic: "If some people in Kashgar are getting richer, more of them will be able to afford to buy good musical instruments. That may help my family's business in the future."

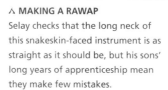

∧ MAKING A RAWAP
Selay checks that the long neck of this snakeskin-faced instrument is as straight as it should be, but his sons' long years of apprenticeship mean they make few mistakes.

> CHECKING THE FRAME
Made from mulberry wood, the frame of the *duttar* – one of the most popular Uighur instruments – must be set into just the right shape before it is strung.

CRAFTSMAN
MAKING TRADITIONAL INSTRUMENTS, KASHGAR

< FAMILY WORKSHOP

Two of Selay's sons now do most of the manufacturing, with Selay restricting himself largely to training, quality control, and playing the finished instruments.

∨ CRAFTING A TAMBOURINE

This tambourine is just one of an array of different instruments made by Selay and his sons, and the workbench is littered with tools and materials.

∧ QUALITY CONTROL

Selay's sons wait for their father's approval as he checks the finish on a recently completed *duttar*, before it goes on sale in the shop.

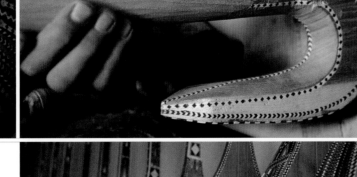

< WORKING ON THE INLAY

An inlay is crafted into the wood of a *rawap*, which has a curious handle at the end of its long neck, allowing it to be hung up out of the way when not being played.

∧ DETAIL OF A DUTTAR

The fine handcraftsmanship that goes into each one of the Selay family's instruments is apparent in the beautifully inlaid wood of this *duttar*.

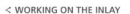

< THE FINISHED WARES

Although many of his instruments are tricky for beginners to play, visitors to Kashgar will often buy Selay's pieces for their sheer beauty alone.

155

∧ PLAYING UIGHUR SONGS
During a break, Selay and his sons,
all accomplished musicians, form a
temporary trio whose sounds attract
curious passers-by to the shop.

讲
述 | Change is good for the development of music, because from the fusing of different styles, something new always emerges. Some music we play now is Chinese, some Kazakh. But we play it on our own instruments, and it sounds good.

讲
述

I feel lucky that I've been able to travel in my lifetime, to Mecca and around China and Pakistan. But Kashgar is my home and I will spend the rest of my days here.

∨ **TESTING AN INSTRUMENT**
Selay plays one of his own designs, a beautifully decorated *gitek*, which was influenced by the early viols of Western music, as well as traditional Uighur musical instruments.

∧ **A CRAFTSMAN'S TOOLS**
Familiar carpenters' equipment such as pliers and set squares lie side by side with other more unusual tools specific to the needs of Uighur instrument-making.

china's ethnic minorities

There are 55 officially recognized different ethnic minorities in China, numbering around 90 million people and making up seven per cent of the population. Some minorities are indistinguishable in appearance from the Han – the largest ethnic group in China – but others are of Indo-European or Turkic descent.

China's minorities mostly live on the fringes of the country, and are often closely related to their cross-border neighbours. Their land was absorbed during periods of expansion, or they are the remnants of invaders who themselves dominated the Han for centuries. Other minority groups are Han with different customs; the Hui people, for example, are Muslim Han. Attempts to absorb minority cultures into the Han mainstream have been met with resistance and there are a growing number of grassroots organizations that are helping to preserve the traditions, customs, and languages of China's minorities. Many ethnic groups have distinctive styles of dress, and their costumes and cultures have become a major tourist attraction in some areas of the country.

∧ **PLAYING IN A TEAHOUSE**
Tea and music are Selay's greatest pleasures. While he and a friend play the *rawap* in a teahouse close to his workshop, the other patrons get a free concert.

> **GETTING A LIFT HOME**
A friend from the teahouse gives Selay a ride home on his motorized cart, which is usually used to transport dry goods and sheep to the market.

< PRAYING AT HOME
A devout Muslim, Selay prays several
times a day, either visiting his local
mosque or, as here, on a prayer mat
in the tiled courtyard of his home.

∧ DINNER WITH FAMILY AND FRIENDS
Selay eats his evening meal with his
sons and neighbours in the traditionally
decorated main room of his house.
A tower of *nan* bread, a local staple,
dominates the table.

∧▷ EVENING MARKET
After dinner, Selay makes an early evening
trip to the market with his wife. Kashgar is
most famous for its huge Sunday bazaar,
which attracts thousands of people each week.

< UIGHUR INSTRUMENTS
In the 7th to 10th centuries, Uighur musicians (from present-day Xinjiang) and their instruments were permanent fixtures at Tang and Song dynasty courts.

乐
器

Traditional Chinese instruments are classified not by the way they are played, but according to the materials from which they are made. They mostly fall into eight groups: silk, stone, wood, bamboo, metal, clay, gourd, and hide. The oldest of all are percussion instruments, mentioned in the earliest surviving examples of written characters, including the *bianqing* with its rows of L-shaped stones suspended on strings from a frame, and struck with mallets. Percussion in general plays a larger role in Chinese music than in Western,

and is often used repeatedly for dramatic effect in orchestral pieces, and for driving along the martial arts scenes of Beijing opera (*see page 277*). The player of the *bangu*, a high-pitched drum of the hide group, sets the pace.

Wood instruments are also percussive, while those blown, like flutes, or using double reeds, like an oboe, fall into the bamboo category. While the clay group has only one member, a kind of ocarina called the *xun*, the silk group runs to dozens of plucked, bowed, and struck stringed instruments.

TRADITIONAL MUSIC-MAKING

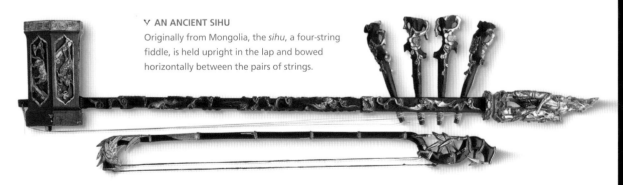

∨ AN ANCIENT SIHU
Originally from Mongolia, the *sihu*, a four-string fiddle, is held upright in the lap and bowed horizontally between the pairs of strings.

The instruments of a touring band moving
from festival to festival include a *yangqin*
(similar to a zither), two *erhu* fiddles, and
two *suona* double-reeded horn pipes.

> LUGU LAKE
Lacuo's home sits on Lugu Lake, which provides the villagers with plenty of fish, water for their crops, and water-plant fodder for their livestock.

"Men are like children," says 22-year-old Muze Lacuo, "they are

摩
梭

our family, so we take care of them." For Lacuo that caring begins most days at 8 a.m. with three hours in the forest collecting firewood, or in a boat on nearby Lugu Lake cutting water plants as fodder for her family's pigs. She helps with the ploughing, shops at the market, and cooks for the family, too.

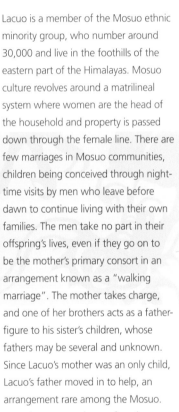

Lacuo is a member of the Mosuo ethnic minority group, who number around 30,000 and live in the foothills of the eastern part of the Himalayas. Mosuo culture revolves around a matrilineal system where women are the head of the household and property is passed down through the female line. There are few marriages in Mosuo communities, children being conceived through night-time visits by men who leave before dawn to continue living with their own families. The men take no part in their offspring's lives, even if they go on to be the mother's primary consort in an arrangement known as a "walking marriage". The mother takes charge, and one of her brothers acts as a father-figure to his sister's children, whose fathers may be several and unknown. Since Lacuo's mother was an only child, Lacuo's father moved in to help, an arrangement rare among the Mosuo.

Lacuo moved away from home, but as the eldest female she was recalled to help with the farming and to become head of the family in her turn. "The village is poor and boring. The city is more fun, and life there is better," she says, dreaming of Beijing rather than the nearby city of Lijiang, where two of her siblings work in the tourism industry.

Perhaps Lacuo envies the celebrity Yang Erche Namu, who at 13 ran away from the Mosuo community to join a song and dance troupe, eventually finding fame as a singer and model. Namu's best-selling autobiography detailing Mosuo sexual traditions, and her appearances on Chinese television, gave notoriety to one of China's more remote and least-known ethnic groups. Tourism to Lugu Lake rapidly climbed from nothing to around 50,000 visitors a year, and the Mosuo now cannily preserve their traditions by dramatizing them to educate paying visitors. "Our village has few tourists, but we still have better food than when I was young," says Lacuo, "and now we have running water and electricity." It was her siblings' city earnings that paid for the recent addition of three rooms to the house.

Lacuo has little time for the tourist picture of Lugu Lake as an idyll of free love with women in control. Many young people have left for the cities, making the transient relationships of Mosuo tradition harder to come by. "A woman's life is bitter here, and we work too hard," she sighs. "If I find a good Mosuo man, I'll make a walking marriage and stay here. This is the Mosuo way, and I accept that."

∧ BREAKFAST AT HOME
Before the day's work, the family prepares yak-butter tea over the fire, and *tsampa* – barley flour mixed with tea to make a high-energy paste.

> MORNING CHORES
Rather than the traditional long Mosuo skirt, Lacuo dresses in casual clothes that are more practical for her daily work around the family's farm.

∨ FEEDING THE LIVESTOCK
The family lives close to its livestock of cattle and chickens. Lacuo feeds the birds in the yard outside their home.

MOSUO MATRIARCH
HEAD OF A FARMING FAMILY, YUNNAN

⋁ PLOUGHING THE FIELDS
Mechanized farming is for the wealthier farms in the east of China. Lacuo and her parents direct the oxen to turn over the dry soil and make it ready for planting in early spring.

⋗ FAMILY PET
Lacuo's mother, Muze Namu, keeps the family puppy out of the way of the plough. In Mosuo culture, women do the lion's share of the farming work.

⋖ WINTER STORES
Lacuo helps a neighbour who has just slaughtered a pig to salt the meat and prepare sausages. Each family kills a pig every autumn.

⋖ PRESERVING FOOD FOR THE WINTER
Hung out in the morning sunshine, the sausages and various cuts of meat will quickly dry out and be ready for storage. The Muze family will shortly kill a pig for themselves, too, its preserved meat helping to vary their diet through much of the winter.

拉 | We Mosuo women do most of the work. Men only begin to work
措 | hard like us after the age of 40 when they finally become adults.

‹ˆ GATHERING WATER PLANTS
With her friend steadying the boat, Lacuo
pulls up a net, heavy with water plants,
from Lugu Lake. Once the boat is filled,
they transport the plants back to shore.

› CARRYING THE PLANTS HOME
Lacuo carries home the day's haul. There
are few vehicles at Lugu Lake and often
residents must carry loads themselves.

< CHANGING INTO MOSUO DRESS
Free of farming chores for the day, Lacuo dons a distinctive Mosuo headdress in preparation for her afternoon trip to the market.

∨ OUTSIDE THE FAMILY HOME
Wearing the long skirt and embroidered jacket of traditional local dress, Lacuo walks under the beautifully decorated eaves of the family's home.

∧ DRYING PLANTS FOR FODDER
Lacuo lays out the plants in the courtyard. Once the sun has dried them, she will stack and store the fodder until it is needed.

< WITH HER YOUNGER BROTHER
Lacuo steps out into the courtyard with her six-year-old brother. As the eldest sibling, Lacuo is like a second mother to him.

∧ DRYING CORN ON THE ROOF
Lacuo hands ears of corn up to her father. The low pitch of the roof makes it the perfect place for drying the cobs, which will later serve as animal fodder.

< TOWN TEMPLE
Lacuo takes a 40-minute truck ride with
a friend to the nearby town of Yongning.
The town is big enough to support a large
Buddhist temple, which Lacuo often visits.

> MARKET DAY
Lacuo visits the local weekly market in the
centre of Yongning to supplement what the
family grows for itself. Her woven basket
is soon full of fruit and vegetables.

∨ WEEKLY SHOPPING
Peppers, essential in the cuisine of nearby
Sichuan Province, and tomatoes are brought
up from the lower altitudes, where growing
them is more feasible than in Lacuo's village.

∧ A SOCIAL OCCASION
The weekly market brings together Mosuo women
from the villages around Yongning. The town also
provides schooling for the local area, and as a student,
Lacuo lived in dormitories here during the week.

拉 | Sometimes I would like to live and dress like a city girl.
措 | But I am Mosuo and I accept our traditions.

< ∧ **LIGHT LUNCH**
Once their baskets are full, Lacuo and her
friend stop to enjoy a dish of noodles in one
of several small restaurants serving market
shoppers, before looking for a truck ride home.

▷ HEAD OF THE FAMILY

As her mother grows older, Lacuo, as the eldest female of the next generation, will take over as family head, and her brother will play the role of father figure to her children.

∧ LACUO AND HER MOTHER

Decades of outdoor work at high altitude have left Lacuo's mother with the same swarthy complexion as the Tibetans, with whom the Mosuo share cultural and ethnic features.

▷ AFTERNOON TEA WITH THE NEIGHBOURS

In the main (and most elaborately decorated) room of the house, Lacuo and her neighbours chat over yak-milk tea and apples.

∨ **COOKING FOR THE FAMILY**
The heat rising from the simple earthen stove helps to dry the cobs of corn as Lacuo prepares the evening meal in the smoke-darkened kitchen.

> **DINNER SPREAD**
Vegetables are the predominant elements in the meal Lacuo prepares. Pork and other meats are delicacies reserved for special occasions.

∧ **PREPARING THE RICE**
Lacuo prepares the rice on a separate fire. Pictures of Chinese scenery and football players adorn the walls above the table.

< **FAMILY ALTAR**
Images of the secular and sacred combine as Mao Zedong, often called the "red sun", occupies prime position over the family altar.

chinese cuisine

China has several major types of cuisine, but every province has its own dishes, which are almost entirely unknown outside China. Many cities have their own specialities featuring local ingredients, and minority peoples also have their own cuisines. Mosuo cookery, for example, borrows from both Yunnan and Sichuan, as well as from Tibet.

Traditionally, rice is favoured south of the Yangzi River, while to the north of the country the main staple is wheat in the form of pasta or bread. The ingredients for many Chinese dishes are cut small for cooking quickly using the minimum of fuel. In Sichuan, dishes are famously fiery; Shanghainese food is sweeter and more oily; while the dishes of Shanxi are vinegary.

Food is an important part of social life in China, with several dishes such as *yuanxiao* (glutinous rice balls) and mooncakes prepared specially for festivals and celebrations.

Xia steps out in the rain for her daily walk. As well as being a good way of meeting up with friends, a walk in the park is seen by older Chinese as essential to their health.

Shanghai-born Xia Weiqin has spent all of her 74 years in her

退
休
教
师

native city, which in her youth was the foreign-run "Paris of the East". In 1988, Xia retired from her job as a high school teacher of English and Chinese. Far from struggling to fill her days, this soft-spoken yet self-confident woman finds that in retirement, life is just as busy and rewarding as it has ever been.

Xia lives with her engineer son, Maxiao Ke, her daughter-in-law, Rongyi Wen, an accountant, and her grandson, Majia Ji, age 22, who is a university student. The family have a two-room apartment in a crumbling colonial-era mansion. While they have their own bathroom, the kitchen is shared with two neighbouring families.

Xia's pension of 1,500 yuan (US$195) per month is far greater than the income of the average working Chinese, and even in relatively expensive Shanghai it enables her to enjoy a comfortable retirement. For those retiring today, the picture is less rosy: of the three million who leave work every year, only about 15 per cent of urban residents have a pension, and among the rural majority, the percentage of retiring people with any kind of financial safety net is even smaller.

Since retiring, Xia has found more than enough activities to occupy her time. In between exercising, studying, and socializing, she also provides the support at home that enables the rest of her family to get on with working and studying. She not only does housework in the apartment, but also shops in the markets for fresh vegetables, meat, and fish, and prepares the family meals.

In the last few years, Xia has found herself drawn back into the world of education, but this time as a student. She has enrolled at a college near her home for senior citizens – known locally as the "Silver Hair Building" – and has studied painting and cooking. She currently attends the college three times a week to take courses on film criticism and tourism, and also to sing in a choir.

Until a few years ago, when a bad fall put her in hospital for about six months, Xia travelled extensively around China, sometimes with her family and sometimes leading a group of fellow college students. Although she loves travel, her trips have convinced Xia that, for her, Shanghai is the only place to live.

Proud of her city, Xia is delighted with the way Shanghai is changing. Since the late Deng Xiaoping decided to recreate Shanghai as China's financial centre, billions have been invested in new construction and infrastructure projects. Today, Shanghainese have the country's highest per capita average incomes. For Xia, the city's rejuvenation has echoes of the glamorous Shanghai of her youth with a return of foreign businesses and a revived love of foreign amusements, such as playing the piano, which Xia enjoys herself.

∧ > **TAI CHI ON THE BUND**
The Bund, the riverside promenade built more than a century ago by foreign developers, is an ideal setting for Xia's tai chi exercises. The Shanghainese use the Bund for everything from gentle walks and jogging to ballroom dancing.

RETIRED TEACHER
ENJOYING LIFE WITH FRIENDS AND FAMILY, SHANGHAI

∨ SHOPPING AT DA GU LU MARKET
Storage space in the apartment is limited, so Xia has to visit the market daily to buy fresh food; even chickens and fish are usually alive until purchased.

< ∨ ON THE WAY HOME
Xia walks home after a busy morning exercising and shopping. Although tai chi keeps her supple, she still uses a stick to steady herself on the uneven pavements.

∧ A FAMILY DUET
With a deep love of music, Xia enjoys playing the piano and singing while her grandson, Majia, accompanies her on the electric guitar.

< PREPARING LUNCH
Xia makes lunch for the family; like many retired people, she provides invaluable domestic support that allows the younger family members to work longer hours.

∨ TURNING PAGES
With a few spare moments, Xia does some background reading for one of her courses – a rare luxury in her busy schedule.

> VISITING THE HAIRDRESSER
Xia settles back for a *xi jian chui* (wash, cut, blow). Some Chinese women go simply for a hair wash and a shoulder massage.

∧ WINDOW SHOPPING
Xia peruses the wares on display in the window of an antiques shop, trying to distinguish genuine articles from the many fakes offered to Shanghai's shoppers.

∧ CHOIR PRACTICE
At the senior citizens' college, Xia and her fellow choristers are in full voice. As well as being a great social focus, Xia's college activities help to keep her mentally active.

> TIME TO SAY GOODBYE
Bidding farewell to her college friends, Xia sets off to prepare for her monthly night out with another group, eager to catch up on the latest news and gossip.

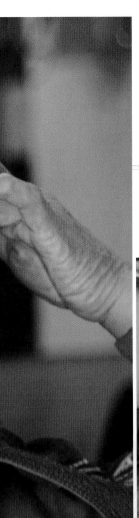

夏 | I think I am busier now than before I retired, but I still have plenty of energy. The most important thing to me is that my grandson graduates and finds a good job.

∨ LEAVING HOME
All ready for an evening of socializing, Xia heads out, umbrella in hand, into Shanghai's rainy alleys in search of a taxi to take her to the restaurant.

⊳ OLD FRIENDS
Xia greets the oldest member of her group, who is 90 years old. Many of the younger friends still travel together regularly on trips around China.

⊲∧ RESTAURANT CIRCLE
Xia and her friends meet at the Wang Xhao restaurant, in a private room that can be secured for an additional fee or a minimum food order, giving them extra privacy.

∧ PREPARING FOR THE NIGHT OUT
Xia gets ready for the night out with her friends. Xia and her contemporaries are proud of their continuing good health and always make a special effort to look good for their monthly dinner.

< **BREAKFAST BEFORE SCHOOL**
Chen rises at 7 a.m. for a breakfast of corn porridge and steamed bread with her grandparents, who encourage her to eat as much as possible.

Xiao Chen was only 15 months old when her parents left her with her grandparents in their Shaanxi village and went off to find work in the booming southern metropolis of Guangzhou, more than a day away by train. Now eight, she has seen her mother only four times, and her father only three times.

小
学
生

Chen's parents migrated to the city to boost the family's income. "We have only 2.4 *mu* (0.4 acres) of land for the whole family," explains her grandfather, "and it only produces about 3,000 yuan (US$390) a year from crops of wheat and corn. Prices at the market are low, and the cost of fertilizer is rising." Although in their mid-60s, Chen's grandparents can easily manage such a small parcel of land themselves, leaving her parents largely without a role. Now they send home substantial sums from their jobs in the big city.

So Xiao Chen walks to school each day by herself, as do most of the other children at the Dong Da Jian village primary school. Although the village has a population of more than 2,000, almost all the adults between the ages of 16 and 45 are away in the growing cities working in factories or in construction, a situation common in rural areas of China.

At school, classes run from 8 a.m. until a break at noon. There are 40 students in Chen's year, and her favourite subjects are Chinese (reading and writing) and mathematics. She has the same teacher for these and for music, and politics is included in the curriculum, even at this young age. Another male teacher runs the physical

education and sports classes for the school, although equipment is very limited – there is only one basketball for the whole school of 200 students.

When she grows up, Xiao Chen wants to be a teacher, too, but her grandparents have other ambitions for her. She's fourth in her class for academic achievement, and they want her to gain a place at a university and then get an office job in the city, where they believe she will have an easier life than in the countryside. There are university places for fewer than one in four aspiring students in China, so the pressure is already on for Chen, and it will intensify in middle school.

The price of being able to fund an education for their daughter is that Chen's parents have become relatively estranged from her. She treats her grandparents as her parents, and prefers their company even when her mother and father come to visit. Her parents have become observers as the grandparents wash, dress, and feed Chen, and help with her homework.

Xiao Chen's parents are now expecting a second child, and it is possible that he or she may also have to join China's estimated 23 million "left-behind children" growing up in their grandparents' care.

∧ **WALK TO SCHOOL**
Insulated against the cold winter day, Chen makes the 10-minute walk to school past the farming land that provides her grandparents' income.

> **CHEN AND HER BEST FRIEND**
Xiao Chen arrives at school early and in time to meet with her best friend, who is in the same class as she is. In the background, the flag of China flies above the main school building.

SCHOOLCHILD
A PRIMARY SCHOOL STUDENT, SHAANXI

> **IN THE SCHOOL PLAYGROUND**
There's time for a little play with friends before the teacher arrives at 8 a.m. The facilities at Chen's school are limited but better than at many other rural schools.

< **LEARNING BY ROTE**
Chen reads aloud from her text-book. Characters are learned by repetitive writing and by regular rhythmic chanting of set passages.

< **WRITING CHARACTERS**
After reading aloud, the students practise writing characters. Each year has a large, single class of around 40 students. The interior of the classroom is unheated and the children stay in their warm winter clothing throughout the day.

∨ **WALKING HOME FOR LUNCH**
The school has no canteen, and at noon all the children return to their homes for lunch. They pass a government slogan painted on a wall advocating "high-quality, all-out development".

陈 | Chen is fortunate. We do not have much land and so we do not need her to help on it. She can spend more time studying.

∧ **FAMILY LUNCH BREAK**
Xiao Chen arrives home from school and eats
a lunch of pork, vegetables, and rice prepared
by her grandmother. Chen's grandfather takes
a break from his farming chores to join them.

> **READING PRACTICE**
After lunch, Chen reads to her grandmother. To help her continue to achieve high grades in school, Chen's grandmother encourages her to study as often as she can.

> **RIDING HER BICYCLE**
Before returning to school for her afternoon lessons, Chen takes a turn around the village on her bicycle. Cars are rare here, and the nearest town is a 15-minute cycle ride away.

∧▷ **A RARE VISIT HOME**
This is the first time in two years that Xiao Chen's parents have been able to visit their daughter together. They are happy with her progress at school under her grandparents' guidance, but miss being able to play a bigger role in Chen's upbringing.

I like learning everything at school, especially Chinese and maths. When I grow up, I'm going to be a teacher myself.

∧ **AFTERNOON LESSONS**
Classes resume at 2 p.m. and run until 5 p.m. The afternoon sun warms the classroom a little, but not enough to allow the students to take off their winter coats.

< **CLASSROOM BLACKBOARD**
Written on the blackboard is the text of a song that the children chant together, learning both the song and new characters at the same time.

education in china

The Chinese education system is structured in much the same way as many other nations, from primary to university level. However, China spends less than 3 per cent of its gross domestic product on education – half the level of developed nations – and as a result the cost of learning is high. Parents in rural areas are often forced to migrate to large cities for work in order to pay for their children's education. However, things are beginning to change; in 2006, the central government instructed municipalities to make education free again in rural areas. This has had a big impact on families such as the Chens. Although they still pay for Xiao Chen's schoolbooks, they have saved about 400 yuan (US$52) a year in school fees. Local government must also now provide an education to children of migrant workers who lack a *hukou* (residence permit). There is still, though, a long way to go before there are enough schools available to take on the growing number of migrant children in China's fast-swelling cities.

◁ WALKING HOME FROM SCHOOL

At 5 p.m., when afternoon classes end, Chen walks home from school with her best friend. Xiao Chen's bag is weighed down with the books she carries home for extra hours of study in the evening.

▽ EVENING HOMEWORK

Back at home, Chen's studies continue as she sits down with her friend in the courtyard of her home to practise reading and writing in the remaining daylight.

△ RECEIVING GUIDANCE

Chen's grandmother makes sure that the strokes of each new character are written in the right direction, and she helps the girls with pronunciation, too.

▷ EATING DINNER

Chen uses the edge of the bed as a table and is distracted by the television as she eats her meal of fried vegetables and *mantou* (steamed bread).

◁∨ **TIME TO PLAY**
As her grandmother eats dinner and her grandfather finishes his chores around the yard, Chen and her friend sit down to a game of cards in the fading evening light.

∧ **TELEVISION BEFORE BEDTIME**
With the television tuned to the children's channel, Chen watches the stories of the cartoon character San Mao (Three Hairs), an enduring favourite with generations of Chinese children.

∧ **FAMILY KANG**
Bedtime is at 10 p.m. and Chen and her grandparents sleep together on a hard, but snug, *kang*, a brick bed heated from underneath by a pipe connected to a wood-burning stove.

< SNACK STAND
Signs for mobile phone cards are almost lost among displays of traditional snacks such as sour plums, dried meats, seeds and nuts, and modern sweets.

China's sweet tooth is big business, with a market worth

中
国
糖
果

more than US$3 billion a year, and in volume terms the largest in Asia. Vendors may still sell sticks of toffee-coated hawthorn berries and crabapples from bicycle-mounted stands, but most of China's traditional sweets, from candied dried fruit to sweetened red-bean pastes, now appear in bright wrappers modelled on Western designs, and are produced in factories. China's one-child policy is said to have produced "Little Emperors" for whom plenty of sweet treats are bought.

Partly through a sense of nostalgia, traditional Chinese sweets still sell better than Western chocolate brands. Perhaps the best-known brand of Chinese sweets is the White Rabbit Creamy Candy. First manufactured in Shanghai in the 1940s, they were given out as gifts for the tenth National Day of the People's Republic of China, and presented to US president Richard Nixon on his 1972 visit to China. They are still among the top-selling sweets today, and one of the only Chinese confectionery brands to be sold outside of the country.

CHINESE CONFECTIONERY

> SOFT DRINKS
Soft drinks packaging imitates the West in slogans and design. Coca-Cola was one of the first brands into China, adapting its name cleverly to *Ke Kou Ke Le* ("very tasty, very happy").

∧ SWEETS, PASTES, AND PASTRIES
From candied fruit and bean paste to flaky
su tarts, traditional snacks compete with
modern sweet brands such as "Flourishing
Son" fruit pastilles (*bottom left*).

> **WASHING BEFORE PRAYER**
Dhongyu rises at 4:30 a.m. and washes in the dim light before going to the monastery to lead the morning chanting session.

∨ **MORNING CHANT**
Well wrapped against the chill morning air, the monks chant the early prayer in the main hall of the monastery, as the first rays of light stream in.

The 300-year-old Atsog monastery, lying deep in rural

西藏僧侶 Qinghai Province in territory that was once part of Tibet, is home to 29-year-old Tibetan Buddhist monk Dhongyu. Both the monastery and its 200 monks – with their cycle of observances and ritual chants – form part of a deep spiritual tradition that for centuries has shaped Tibetan civilization.

Dhongyu joined the monastery when only ten years old, although monks are not officially recognized as such until they reach the age of 18. "Even at ten my family thought I was wise, and that I would make a good monk," he says. It's a matter of pride among many Tibetan families with more than one son to send the brightest one to a monastery.

Beginning as novices, the monks embark on a lifetime commitment to studying and understanding the inner meaning of Buddhist texts. They start as children with prayers, chants, and Tibetan language and literature, and continue as adults with philosophy and analysis of Buddhist scriptures. Dhongyu, like most Buddhist monks, spends much of the day in private study, and in performing personal spiritual exercises. "Training never ends," he explains, "the five key books of Tibetan scripture take a lifetime to learn and understand."

Dhongyu takes the lead in the morning and evening chants. It is a great responsibility, calling for a strong voice and knowledge of the whole liturgy by heart. During festivals, the chanting continues all day as people from the surrounding area come to pray, and to leave the donations of food and money on which the monastery depends.

Although Tibetan monasticism is characterized by a rejection of material possessions, Dhongyu has avoided some of the physical hardship associated with the monastic life, since his family owns large flocks of sheep and yak and can provide him with some luxuries. He has his own courtyard house, and does not sleep in the monastery dormitories. He also owns a car, a television, a DVD player, and an electric heater, which wards off the bitter winter cold.

Tibetans now account for only about one-fifth of the population of Qinghai Province, but most of the monks at Atsog are Tibetan, with a few Tu and Mongolians – both minorities with long histories of Tibetan Buddhism – and a single Han Chinese. The authorities restrict the number of monks and novices at many monasteries including Atsog. However, well away from more sensitive areas such as Lhasa, controls here are relatively light.

Remote Atsog is rarely visited by foreigners, but Dhongyu feels strongly about the influence of his religion on the outside world. "Tibetan Buddhism is a growing faith. One hundred years ago no one had heard of it, but now quite a lot of Europeans practise it, and there are even Tibetan monasteries in America."

> **TIBETAN DECORATION**
The wooden panels lining the prayer hall are beautifully decorated with traditional Tibetan patterns and motifs.

BUDDHIST MONK
PRAYER AND CONTEMPLATION AT ATSOG MONASTERY, QINGHAI

> **OUTSIDE THE PRAYER HALL**
The monks, in a sea of carmine robes, leave the prayer hall after the chants are over. Silk prayer flags hang in the background.

< **LIVING ROOM ALTAR**
Dhongyu's private altar in his house displays a picture of the current Dalai Lama, who was born not far from Atsog monastery.

∧ **READING BUDDHIST SCRIPTS**
Dhongyu takes time to study Buddha's teachings, one of the Three Jewels (the Buddha, his teachings, and spiritual guides).

< **PREPARING BREAKFAST**
Dhongyu carves off pieces of yak butter, which he mixes with ground barley and a little warm water to make a high-energy paste called *tsampa*, essential food in such a cold climate.

< **KNEADING THE TSAMPA**
The process of mixing and kneading the *tsampa* has meditative qualities, and is performed by the monks as a kind of morning ritual.

讲
述 | A famous writer once said that "the twenty-first century is the century for Buddhism and science". So I see Buddhism as the future.

> THE MONASTERY GROUNDS

The monastery is a splash of colour in an otherwise arid, hilly landscape. It is remote enough to encourage contemplation, and the site avoids valuable grazing land.

> OUTSIDE HIS HOME

Dhongyu's modern home sits on the outskirts of the monastery complex. He moved there from the dormitories several years ago.

∨ MAKING CURTAINS

The monks do most of their own maintenance work; here, Dhongyu helps the monastery's leader make new curtains.

∧ CHOPPING FIREWOOD

Dhongyu may have comforts at home, but the monastery still requires manual labour to run, and not all of the monks' time is spent in contemplation.

∧ > CARRYING WATER

The monastery does not have piped water for drinking or washing, and one of Dhongyu's morning duties is to get water from a well in the grounds.

ᐸ A YOUNG NOVICE

Dhongyu stops to speak to a boy, sent to the monastery at a young age to receive the guidance of the older monks. He will be recognized as a monk when he is 18.

ᐯ SPINNING THE PRAYER WHEELS

Each prayer wheel, or drum, that Dhongyu spins is carved with the text of a chanted prayer. Each revolution of the drum counts as one iteration of the chant.

ᐸ IN TOUCH WITH THE WORLD

Few corners of China are now remote enough to be without a mobile phone signal, and Dhongyu is able to keep in touch with his distant family.

ᐱ WALKING TO THE PRAYER HALL

Chiming bells call the monks to afternoon prayer. During Buddhist festivals, the usually quiet grounds are filled with thousands of pilgrims.

∧ THE AFTERNOON CHANT
After the morning chores are completed,
the monks file into one of the monastery's
many halls for an afternoon prayer session.

讲
述

Buddhism is wide and deep. A monk's training will last a lifetime; you can never learn enough.

∨ OUTDOOR COOKING AREA

The monks use a basic range of metal cooking utensils to prepare tea and food on coal- and wood-burning stoves.

> GROUP STUDY

At the modest home of a fellow monk, Dhongyu and a visitor to the Atsog monastery – a Tibetan pilgrim – read Buddha's teachings together, and drink tea.

∧ SMALL PRAYER WHEEL

The hand-held Tibetan prayer wheel has the same functions as larger drums, with each revolution of the wheel serving as one iteration of the chant.

> THE TEXT

While the group listens and prays, Dhongyu reads aloud from one of the five key books of Tibetan scripture, which Buddhist monks believe take a lifetime to learn and understand.

> TRAVELLING TO A NEARBY TEMPLE

In the luxury of his own vehicle, Dhongyu travels to another monastery nearby to visit a friend. The monastery is so remote that he must leave his car at the bottom of the track and walk the remaining distance.

< ARRIVING AT THE TEMPLE

The Kumbum monastery, near the provincial capital of Xining, and much larger than Dhongyu's own, is the most important Tibetan Buddhist monastery outside Tibet.

∨ MAKING A RITUAL OFFERING

Dhongyu makes an offering of water at the temple. When visiting, offerings of water, food, or flowers are made, or yak butter, brought in a jar, is added to the lamps.

> AT A TIBETAN MARKET

On his way back to the Atsog monastery, Dhongyu stops at a market in Xining to pick up supplies. Although the majority here is Han Chinese, there are also many Tibetans who still dress in traditional clothing.

∧ BACK AT HOME

Dhongyu takes time out from study and prayer to enjoy an evening watching television in his electrically heated house.

< EARLY MORNING HERB SEARCH
Early each morning, Chen goes out to search for natural ingredients before returning to the town of Mengyang to open his clinic for the day.

When his grandfather was 90 years old, Chen Yihe received a

草
药
师

summons to return from Yunnan to his home town in Hunan Province. "My grandfather was a doctor, and from when I was six he would take me to look for herbs in the woods. He was worried that his knowledge of traditional Chinese medicine would shortly be lost," remembers Chen.

At the age of 16, Chen's informal education in traditional medicine was interrupted by a government drive to develop China's impoverished border areas. This saw Chen despatched to the remote subtropical region of Xishuang Banna, which borders Laos.

Chen Yihe was assigned to a clinic at a rubber factory, but after recovering from a near-fatal accident, he resolved to take up traditional medicine himself. He worked hard, learning all about the herbal lore of local ethnic minorities and as much as he could from his elderly grandfather during occasional visits home. To become an all-round medical practitioner, Chen also had to become an expert in other techniques, such as acupuncture, acupressure, and cupping.

Now 60, Chen rises at 7 a.m. in a house that doubles as a storage space for the herbs he collects or buys in local markets, and prepares for the 8:30 a.m. opening of his busy clinic, the only one of its kind in three districts. China has 1.75 million doctors trained in Western medicine, compared to only 270,000 practitioners of traditional medicine. Although support for traditional medicine is enshrined in the Chinese constitution, its survival is based on cultural pride rather than on science.

Some aspects of traditional Chinese medicine have gained a certain amount of acceptance in the West. Particularly popular is acupuncture, which is based on the belief that the human body is controlled by a life force called qi that flows through channels between the organs of the body. However, the herbal side has drawn fierce criticism. In 2006, university professor Zhang Gongyao proclaimed that "Chinese traditional medicine has neither an empirical nor a rational foundation. It is a threat to biodiversity." It is undeniable that the use of tiger bone in remedies has helped to reduce China's wild tiger population to only 50 animals, and ingredients do include substances banned in developed nations.

Chen keeps meticulous records of his patients' responses to treatment, and insists that traditional medicine works – although why it does remains a mystery to him. He leaves the theory to his three children, all of whom have been to medical school. Chen has insisted on passing on his knowledge and techniques to his children, since he, too, fears that what his grandfather considered China's greatest invention, and a vital part of Chinese culture, is in danger of being forgotten forever.

∧ > GATHERING ROOTS AND BARK
Chen chops bark and roots for his remedies. Chinese herbal medicine employs leaves, stems, bark, roots, seeds, flowers, and all other parts of plants large and small, as well as animal and mineral material.

CHINESE HERBALIST
A DOCTOR OF ALTERNATIVE MEDICINE, YUNNAN

< RETURNING HOME WITH HIS FINDS
Most of Chen's herbs are gathered from the woods near his home. What he cannot find he buys at a local market.

∨ HAVING BREAKFAST AT HOME
Having built up an appetite, Chen breakfasts in his courtyard at home, surrounded by bundles of roots and herbs in various stages of preparation.

< CHEN'S MENGYANG CLINIC
Chen's clinic is the only one in the area offering alternative Chinese medicine, and it is particularly popular with those who can't afford expensive modern treatments.

∧ INGREDIENT BANK
In Chen's clinic, each of the neatly labelled compartments in this bank of drawers contains a different ingredient. In total, Chen uses around 800 herbal and other ingredients to prepare formula remedies for his patients.

∧ TENDING TO A PATIENT
Listening to a patient's pulse is one of Chen's crucial diagnostic techniques. Practitioners claim to be able to identify many pulse types unknown to mainstream medicine.

193

∨ WEIGHING INGREDIENTS
Chen weighs an ingredient with an old-
fashioned stick balance, which is still in
use in markets and shops across China.

< TAKING STOCK
Checking through his vast bank of storage
drawers, Chen takes note of which of his
many herbs and other ingredients need
their stocks replenished or replaced.

< PULVERIZING ROOTS
Much of the preparation work is done at
the clinic. Most ingredients are dried and
then ground up using a mortar and pestle,
one of the herbalist's most important tools.

∧ POTIONS OF SNAKES AND INSECTS
Such is the range of natural ingredients
that Chen's shop, like those of many
other herbalists, seems part pharmacy,
part natural history museum.

> SELECTING INGREDIENTS
After a diagnosis, Chen draws up a list of
ingredients needed to make the patient's
remedy. He then gathers the appropriate
amount of each one from his stores.

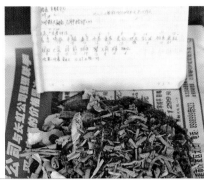

< **A PATIENT'S REMEDY**

Patient remedies are given as mixtures of ingredients wrapped in twists of paper with hand-written instructions. Most are made into bitter soups using boiling water.

∨ **CICADA SKINS**

Herbalists don't only deal in herbs: the dried parts of a vast range of insects and animals, including endangered species, are all part of the Chinese pharmacopoeia.

< **SLICING WOOD**

Chen cuts fine slices from the wood of various trees with chemically active ingredients in their sap. The slices are later dried and crumbled or ground up.

∧ **SUN-DRIED MEDICINES**

Chen places flat baskets of fruit peel, leaves, and other medicinal ingredients in the sun to dry outside his clinic. They are then stored in sacks and bags, ready for use.

陈 | I am one of the last generation to be properly
trained in the knowledge of Chinese herbs.
When we've all died – what then?

∧ **TURTLE SHELLS AND CICADA SKINS**
While cicadas can be obtained locally, farmed-turtle shells, dry-climate plants, and parts from wild animals and sea creatures are all bought by Chen from specialist vendors at local markets.

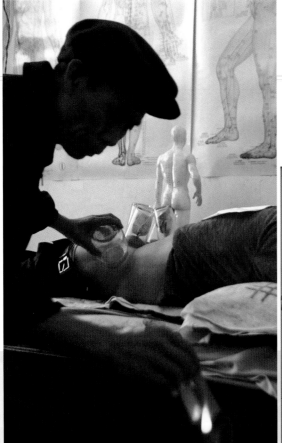

< APPLYING HOT CUPS

Chen administers cups to a patient. A form of massage, cupping is thought to detoxify the body. The air inside each cup is heated, creating a vacuum that sticks to the body.

∨ ACUPUNCTURE CHARTS

Wall posters show the channels of energy that Chinese medicine practitioners claim flow around the body, and the points at which to insert needles in order to affect these flows.

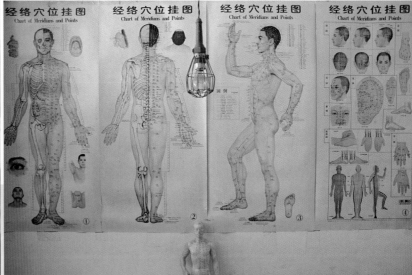

∧ ADMINISTERING ACUPUNCTURE

Chen treats a patient using the famous technique of acupuncture to try to reverse the facial paralysis caused by a stroke.

> ACUPRESSURE POINTS

Chen also uses acupressure, which, in addition to the acupuncture, applies pressure to key points with specially designed suction cups.

∧ STAGES OF CUPPING

Chen uses a range of bowls, jars, and cans from around his clinic as "cups". Each cup increases blood flow to the area of skin beneath it, leaving temporary red welts on the patient's back.

> HOUSE CALL

Sometimes the service goes beyond the treatment itself. Chen gives one of his patients a ride home on the back of his motorcycle at the end of the clinic session.

< RETURNING HOME WITH BRUSH
After closing his clinic, Chen spends an hour collecting more bark, returning home with a substantial bundle of trimmings from a shrub with important medicinal properties.

∨ TIME OFF
At the end of a long day, Chen relaxes by playing traditional music. His instrument of choice is the *erhu*, the bowed lute whose soaring, plaintive sound characterizes much of Chinese folk music.

书 | I feel that, as a doctor, I should regard other people's pain as my pain, and I try my best to bring happiness to people.

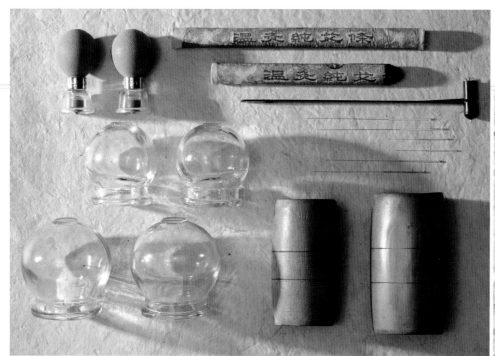

< ALTERNATIVE TREATMENTS
Moxibustion sticks (*top*) and acupressure tools (*top left*) are used as alternatives to acupuncture. The practice of cupping is thought to rid the body of toxins.

中
药

Traditional Chinese Medicine (TCM) has a history that dates back over 4,000 years. It is based primarily on the principle that imbalances in the flow of energy (qi) in the body are the cause of ill health and disease, and doctors of traditional medicine use a combination of methods to rechannel these energies. The two main treatments used are herbal medicine and acupuncture, and these are often combined with moxibustion (heat treatment), acupressure, cupping, *tui na* (massage therapy), and exercise such as *qigong* and tai chi.

Chinese medicine holds that there are 12 meridian lines in the body – one for each of the 12 main organs – along which qi flows. Acupuncture points are located along these lines, into which needles are inserted to alter or unblock the flow of qi.

There are around 11,000 herbs, minerals, and animal by-products in use that are prescribed in combinations to treat a variety of common illnesses. The controversial use of parts of endangered species in TCM has been heavily restricted in recent years, and is illegal in most parts of the world.

ANCIENT HEALING

> **BOOK OF REMEDIES**
A copy of an ancient manuscript, this book lists hundreds of "recipes", giving the right combinations and quantities of herbs to fight various illnesses.

Ingredients are grouped according to their ability to "heat" or "cool" the body. Herbs and bark are crushed to a powder or boiled and served in soups.

Before the sun can climb high enough in the sky to reach into

蟋
蟀
贩
子

the narrow grey-walled alleys surrounding Beijing's Guanyuan Market, Lan Yindong sets out his stall, hanging miniature cages from bamboo poles, and building columns of small ceramic pots on a table, labelling them with spidery characters: Golden-Headed Emperor and Black Dragon with Open Wings.

Lan stacks rows of polystyrene crates and, removing the lids, places sheets of glass over the top, revealing dozens of small bright-green crickets. "These are famous for their mournful song," says Lan. "But they also make good body-building bird food."

On leaving a factory job, Lan chose to follow his father into the centuries-old trade in crickets and grasshoppers, a business that is currently experiencing a revival in Beijing. "My customers include everyone from children to the retired." He sets out lines of matchbox-sized transparent containers, pushing rations of apple flesh into small holes in their sides. They contain tiny crickets that are smaller than a housefly but sing with such loud voices that they are known as *jinzhongr* ("golden bells").

Market vendors are often migrants from elsewhere in China, but Lan is a true Beijinger, as the extra "r" sound at the end of some of his words gives away. "Keeping crickets for their song and for fighting goes back to the Tang dynasty," he explains. "And crickets were a common subject of tea-shop discussion during the Song."

Nearby, another man sells gourds with perforated wooden caps. These are portable grasshopper living

quarters, which can be slipped inside a jacket to keep the insects alive during walks in Beijing's chilly winter. The perforations allow air in, and let the metallic chirping of the cricket's song out. It seems the Chinese, not the Japanese, produced the first Walkman.

One of Lan's customers causes a mass escape, and others rally round to help catch the excitable insects. They question Lan about his crickets. "They're from Shandong," he claims. This is traditionally the home of the best fighting crickets, known as *xishuir* or *ququr*.

In the alley behind the market, men are bunched around a low table where two *ququr* in a clear plexiglass arena are being tickled with rats' whiskers on slender sticks, encouraging them on towards one another. Bets are called and money flashed discreetly, and the insects chirrup piercingly and lock mandibles, pushing each other to and fro. When one disengages and runs away, the fight is over. Some of the winning crickets sell for as much as an average weekly wage, and by the end of the day, Lan has done well.

"I wanted my daughter to do this, too," says Lan. "But," he adds proudly, "she already owns a restaurant."

> AN EARLY START

Lan leaves home around 6 a.m. and breakfasts on fried pancakes at a small cafe close to the covered market. The rest of the day will be spent at his stand, where he'll eat *hefan* (a boxed lunch) so as not to miss customers.

> TRAVELLING TO WORK

Lan catches the bus to work. Although car ownership in Beijing is rising dramatically, the vast majority of the city's population travels by bicycle or mass transit.

> CROSSING THE RING ROAD

The Guanyan Market, where Lan's stand is located, is on Beijing's Second Ring Road, which follows the route of the city walls torn down by Mao Zedong in the 1950s.

ᴠ GUANYUAN MARKET

The indoor market specializes in everything for both traditional and modern hobbies; not only insects but also songbirds, fish, flowers, and kites.

CRICKET SELLER
A VENDOR AT GUANYUAN MARKET, BEIJING

< A CLOSER LOOK
A large grasshopper is temporarily set free from its miniature cage so that an interested buyer can give it a closer inspection before purchasing.

兰 | My customers used to be the older generation, but now more and more younger people keep crickets, too.

∧ TAKING STOCK
Beneath rows of tiny cages, Lan wields a small net used to catch crickets. His sign says *ming chong chong ju* – "singing insects and insect utensils".

> FEEDING TIME
Lan uses a long-handled miniature spoon to transfer ant eggs into the feeding dish in a cricket's pot.

∧ CRICKET IN ITS QUARTERS
The *xishuir* cricket, kept for fighting rather than song, is "tickled" with a fine stick in its ceramic pot, to agitate it before a match.

三 | Crickets are known for their mournful song, but they also make good bird and fish food.

> **FOOD FOR PETS**
Smaller insects are sold in bulk to fish and bird enthusiasts, who believe that the crickets provide good, fresh protein for their pets.

∨ **SINGING GRASSHOPPER**
Lü guoguor (green grasshoppers) like this specimen are among the cheapest and most common singers, and are priced according to size.

> **READY FOR PURCHASE**
Lan shows an interested customer one of his many crickets for sale. Much time may be spent studying dozens of insects before a choice is made.

∨ **OIL GOURD CRICKETS**
The small and expensive *youhulu* (oil gourd) cricket is said to have the most haunting song of all the singing crickets and grasshoppers.

∧ **CHECKING THE GRASSHOPPERS**
Lan has a substantial collection of insects. The best singing grasshoppers come from Tianjin, so naturally the vendors claim this origin for their stock.

traditional chinese pastimes

It's a common saying among the older generation that China's four great pastimes are *hua*, *niao*, *yu*, *chong* – flowers, birds, fish, and insects. Many balconies sport a ceramic bowl with lump-headed *longjingr* ("dragon eyes") and *wang tianr* ("skygazers") fish, their eyes black dots in the very tops of their heads. Often, older homes are topped with makeshift pigeon lofts that house birds trained to fly in circular formations called *panr* ("plates"). Small flutes are attached to their tails which produce an eerie humming sound as they pass overhead. Black-headed, yellow-beaked birds called *wutong* are trained to perform the trick of *dadanr*, streaking aerobatically to collect pea-sized balls fired into the air.

Pastime markets are also well stocked with fishing line, reels, and a special translucent paper called *wufangbu*, for enthusiasts who have returned to making traditional *shayanr* ("sand swallow") kites.

China's new commercialism may have brought the wrecker's ball to traditional housing in the cities, but it has also lifted suspicion of bourgeois possessions, and provided the disposable income to fuel demand for pets and playthings and for the market vendors, like Lan, to fulfill it.

< TINY DISHES OF FOOD
Crickets and grasshoppers are relatively expensive, so buyers take much care in feeding them the right food in order to extend their short life span.

∨ TICKLING THE CRICKETS
Onlookers watch as sticks tipped with a rat's whisker are used to encourage the near-sighted crickets towards one another so that the fight can begin.

∨ HEADING HOME
After closing up his stall at 6 p.m. at the end of a successful day's trading, Lan waits at the side of the road for a bus to take him home, where he will have dinner with his family.

∧ CRICKET FIGHT IN ACTION
A hollow tube transfers the cricket to the arena, where it is goaded towards its opponent until the pair lock jaws. The first to roll onto its back, or run away, loses the fight.

> WATCHING THE FIGHT
Cricket enthusiasts take a close look at a fight in progress behind the market. Gambling in China is illegal, but much money may change hands on the result.

∧ FAMILY BUSINESS
Over dinner, Lan reminisces about his father, also a cricket seller, whose photograph is in a book about Old Beijing. His daughter has chosen a different career, so on retirement Lan will sell his business rather than hand it down.

< LIVING QUARTERS
Many crickets are kept in simple teapots or jam jars. The best fighters, however, are housed in expensive ceramic cylinders moulded with auspicious symbols.

For more than 2,000 years, the Chinese have listened to the songs of crickets and grasshoppers and written about them as lyrically as Western poets have written of birdsong. The awakening of cricket song traditionally marked the start of the ploughing season, and the singing of different varieties punctuated the summer and early autumn months. The cricket's activities were often immortalized in rustic proverbs, and their ability to lay hundreds of eggs earned the respect of a people who equated fecundity with good fortune.

蟋
蟀

By the Tang dynasty (618–907), crickets were being kept for their song, and by the Song (960–1127) they were also used for fighting. In the Ming dynasty (1368–1644), the Chinese discovered how to hatch cricket eggs out of season so that their song and fighting abilities could be enjoyed year-round.

Today, keeping crickets is a pastime well suited in scale to the small living spaces of most ordinary Chinese, and there's a market for the myriad accessories that go with them, from miniature feeding bowls and spoons to ornate carved gourds.

CRICKET-KEEPERS' TOOLS

> GRASSHOPPER HOME
In warm weather the prettier singers are displayed in miniature cages made of anything from common bamboo to sandalwood and silver.

∧ **CRICKET-KEEPING EQUIPMENT**
Tools for catching crickets, for
transporting them, and for goading
them to fight are available alongside fine
feeding dishes and other paraphernalia.

< **SPECIAL BREAKFAST**
Wu and his family share a special sweet cake of pounded sticky rice, sugar, and peanuts called *ciba*, made especially for the festival celebrations.

Such is the respect of the residents of Quekenba village for

风
水
师
傅

their 37-year-old feng shui master or geomancer that this year they've asked him to organize their *miao hui* or temple festival, a rare honour for someone so young. An important religious and cultural event, the festival takes place only once every eight years, and is unique to the area. "It's a big thing for the village and it means that the villagers trust me," says Wu Jianxin proudly.

The villagers are Kejia people, Han Chinese who moved south from central China and reached the mountainous interior of Fujian Province during the Tang dynasty (618–907). These internal migrants, known as "guest people", were often driven by earlier settlers to the poorest farming land on the highest ground. They still speak a language they claim is close to an early form of Chinese, and one that is incomprehensible to their neighbours.

Every eight years, the Quekenba villagers gather to carry a small statue of Guanyin, the Buddhist goddess of mercy, from the 700-year-old Chao Tian Temple to their own village temple. They return the statue a year later for one of the other neighbouring villages to take, in a tradition nearly as old as the temple itself. According to local folklore, the festival began when a local official saw that the Chao Tian Temple had become dilapidated and offered to fund repairs. In return, the official wanted to take the temple's Guanyin image home to provide protection for his own village. The nearby villagers, wishing to retain the goddess's benevolence, negotiated a compromise in which each village would house the statue for a year at a time.

As the festival host, Wu has raised the funds, organized the events, and helped to prepare special food for the occasion. He spends most of his time, as the local feng shui master, choosing auspicious dates for weddings and funerals, and suggesting propitious locations on which to build houses and tombs for fee-paying customers. At the age of 15, having lost interest in school, he began to study feng shui with his uncle, and now his fame has spread not only to the eight villages in the area, but even to the town of Longyan, 100km (60 miles) away.

Wu is one of the few people of his generation left in the village, the rest having gone south to Guangdong Province to work, and it's the funds they send back that have boosted the local economy. More and more people can now afford Wu's services. "When I was a child we didn't even have enough food." He gestures to the village around him. "But now nearly every family has a motorcycle, television, and refrigerator." Wu can afford to send his two sons to school without migrating to Guangdong Province himself. "My income as a feng shui master is good, and it's gradually getting better as both villagers and city businessmen begin to believe again."

∧ **SHOPPING FOR THE FESTIVAL FEAST**
With his 10-year-old son, Ming, Wu visits a nearby town to buy the ingredients for an assortment of special dishes to be eaten during the festival celebrations.

∨ **RETURNING HOME**
Wu travels home with the goods on his motorcycle, an increasingly popular way to get around in rural communities, since they are cheaper to run than cars.

> **ROLL OF HONOUR**
The contributions made by each villager to the cost of the festival are listed by Wu and an elder villager by name and amount, and later posted up to honour all concerned.

FESTIVAL HOST
ORGANIZING A TEMPLE FESTIVAL, FUJIAN

< MAKING FESTIVAL SWEETS
Helped by his wife, Wu pounds rice into a sticky paste, ready to make more special *ciba* for breakfast the next day.

∨ PLANNING FESTIVAL EVENTS
At a neighbour's house, Wu discusses the events of the festival with village elders and those who will participate in the procession and ceremonies.

< WELCOMING THE BUDDHA
Offerings of tea and fruit are placed on the street outside each home to welcome the arrival of the Guanyin image to the village.

∨ AN EXPECTANT CROWD
The older residents of Quekenba await the arrival of the procession. In their younger days, many took part themselves, carrying the statue from village to village.

∧ DISPLAYING THE CONTRIBUTORS
Wu puts up a poster listing the names of the villagers who have offered to take on tasks during the festival. The poster to his left announces that an opera performance will take place in the village square.

< JOINING THE PROCESSION
Wu takes his place among the celebrants in the colourful procession as they make the three-kilometre (two-mile) walk from Chao Tian Temple back to Quekenba village.

∨ CARRYING THE STATUES
The village temple's own Buddha image and six other statues have been taken from Quekenba to accompany the Guanyin image in the procession back to the village.

∧ **WINDING THROUGH THE FIELDS**
Religious figures from both Buddhism and Daoism
are among the eight statues carried in the procession.
The villagers choose the deities from both religions
who seem most responsive to prayers.

吴 | In the cities, people do not have enough belief. I think belief is good, it helps to bring communities together.

< PASSING A RICE PADDY
The procession follows raised causeways through the flooded rice fields that provide much of the food, and income, of the local villagers.

∨ WELCOMING FIREWORKS
On the outskirts of the village, loud explosions mark the passage of the procession and are believed to scare away any harmful demons.

∨ PRAYING TO THE BUDDHA
Wu lights incense and prays to the statue of Guanyin. Originating in India as a male figure, in China she was transformed into a female deity often known as the "goddess of mercy".

∧ ARRIVING AT THE VILLAGE
Musicians compete with a cacophony of firecrackers as the procession arrives at Quekenba village, winding between mud-walled houses.

> ALTAR FOR THE BUDDHA
The villagers leave offerings at the altar in expectation that the arrival of the Guanyin will increase the good fortune, happiness, and prosperity of the village.

< VISITING THE ALTAR
Since the Guanyin is only brought to
Quekenba once every eight years, it
is a sombre occasion for the villagers,
whose belief in the deity runs deep.

< FINAL PROCESSION
The following morning, the statue is taken
down to the river to pray for plentiful rain
and no floods. Little is of more importance
to the village farmers than the weather.

∨ VILLAGE ELDER PAYS HOMAGE
One of Quekenba's most respected
figures leads in making obeisance to
the Guanyin statue, on the banks of
the local river.

∧ FOOD OFFERING
Below the Guanyin statue, the villagers
offer the best food they have to the deity,
including expensive meat dishes they can
rarely afford to eat.

< FAMILY ENTERTAINMENT
The festival celebrations conclude with a
performance in the village square by a local
opera troupe. The traditional music and
dance attracts all generations.

< PENDANTS OF PROSPERITY
Gifts of tasselled pendants called *guajian*, hung on walls, incorporate symbols of wealth, health, and good fortune, wishing these on the recipient.

Spring Festival, the lunar New Year, is the most important festival of the Chinese calendar, setting hundreds of millions off on journeys to return to their home towns and villages with debts settled and bearing gifts for family members.

节
日
装
饰

Many of the traditional New Year decorations and gifts have to do with wishing others the prosperity and fecundity you hope for yourself: enough money, many sons, and plenty to eat. Gold and red diamonds with the upside-down *fu* character appear pasted on walls and doors. *Fu*, meaning "good fortune", and *dao*, meaning "inverted", sound together in Mandarin like "fortune arrives". Fish-shaped snacks also depend upon punning for their impact: *yu* can mean both "fish" and "surplus", and the small Chinese *guizi* (date), another seasonal gift, also sounds like the word for "sons".

Red, the colour of luck, and gold, the colour of money, predominate in festival decorations, especially in the paper *fa cai shu* or "get rich trees" with their coins and gold ingots, and labels wishing health and good fortune.

FESTIVALS AND GOOD FORTUNE

> NEW YEAR BASKET
This delicate basket, a luxurious New Year gift, contains seasonal snacks, such as sweets and dried fruits, wishing the recipients full stomachs for the coming year.

△ GIFTS AND DECORATIONS
Children are the lucky recipients of *hong bao*, red and gold packets of money. Hanging decorations bring good fortune from Guanyin, the goddess of compassion.

> **MORNING MEAL**
Li breakfasts on porridge and steamed bread with her boyfriend and his mother, with whom she lives, in a small cafe close to their house.

"My parents were astonished when I told them I wanted to
企
业
家
open a shop," says 23-year-old Li Qinghe. "My father's a Chinese teacher, and my mother's a nurse, and both are still working hard. They would never have thought of doing anything like this themselves." Understandably, perhaps, it took them some time to come to terms with their daughter's ambition.

After much persuasion, Li's mother lent her 3,000 yuan (US$388) and her father gave her 2,000 yuan (US$260), which together was enough to cover all her start-up costs. Li eventually opened her business in a waterside house in the old part of Suzhou, in Jiangsu Province, selling porcelain and jewellery to tourists.

Canal-laced Suzhou, one of many places in the region labelled the "Venice of China", has held a reputation as a beauty spot for centuries. Now one of the wealthiest cities in south-east China, its transformation into a centre for manufacturing and the development of high-technology products has done nothing to reduce its appeal to tourists. Visitors swarm into the elaborate ornamental gardens built by retired officials and literati during the Ming and Qing dynasties, and wander the narrow streets of the "old city", lined with ancient whitewashed buildings, looking for souvenirs.

When Li first opened the shop, she whiled away the time between customers by making jewellery for herself. When those same customers started to show an interest in her creations, she began to sell these, too. Today, she operates principally as a jeweller, making a wide range of items.

Li rises for breakfast before noon, then checks her e-mail before taking the hour-long bus journey to Suzhou. She buys something for lunch as she walks along the flagstone lanes to the shop, often pausing to look in the antiques or jade markets on the way.

The afternoon is spent working on her designs, and after going out to dinner with her boyfriend or eating a meal he brings into the shop, Li works through until about 10 p.m.

Li is aware that she has a degree of freedom unimagined by her parents, not only in being able to start her own business, but also in having the time and resources to study for an MA in film animation, which she hopes will one day help her to realize her dream of making short films using clay figures. Sometimes Li closes her shop for a few days just to go travelling, and she's currently considering a trip abroad. Before going to sleep each night, she tries to learn three new French and Spanish words.

"When my parents were working hard to support the family, they had no time to think whether freedom was precious to them or not." She laughs: "Sometimes I'm dissatisfied with what I have simply because I am free enough to be able to think about it!"

∧ **STUDIO AT HOME**
Li paints experimental designs on ceramics in her home studio, which she shares with her boyfriend. She often works in the studio before leaving to open her shop.

> **WALKING TO THE SHOP**
After a long bus ride, Li reaches the historic quarter of old Suzhou. She takes the canalside path to her shop, which is based in an old traditional-style house.

ENTREPRENEUR
CRAFTING AND SELLING JEWELLERY, SUZHOU

▷ COMMISSIONED WORK
Such is the demand for Li's jewellery that she is often commissioned to make new pieces for regular customers, as well as selling the ready-made pieces on display.

∨ FINISHED PIECES
Li's jewellery is modern and global in style, rather than typically Chinese. It is popular with upwardly-mobile Chinese who want to associate themselves with "foreign" things.

∧ OUTSIDE HER SHOP
Li fell in love with the shop and the old building even before she had decided exactly what kind of business she wanted to start.

∧ LI'S WORKSHOP
With pliers, wires, and beads littering the work surfaces, Li begins work on new pieces to maintain the shop's stock. Soon she hopes to establish a brand name for her designs.

李 | I feel lucky in my success and try to remember everyone who has helped or encouraged me.

> **SEARCHING FOR INSPIRATION**
Li finds the inspiration for some of her ceramic designs from traditional Chinese motifs, and browsing in Suzhou's many antiques stores provides her with a rich supply of creative ideas.

∨ **A ROMANTIC BREAK**
Despite combining business with being a student, Li still finds time each day to have dinner with her boyfriend, or at the very least to pause for a tea break and a chat.

∧ **STUDYING IN THE LIBRARY**
Li closes her shop for a few hours to study in the university library. Post-graduate students like Li have access to a wide range of materials.

> **SHOPPING BREAK**
Like many young Chinese women her age, Li likes to keep abreast of the latest fashions, which she finds at Suzhou's large department store.

∧> **TRYING ON NEW CHINESE DESIGNS**
The success of Li's business allows her to enjoy new clothes. While most items are designed by foreigners and sent for export, Chinese retailers are fast catching up.

∨ TRYING DESIGNER PRODUCTS
Li tries on make-up before her night out.
Expensive international brands, sold in
large, urban stores, appeal to the new
wealthy class of businesswomen in China.

china's young entrepreneurs

In the early 1980s, permission was given for individuals to
start their own one-person businesses. Bicycle repair shops,
food stalls, and sewing services sprang up rapidly. Then
permission was finally given for private businesses to hire
as many as seven non-relatives, and restaurants opened
everywhere. Suddenly everyone wanted to *xia hai* – "jump
into the sea" of commerce. While about 85 per cent of the
population is still employed by the state in some way, this
new economic freedom has allowed young entrepreneurs
like Li to open thousands of new businesses around the
country. Now the private sector produces around ten per cent
of China's gross national product, and businessmen and
women are even allowed to join the Party.

However, this growth in private enterprises means
that the wealth gap between the better educated and
more entrepreneurial Chinese, and the farmers and migrant
workers, is now even greater than ever, and it is still growing.

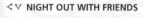

< ∨ NIGHT OUT WITH FRIENDS
Li enjoys an evening with her boyfriend and
friends in a Suzhou night-spot. Western-style bars
in China's major cities are the first choice for many
young Chinese on a night out, even though a
single drink may cost more than a hearty meal.

张

> The fish are getting smaller and fewer. But thankfully, freshly caught wild sea fish are still in demand.

The coastal waters of Zhejiang Province, in eastern China,

渔
民

are dotted with islands, one of them a banana-shaped speck less than 4km (6½ miles) long called Ji Shan Dao. The harbour is full of deep-water trawlers that go out into the East China Sea for long periods, but Zhang Zhiping's three small fishing boats venture no more than an hour from his island home.

"I only fish in relatively nearby waters," says Zhang, "and though the fish seem a little better this year, for the last two years they've been smaller than average, and they fetch a low price. For big fish you have to go much farther out now." Zhang worries that there are too many fishermen now. He himself only has four employees, who all originate from the landlocked Sichuan Province, which, as China's most heavily populated province, is a major exporter of labour to the wealthier coastal areas.

The industrialization that has made Zhejiang the country's wealthiest province is adding to Zhang's problems. Manufacturing plants, which produce an array of consumer goods that are exported around the world, pollute the rivers, and the poisons are swept out to sea, stunting the development of the fry. "The pollution makes the water less nutritious for the fish," he complains.

In 2000, over-fishing in China's exclusive territorial waters led to the passing of a law forbidding further growth in catches of both freshwater and sea fish. Although often ignored, a June-to-September moratorium on fishing in certain sensitive locations was also introduced to allow the fish to breed and stocks to grow.

Fish cultivation is a growth industry along coastal areas, and more than 60 per cent of China's fish consumption is now of farmed products. But for now, most of the fish in Zhang's area is freshly caught. "People prefer wild fish," he insists. "They taste better and sell for a higher price." But fishing is a risky business, and one that Zhang would happily give up. "It's hard and dangerous work," he says. "Accidents happen, and lives are lost."

It's a gamble, too. In addition to salaries, maintenance, and fuel, Zhang has to pay 100,000 yuan (US$13,000) a year in assorted fees to the government. While he hopes to make around double that this year, catches were so small last year that he lost an equivalent amount.

However, under the policy reforms that were initiated by the late Deng Xiaoping, life has improved for the island's fishermen. "We're not poor," Zhang maintains. "We have everything we need. But I'm not rich enough. If I were richer, I wouldn't stay here." He hopes his only son, a migrant worker in Shenzhen, will get a safe and reliable job in the city, and that when Zhang and his wife are ready, they will be able to abandon their island home and move there to join him.

∧ **TRAWLERS IN THE HARBOUR**
Zhang's fishing operation is on a small scale, but other residents of Ji Shan Dao operate larger deep-sea trawlers such as these, moored in the harbour.

> **ENGINE TROUBLE**
The morning's fishing is cut short, as the engine on one of Zhang's boats fails, and he must tow it back to the harbour for repairs.

∨ **AT THE HELM OF HIS BOAT**
Zhang rises at 4 a.m. to reach the fishing grounds, and it is frustrating when his equipment lets him down, as it takes an hour to return to harbour.

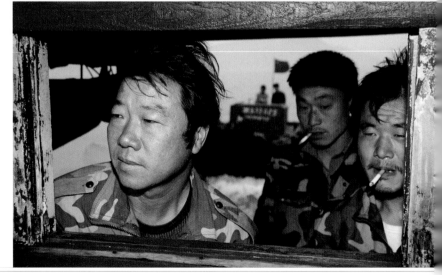

SEA FISHERMAN
TRAWLING OFF JI SHAN ISLAND, ZHEJIANG

< **THE MORNING'S CATCH**
Zhang unloads the morning's meagre haul. Despite regulations, over-fishing and pollution in the area means that the remaining fish are small.

∨ > **MENDING NETS ON THE HARBOUR**
Zhang's wife, like many of the island's women, handles repairs to the nets and other maintenance. Once a catch is landed, she will sell it at the dockside.

∧ **OFF TO FIX THE ENGINE**
Zhang sets off with the faulty part to arrange repairs. The cost of routine maintenance is not something the fishermen's tight margins permit.

< **LEAVING THE HARBOUR**
Zhang's competitors from a large commercial trawler wait as their vessel is loaded with ice for a trip that will last several days.

< IMPROVING HIS GAME
In better times, Zhang was at sea from 5 a.m. to 10 p.m., but now, with smaller catches, he has more spare time than he would like but uses it to improve his chess game.

< ∨ CARING FOR HIS GRANDDAUGHTER
Making fewer trips to sea also means that Zhang can spend more time with his granddaughter, in turn freeing his son to pursue a career in the city.

> CHESS PIECES
Chinese chess, one of Zhang's great passions, is very similar to the Western version, and these red pieces equate to pawns in the Western game.

DOMESTIC CHORES
Zhou catches up on some duties at home, refilling a large clay vessel with preserved vegetables and a smaller one with locally made spirit.

MAKING A TOAST
Zhang raises his glass in a toast. The family usually drinks beer with dinner, reserving the potent *bai jiu* spirit for special occasions and banquets.

FAMILY DINNER
Unsurprisingly, fresh fish is often on the menu for Zhang's family. If all the catch has been sold, then there will always be plenty of dried fish to eat instead.

A GAME OF MAHJONG
Zhang takes on a friend at mahjong. The game is very popular in the area, since Ningbo, in the north of Zhang's home province, claims to be its birthplace.

Across China, the first hint of spring warmth brings people
打
牌
out to sit on tiny stools at low tables for roadside or courtyard sessions of Chinese chess, go, mahjong, Chinese dominoes, and modern card games, often attracting a crowd of onlookers.

At first sight, many traditional Chinese games look similar to those played in the West, but Chinese dominoes, for example, are longer and thinner, and used in the same way as playing cards, rather than laid out in connecting lines on the table. China's best-known game export is mahjong (majiang),

created in around the 1850s from much older domino and card games. A craze for the game swept through Europe and North America in the 1920s, and at some mahjong parties players would even dress in Chinese costume. Nowadays, the computer-game form of mahjong is also popular in China.

Chinese chess (xiangqi), which has been played for more than 2,000 years, differs from the Western variety in having fewer pawns and in restricting the "general" (the West's "king") to a limited "palace" area, making for a faster game.

GAMES OF CHANCE AND SKILL

> SET OF DOMINOES
Chinese dominoes, which date from the 12th century, are more like playing cards and have no blanks. The Chinese also appreciate the Western game, making their own sets, as shown here.

∧ **AN ARMY IN A BOX**

In Chinese chess and *banqi* (half chess) –
played on only half the board – weapons,
chariots, and soldiers are indicated by the
characters displayed on each of the pieces.

> **TRAVELLING TO WORK**
> The troupe is performing at a village a short distance from Shaoxing, and Zhang sets out from the company's headquarters carrying her costume and make-up kit.

> **REVIEWING HER LINES**
> Although she has performed this role many times before, Zhang still feels nervous before a performance and takes time to go over her lines before the matinee.

When Zhang Lin was only three years old, she began to learn

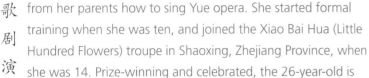 from her parents how to sing Yue opera. She started formal training when she was ten, and joined the Xiao Bai Hua (Little Hundred Flowers) troupe in Shaoxing, Zhejiang Province, when she was 14. Prize-winning and celebrated, the 26-year-old is now one of the most esteemed performers in her field.

Zhang comes from the city of Shenzhou, two hours by car from Shaoxing, and the birthplace of this form of Chinese opera. "Back in my home town when I was growing up, 90 per cent of the people could sing *Yue ju*." While Chinese opera can trace its origins back at least as far as the 12th-century Song dynasty, the best-known forms today have very brief histories. Even world-famous Beijing opera (*Jing ju*) only dates back to the late 18th century, and Zhang's *Yue ju* style only to the 1930s.

The roots of Yue opera lie in early-20th-century farmers' songs that were more chanted than sung, using the local dialect. The accompaniment was principally a wooden clapper, but the farmers' pungent and vivid language made this new form quickly popular. In the early 1920s, it caught on in nearby Shanghai, gradually gaining a more tuneful musical accompaniment.

As recently as 20 years ago, opera was one of very few entertainments available to the Chinese, but now it faces vast competition from television, film, and modern nightlife of all kinds. "Yue opera is very slow, not as exciting as a Hollywood movie, and not really in step with the pace of modern life," says Zhang. "But if people just calm down

and listen to it, they find it very tasteful and beautiful." There are few opera writers now. "Most of the good writers would prefer to write soap operas for television – it makes more money," Zhang explains. So the opera troupe's repertoire consists mainly of established classics based on mythologized history and well-known love stories.

State subsidies for opera are withering away, and the Xiao Bai Hua troupe is now required to make at least 150 commercial performances a year in order to make a profit. This means that the 25 performers and many of the 50 support staff spend much of the year on the road, travelling as far as ten hours from their Shaoxing base, and spend little time at home. "My parents and my younger sister are still in Shenzhou, and I see them about four or five times a year," says Zhang. "The troupe spends so much time living and travelling together, that if we have any problems, we tend to talk to each other first."

When she won first prize in a national *Yue ju* competition in 2005, Zhang's face was often on local television, and the public recognition of her skills seems to make her content. "I feel happiest when my audience gives me big applause. That's enough for me."

> **GETTING READY FOR THE SHOW**
> Zhang's preparations start two hours before the show. Her heavy make-up is designed to make her look more masculine for her male role in the play.

OPERA PERFORMER
ON TOUR WITH A TRAVELLING YUE OPERA TROUPE, ZHEJIANG

< IN THE WINGS
The Xiao Bai Hua is an all-female troupe, so the women also take the male parts. Dressed as a general, Zhang waits in the wings, ready for her cue.

张 | Being part of a travelling opera troupe is a special job and life experience; the troupe is like my family now.

< ∨ AT WORK ON STAGE
Zhang performs in front of a large audience. A successful textile dealer based just outside Shaoxing has paid for a performance by the troupe in honour of his father's 70th birthday.

∧ WAITING BACKSTAGE
In their elaborate costumes and carrying props designed to make their roles clear to the audience, the cast members chat backstage as they wait to go on.

< ∧ A FULL HOUSE
As the show is performed in a public square, it is open to the villagers, as well as the family members, and many take advantage of the opportunity to see a well-known performer for free.

< COSTUME SHOES
Each change of costume requires a change of matching, and equally elaborate, footwear befitting the character's status. The platform soles give the actors more presence on stage.

张 | Yue opera is part of our cultural heritage, and we need to preserve it, otherwise it will disappear.

∧ CENTRE STAGE
Opera performers need to be multi-talented
artists, matching the swirling music with
colourful dances, occasional martial arts,
and equally impressive voices.

229

< ∨ GETTING INTO COSTUME
Beneath her bright costume, Zhang dresses warmly, adding extra layers for the evening's open-air production, the second performance of the day.

∨ THE OPERA OF MENG LIJUN
Meng Lijun tells the story of a young girl betrothed to a general (played by Zhang), who is forced to flee her home, leaving her portrait behind as a memento.

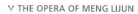

∧ > READY TO GO ON STAGE
Zhang checks the final addition to her costume, an imposing headdress that signifies the status and rank of the character she plays.

∧ PLAYING THE PART
The general (Zhang) pines for his beloved, little knowing that, disguised as a man, she has passed examinations leading to a senior post in the imperial civil service.

< ∨ **THE PLOT THICKENS**
At court, the general recognizes the new Premier as the disguised Meng Lijun, while the emperor has also recognized that she's a woman and has fallen in love with her.

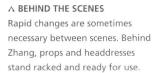

∧ **BEHIND THE SCENES**
Rapid changes are sometimes necessary between scenes. Behind Zhang, props and headdresses stand racked and ready for use.

∧ **THE FINAL ACT**
The performance finishes with a wedding scene between the general and Meng Lijun. Television soaps may be more popular, but can offer little more in the way of plot.

mass entertainment

While opera is still a popular choice for traditional occasions, such as village festivals, it is no longer China's main form of entertainment. As the economy has grown, so have the entertainment choices, from spectator sports to stadium rock concerts, karaoke bars, and the Internet.

Television is now almost universally available, with a host of national channels competing for advertising. Foreign sports have a big following, as do soap operas, their plots laced with pro-socialist messages approved by the censors. Recently, some reality television formats, such as the *Supergirl* talent contest, have been hugely successful.

In cinema, although the government restricts the distribution of foreign films to 20 a year, the Chinese box office record is still held by the 1997 Hollywood blockbuster *Titanic*. But DVD players are common, and almost every foreign title is available on pirate DVD within a week of its opening overseas.

王逸少書不可多得於好
事家蓋見之一二焉此
秘閣所藏快雪時晴帖墨
本乃真蹟也尤為奇特翰

雪書云可年前二白過迷離融日彩雲漢妻和冰
毛筆細銀花纈樹朵時臨縮牽玉枕枝好月
庚午新正雪晴有作作為澤玉石子命工製為卷之玩鴛曾縮臨是
帖於上故末句及之再書於冊清淺

盼雪遠冬來一朝甚一朝三更殘靄集四
鼓拆雲飄出沃心芽潤深培麥本饒惟期
盈尺積寧祇百憂消夜雪一律
癸卯嘉平月下游洪筆

右軍此帖跋語俱佳紙亦清瑩可玩膜
題識數番至與筆墨相和愛不釋手
得意輒書無為次苐也乾隆偶記

己巳臘日雪後委典帖臨此帖遜命失衆
劉於姬宋右所製玩鴛玉吴尓佳話也
三希堂子誠識

不勝欣羡至延祐五年四月二十一日
翰林學士承旨榮祿大夫知制誥兼修國史臣趙孟頫奉
勅恭跋

CULTURE

文化 THE SPIRIT OF CHINA

China is one of the world's most remarkable and enduring civilizations, and its cultural, spiritual, and artistic traditions are the foundation stones of the modern nation. The Chinese are justifiably proud of their great heritage, and many are concerned that the tides of modernization and globalization may sweep away their traditional values and ways of life. However, the resilience of Chinese culture over the past 4,000 years suggests that those fears are groundless. Despite the ethnic and linguistic variety found within the country's borders, a shared language and worldview has linked the Chinese people for millennia. As China begins to play a growing role in the international arena, it is important for anyone who seeks to understand the country to be aware of the traditions that have shaped it. This chapter focuses on China's religious and philosophical beliefs and practices and its artistic and literary heritage, opening a small window into the culture of a fascinating and unique civilization.

In spite of formidable geographical and linguistic barriers,

三
教 as well as violent regime changes, civil wars, foreign invasion, and natural disasters, Chinese culture has remained remarkably unchanged over four millennia, providing a clear and incredibly unified picture of what it really means to be "Chinese". In order to understand the cultural heritage of this complex and fascinating nation, it is important to go back to the ancient belief systems, creation myths, and traditional philosophy that underpin the whole of the Chinese way of life.

道 the dao

The Dao, or "The Way", is central to Chinese thinking. It can refer to the path an individual should take in life, or to a vision of cosmic, natural, and social order. Disorder, caused by lack of virtue, could bring about natural disasters such as earthquakes and floods. The ruler and his officials were charged with maintaining harmony and could lose the mandate of heaven (*tianming*) if they did not follow the way of virtue.

The earliest anthology of Chinese poetry, the *Shijing* or *Classic of Poetry*, which dates back to at least the 10th century BCE, portrays an idealized ancient world, where people lived in close harmony with the land and the agricultural seasons, understanding and controlling their environment. The ancient society was hierarchical and often violent, but ideals of social harmony, shaped by the Dao, became a defining part of the relationship between Chinese people and their world.

Traditionally, the family was the major unit of social organization, a concept that endures in Chinese society. The ideal family is strongly patriarchal, with the father as the central figure to be honoured and obeyed (although sons are expected to respect their mothers). The father, like the ruler, has an obligation to preserve harmony, and to lead by moral example, by following the Dao. Each family member is aware of their status, but roles change: sons become fathers, and daughters-in-law become mothers-in-law, preserving the natural patterns (or Dao) of society.

盘 pan gu

古 The Chinese have various myths about the creation of the world and human beings, one of the most popular being the story of Pan Gu. It tells that in the beginning there was nothing in the universe except a formless chaos, which over time coalesced and formed the perfectly opposed principles of yin and yang. From in between the two, a giant by the name of Pan Gu was born, representing the human element in the cosmic triad comprised of *Tian*, *Di*, and *Ren* (Heaven, Earth, and human beings).

Pan Gu created the world by separating Yin (Earth) from Yang (Sky) with his axe, and to keep them separated he stood between them. This process took 18,000 years, and "each day the heavens rose ten feet higher, each day the earth grew ten feet thicker, and each day Pan Gu grew ten feet taller".

"When he was approaching death, Pan Gu's body was transformed. His breath became the wind and clouds; his voice became peals of thunder. His left eye became the sun; his right eye became the moon. His four limbs and five extremities became the four cardinal points and the five peaks. His blood and semen became water and rivers. His muscles and veins became the Earth's arteries; his flesh became fields. His hair became the stars; his bodily hair became plants and trees. His teeth and bones became metal and rock; his marrow became pearls and jade. His sweat became rain. All the mites on his body were touched by the wind and were turned into the black-haired people".

WAYS OF THOUGHT
THE ANCIENT ROOTS OF CHINESE CULTURE

女 nü wa

娲 In some myths predating the story of Pan Gu, the goddess Nü Wa (also known as Nü Kua) formed human beings out of yellow clay in order to populate the Earth. However, she grew

> She rides in a thunder-carriage driving shaft-steeds of winged dragons and an outer pair of green hornless dragons.

tired of this lengthy task, so instead she drew a rope through the mud and flicked blobs of it to make more people. Some stories claim that the handcrafted clay people became noblemen and rulers, while the mud men were commoners. Other tales tell that the mud men melted in the rain, introducing sickness and abnormality to mankind. Nü Wa is also credited with saving

Heaven and Earth when fire and floods raged out of control and the pillars supporting Heaven were damaged by the water god, Gong Gong. Nü Wa smelted five-coloured stones to mend the heavens – a story that features in the great 18th-century novel, *The Story of the Stone* (*see page 274*). Nü Wa replaced the four pillars holding up the sky using the severed feet of a giant turtle she had slain, but she was unable to straighten the tilted sky and, as a result, to this day the sun, moon, and stars move toward the northwest, and Chinese rivers flow southeast into the Pacific Ocean. Nü Wa also slaughtered a black dragon to save the region of Ji, and dammed the floodwaters, so that peace reigned everywhere in the world. For these deeds she earned the unending gratitude of the people.

< NÜ WA AND FU XI
Nü Wa and Fu Xi had human torsos but their lower bodies were those of dragons or snakes.

FU XI

In later stories, by the Han dynasty, Nü Wa finds herself demoted to a less important role and is closely linked to her elder brother and consort, Fu Xi. Together, they are referred to as the "parents of humankind". Fu Xi is considered to be a Chinese cultural hero and is credited as the creator of many of the world's greatest and most important inventions, including writing, nets for hunting and fishing, and music. Fu Xi observed the natural world in order to develop his inventions. After watching a spider spin a web, he wove fishing nets, and having noticed the markings of a mythical dragon-horse (sometimes said to be a turtle), he developed the Eight Trigrams. The trigrams are the basis of the divination classic, the *Yi Jing*, or *Book of Changes*, so Fu Xi is believed to be the inventor of divination. He also knotted cords, with which he is often depicted, for calculations of time and distances, and as a form of writing.

∧ CONTROLLING THE NATURAL LANDSCAPE
Early Chinese people believed that the relationship between the human and natural worlds, as seen in the agricultural landscape, created a triad of Heaven, Earth, and humans.

黄 the yellow
帝 emperor

The mythical Yellow Emperor (Huangdi) is said to be the ancestor of all Han Chinese. According to legend, the Emperor's mother witnessed a strange flash of lightning, and 23 months later the Yellow Emperor was born. The Emperor was the creator of Chinese culture and civilization – a warrior and peacemaker who fought only to preserve his state when under threat. His reign is considered a Golden Age.

The Yellow Emperor fought several terrifying enemies, beginning with his rival half-brother, the Flame Emperor, as well as the monster war god, Chi You, against whom the Yellow Emperor was almost defeated until he marshalled the rain and wind gods and his own daughter, Goddess of Drought, to his aid. He also killed the one-legged Kui Monster and used his hide to make a drum to strike terror into his enemies. After defeating his other enemies, the Four Emperors, this reluctant warrior was able to restore peace and harmony.

The Yellow Emperor is credited with bringing to the Chinese people fire, weapons, boats, agriculture, musical instruments, clothes, palaces, houses, and the equitable distribution of land through the wells and fields system. He is said to have lived to 100 due to his interest in natural health and treating illness, and is considered the father of Chinese medicine. After his physical death he became immortal, and in later centuries he became a supreme deity in religious Daoism (*see page 248*).

∧ **THE FATHER OF MEDICINE**
The Yellow Emperor, seated in the Hall of Brightness, presents medical books to the Thunder Duke, Lei Gong.

尧
舜
禹 the three demigods

The three mythical "demigods", Yao, Shun, and Yü (also known as the Three August Ones), were ancient Chinese rulers revered by the philosopher Confucius (*see page 242*).

According to legend, Yao, the son of a red dragon, was a shadowy figure who ruled from the age of 20 until he was 119 years old. He bypassed his sons to give his throne to the worthy Shun, thus establishing the concept of merit over heredity that became central to later Confucian ideals of rulership.

EMPEROR SHUN

Shun was the epitome of the filial son who always honoured his father despite that father's cruelty. Shun's father was blind and favoured Shun's stepbrother, Xiang (Elephant – known for his long nose), who hated Shun. Shun's father and stepbrother plotted to kill him three times, but each time he was rescued through the magic intervention of his two wives, the daughters of Yao. They gave Shun magic robes that transformed him into either a bird or a dragon in times of extreme danger, and saved him from being poisoned in Xiang's third attempt on his life. Despite his family's cruelty, Shun forgave them and looked after them when he became ruler at the age of 53. Shun was a great emperor and his fifty-year reign was one of the longest in Chinese history.

On his death, his two widows wept so much that their tears marked a type of bamboo still found in south China and known as a poetic symbol of grief for a loved one. On their journey south to mourn at their husband's grave, the two sisters drowned and became river goddesses in Hunan Province. Shun's stepbrother, full of remorse, transformed himself into an elephant and was set to work in the fields.

THE GREAT YÜ

Shun in his turn passed his throne on not to one of his nine sons, but to the Great Yü. During Yao's time, floodwaters

> Born out of his father Gun's dead body, Yü was the last ruler of the Golden Age and founder of the Xia dynasty, most ancient of the Chinese dynasties.

covered the Earth, and the people suffered terribly. Yü's father, Gun, was charged with controlling the Great Flood and mapping the world, but he failed and was executed. Yü took over his father's task. The main myths about Yü deal with his heroic role in controlling the floodwaters inundating the world, sometimes alone and sometimes with the aid of deities and mythical creatures. Once the Great Flood had subsided, Yü restored civilization to the world and rewarded the worthy.

Yü is also credited with measuring the world and dividing it into the Nine Provinces (nine is a symbolic number associated with the male principle Yang, and Heaven). He was a warrior-emperor who brought peace to his empire and cast Nine Sacred Cauldrons. Ownership of these magical bronze vessels became a symbol of imperial moral worth and a sign of Heaven's favour. Yü chose his wife, Nu Jiao, through the omen of seeing a white fox with nine tails, a creature associated with her people. Nu Jiao turned to stone from fear while pregnant when Yü transformed himself into a bear. Yü ordered the stone to split open and his son, Kai (meaning "to open"), was born. Kai is said to have introduced the music of Heaven ("the Nine Counterpoints and the Nine Songs") to Earth.

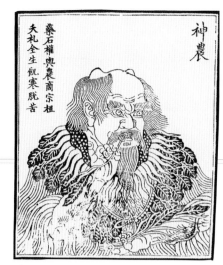

> SHEN NONG
Shen Nong (meaning the Divine Farmer) showed the Chinese people how to grow grains, thus avoiding having to kill any animals for food.

神
农 agriculture gods

One of the most important cultural figures in Chinese tradition is Shen Nong, the farmer god who taught the Chinese people about agriculture. He introduced the plough to the Chinese people and showed them how to plant millet. He is also known for his role in helping people distinguish between poisonous and harmless plants and shellfish. He himself tasted every plant and water source, suffering poison 70 times in a single day, so that the people would know what was safe to eat and drink. He is often depicted with a rust-red whip that he used to thrash plants until they revealed their characteristic flavour and use.

Another farmer-god whose role overlaps with that of Shen Nong is Lord Millet, conceived when his mother trod on the giant footprint of a god, and brought up by the birds and beasts of the field when abandoned by his mother's family. There is a famous hymn about Lord Millet in the *Classic of Poetry* that details his miraculous birth and childhood and his introduction of agricultural skills to the people. Lord Millet, who is depicted as female in some early texts, is also believed to have been the founding ancestor of the Zhou dynasty.

< THE DRAGON'S CHILD
The first of the three demigods, Yao was the son of a red dragon. His throne was inherited by Shun, who was able to transform himself into a dragon's shape.

后羿 yi the archer

Legend tells that the ten children of the goddess Xihe and the god Dijun were suns, one for each day of the ten-day-week cycle. Every day the suns would bathe in the sea beyond the Eastern Ocean and roost in the enormous fabled Fusang tree, taking turns shining down upon the world. However, one day, tiring of their usual routine, they all decided to shine together. This caused great hardship and suffering for the people on Earth below. The world's waters and plant life began to shrivel up and it became so hot that the people and animals found it hard to breathe. Monsters began to appear out of the dried-up lakes and forests.

The suns ignored the pleading of the people, but their father, Dijun, decided to take action to save the world and gave the heavenly archer, Yi, also known as Houyi, a vermilion bow in order to persuade his children to stop what they were doing. They refused to yield, and when Yi saw at first hand the devastation the suns had caused, he was filled with rage. He seized his bow and shot down nine of the suns in turn.

> Yi was supposed to scare the suns into resuming their original cycle, but they refused to listen, and Yi was so enraged that he shot them down to bring an end to their destructive power.

One by one they fell to the ground, each taking on the shape of a three-footed crow as they died. The last sun, warned by the others, remained in the sky, where it continues to carry out its duties to this day, warming and shining light upon the Earth.

Yi went on to fight many of the monsters now roaming the Earth as a result of the suns' actions and was rewarded for his role in saving the world from destruction. However, Yi had so angered Dijun by killing his sun children, rather than persuading them to resume their normal duties, that he was banished from the heavens down to Earth with his wife, Chang E, and commanded to live out the rest of his days as an ordinary mortal man.

Chang E was extremely unhappy at being cast out of Heaven and she persuaded her husband to ask the Queen Mother of the West (Xi Wang Mu), a dangerous goddess who lived on Kunlun Mountain, for some of her elixir of immortality. Yi endured many hardships in his attempts to do his wife's bidding, but ultimately he received the elixir and brought it back. Then, however, his wife stole it from him and, after drinking it, floated up to the moon, where she became the Moon Goddess, living in a palace with a hare and a cassia tree. In some versions of her story she is punished by being turned into a toad, and to this day many people still claim to be able to see the image of a toad reflected in the moon.

THE QUEEN MOTHER OF THE WEST

The Queen Mother of the West was originally portrayed as a wild and dangerous goddess who had animal features and bird and beast helpers and guardians. She lived in a remote mountain far to the west of China and terrified those who saw her. Over the centuries her character was transformed into something more benign, a queen with the power to confer eternal life. The Queen Mother of the West appears in later fictional narratives, notably in the *Journey to the West* (*see pages 271–72*) when Monkey steals her peaches from the tree of immortality, which only ripen every 3,000 years.

∧ **YI THE ARCHER**
Yi spared the last of the ten suns from destruction so that the world was not left in complete darkness.

卜 diviners and 筮 shamans

During the Shang dynasty (c.1766–1122 BCE), Chinese people communicated with their gods and ancestors through divination, using oracle bones made of incised cattle bones and turtle shells to ask questions on matters related to auspicious days for hunting, battles, harvesting, and ritual occasions, and even which spirit might have caused the king's toothache. Diviners interpreted the cracks made by burning along drilled holes.

During the Zhou dynasty (1122–221 BCE), people carried out ritual sacrifices using extraordinary bronze vessels incised with meticulous written records, though the exact nature of the sacrifices has been lost over the centuries.

The Chinese affinity for nature meant that many minor deities were associated with natural phenomena such as wind and thunder or physical features such as lakes, rivers, and mountains, even taking the form of dragons in underwater kingdoms. The ancient Chu culture of Hunan is known for its mountain and water spirits and river gods. These spirits needed to be appeased by shamans who made spirit-journeys to find them or who offered up human sacrifices as consorts to prevent flooding. Shamans performed rituals involving music, dance, and plants to prepare themselves to enter trances to encounter the gods.

The poet Qu Yuan (c.340–278 BCE), the earliest of China's poets known by name, is said to have written a series of songs in shamanistic style, the most famous of which is "On Encountering Sorrow" ("Li Sao"). Banished from the Chu court by the actions of malicious rivals, Qu Yuan spent his time observing the rites of the shamanistic folk in the south of China. He eventually drowned himself, and China's famous Dragon Boat Festival originated as a search for his body. Traces of shamanism are still found in Daoist poetry and popular religion.

∨ THE LANDSCAPE OF THE GODS
Living closely with nature meant that the Chinese associated many minor deities with features of the landscape.

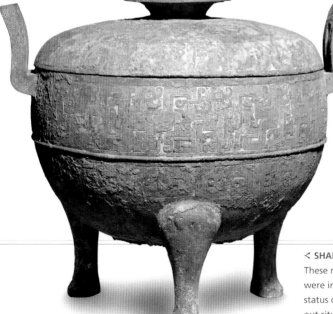

< SHANG RITUAL BRONZE
These magnificent bronzes were indicators of the status of those carrying out ritual sacrifices.

> **PHOENIX AND DRAGON**
These two mythological creatures represent the opposites of yin and yang.

气 the concept of qi

Qi is a fundamental part of Chinese culture. Qi is present in all things, and at a simple level it means air, breath, and vapour or steam, and is associated with vitality, the life-giving breath of the cosmos, and the energy that is found in, and animates, all living things. Qi is believed to work in regular cycles of waxing and waning, and these are mirrored in the rise and fall of ruling dynasties and the ever-changing transformations of the natural world, as well as the life cycle of human beings. It has negative and positive properties relating to emotions and moral behaviour, and excess qi can cause disorder in the physical, mental, governmental, and cosmic worlds. Medical, meditation, and tai chi (*Taijiquan*) practitioners all emphasize the importance of maintaining the balance of qi in the body for spiritual and physical health and strength. Chinese traditional medicine, including acupuncture and use of pressure points, is based on the ways in which qi moves through the body via channels, or "meridians". Imbalances or blockages of qi need to be cleared to restore good health.

阴阳 yin and yang

The complementary pair of yin and yang arise from qi, and explain how natural patterns (or Dao) shape the world, society, and the human body. Originally referring to the shady (yin) and sunny (yang) sides of a mountain, these terms encompass cycles of opposing yet complementary polarities, including female and male, dark and light, moon and sun, wet and dry, cold and hot, waning and waxing, latent and active, the worlds of ghosts and human beings, and north and south. Although opposing, yin and yang need each other to exist, and when balanced can work together in perfect harmony. According to legend, Heaven was formed by accumulating yang floating up, and Earth was created by turbid yin settling down. Traditionally, dragons are used to represent yang, and the phoenix to depict yin. Human bodies comprise yin and yang aspects, which need to be kept in the correct balance in order to maintain good health.

∧ **TAI CHI AT DAWN**
Many Chinese practise tai chi as a martial arts therapy to help balance the levels of qi and maintain a healthy mind and body.

∨ **THE PATHS OF QI**
Traditional Chinese medical practitioners
believe that the paths of qi through the
body are essential for good health. Maps
of the body show the channels it follows.

While yin and yang are interdependent, with elements of each always present in the other, there is, however, a hierarchy of yang over yin.

THE HIERARCHY OF YIN AND YANG

In general, yang has more positive connotations than yin, and refers not only to the hierarchy of male over female, but also to master (or mistress) over servant, or ruler over official. Excesses of both yang and yin can cause disorder in the physical or governmental world, but too much yin is perceived as more

> Chinese concepts of how the universe was formed are closely linked to traditional theories of natural science and a belief that the processes of the natural world (the Dao) are mirrored in human society and government.

dangerous, often signalling the untoward power of women or the presence of a woman ruler. Such an imbalance is often revealed by omens such as flooding.

Yin and yang are found in everything from food, feng shui, health, social relationships and customs, fortune-telling, and popular religions, to the workings of the universe.

五行 five phases

The concept of classifying the world according to five natural elements, or phases, is fundamental to the belief systems of many traditional philosophies from around the globe. According to Chinese philosophy, the Five Phases, also known as *Wu Xing* or the "Theory of Five Transformations", develop, like yin and yang, out of qi. The way in which the phases interact and change helps to explain how natural phenomena influence a variety of areas, including human society, the cycles of history, and the natural world.

CYCLES OF THE PHASES

The Five Phases are wood, fire, metal, water, and earth. These elements are cyclical in nature, with each phase overcome or "conquered" by the succeeding one – water overcomes fire; metal (in the form of an axe, for example) overcomes wood. Each phase also gives birth to the next: water produces plants (wood); wood causes fire, and so on. Each phase is linked to a particular direction and animal as well as a colour: for example, wood is represented by green-blue, fire by the colour red, earth by yellow, metal by white, and water by the colour black.

HOW THE PHASES ARE USED

Five Phases theory can be used to correct imbalances of the qi energies of different elements. Traditionally, the Five Phases are used to interpret events in many

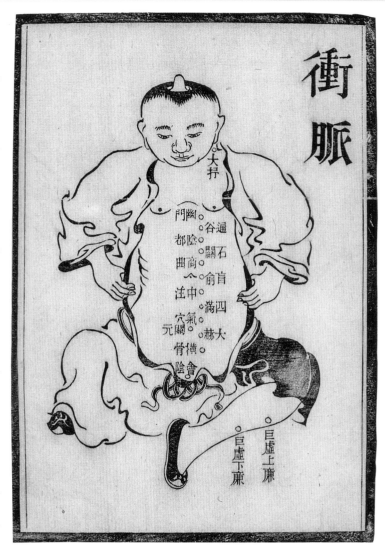

disparate fields, including the rise and fall of ruling houses, with early Chinese dynasties being assigned a particular phase by later historians.

Ancient physicians used Five Phases theory to discover more about the relationship between the human body and the natural world, and this system can still be seen today in

disciplines such as acupuncture. The phases play a central role in descriptions of how the human body works, and these interpretations influence the choice of medicines used in order to correct imbalances and cure illness. In addition to this, the Five Phases are used in Chinese astrology, feng shui, martial arts, and even music.

< **FENG SHUI COMPASS**
The ancient art of feng shui, the auspicious placing of objects, is based on the flow of qi, yin and yang, and the interaction of the Five Phases.

In contrast to the more spiritual and mystical practices of

哲 Western religions, Chinese religions tend to be based around
学 moral and ethical codes, linked to varying conceptions of the
与 Dao or Way (*see page 234*). The development of the major
宗 Chinese philosophies and religions can be traced back to the
教 turbulent "Spring and Autumn" era (c.771–481 BCE), when The
Hundred Schools of Thought emerged. Appearing at the same
time as Greek philosophy, the most significant of these "ways
of thought" are Confucianism, Daoism, and Buddhism.
Confucianism and Daoism are often seen as two sides of the
same coin, with Confucianism representing the public world
and Daoism contemplation and artistic creativity. Alongside
these more established philosophies or religions, a host of
folk beliefs and local customs remain popular.

孔子 confucius and
与儒家 confucianism

Confucianism was the Chinese
state ideology from the second
century BCE until around 1911,
and still plays a major role in the
governments and societies of East
Asia. Beliefs in the importance of moral
persuasion over force, of the power of
civilized learning to transform people,
and the need to honour the traditions of
the past, are preserved in the spirit of
Confucius's own optimistic ideals today.

Confucius, or Kong Fuzi (551–
479 BCE), was born into an impoverished
scholarly family in the state of Lu,
now Shandong Province, where his
descendants still live. He had minor
government jobs but never held a
high position. He was also a
teacher, and was so profoundly
inspirational that his way of
thought came to influence the
people of East Asia for over
2,000 years. His philosophy has
become one of the most
prevalent world views, having a
profound effect on the governments,
societies, cultures, educational practices,
and family and spiritual life in East Asia.

THE ANALECTS OF CONFUCIUS
Compiled in the form of unconnected
sayings, *The Analects*, which
are also known as *Selected
Conversations*, represent the
most important values of
Confucianism. These teachings were
recorded by Confucius's disciples one or
two generations after his death. Perhaps

the most important of all the Confucian
virtues is *Ren*, which means humanity
and benevolence: "To bring comfort to
the old, to have trust in friends, and
to cherish the young".

Confucius and his followers
believed that a ruler of the true Way
(Dao) should be benevolent and lead by
moral example rather than through
force, and that an individual had an
obligation to live a life of virtue so that
all society could learn and benefit.
Confucius also believed that people
should work toward improving
themselves, a process that in turn
would benefit the family and the state.
The moral leader of society was the
junzi, or noble person, who through a
hard and continuous process of
education and constant emphasis on

> The Master said, "The rule of virtue can
> be compared to the Pole Star which
> commands the homage of the multitude
> of stars without leaving its place".
>
> *The Analects*, Confucius

living a moral life taught others how to
behave. To be a *junzi* and to practise
benevolence, one must first of all be a
filial son, one who honours, respects,
and obeys his parents (women were not
considered to be particularly important
according to Confucian philosophy).
Filial piety (*Xiao*) and the emphasis on
the importance of knowing your proper
role and status within the family and
society are key to an ordered and
harmonious world. Linked to this is the
concept of *Li*, ritual decorum or correct
behaviour, whereby people behave

PHILOSOPHY AND RELIGION
THE HUNDRED SCHOOLS OF THOUGHT

properly and with genuine acceptance of their status and give true respect to their elders to prevent discord. Social harmony and order are the linchpins of the Confucian world view, and represent an idealized vision of the role of the individual working to ensure the collective good, enshrined in the Way.

MENCIUS

Mencius, also known as Master Meng (c.372–289 BCE), was Confucius's most eminent disciple and very influential in his own right, developing the aspects of

> The Master said, "Yu, shall I tell you what it is to know? To say you know when you know, and to say you do not when you do not, that is knowledge".
>
> *The Analects*, Confucius

Confucianism that were to transform it into a state ideology. While Confucius never had the influence over rulers he had hoped to achieve in his own lifetime, Mencius was the admired and trusted advisor to several rulers.

Mencius saw it as his task to educate a ruler in the art of governing humanely, or the "Kingly Way". A good

ruler who cared for the welfare of his subjects would win their hearts, but the people had the right to depose any bad rulers. Unsurprisingly, the latter idea was not at all popular with those in power. Mencius also developed a fuller conception of human nature than that found in *The Analects*. He considered people to be basically good but vulnerable to corruption by external influences shaped by qi (*see*

page 240). Mencius's mother is famous for her role in her son's education, moving house three times to protect him from what she considered to be the negative influences of bad neighbours.

Both Confucius and Mencius were profoundly optimistic about the potential for all people to perfect themselves and, by extension of this, for human society to exist in harmony rather than discord, and without the need for rule by means of laws and punishment.

∧ SAGES AT WUYU

This 19th-century painting depicts one of *The Analects* in which a pupil relates his desire to meet with educated men and engage in cultivated conversation.

道 家 daoism

The philosophy of Daoism advocates living according to the Dao, literally "the Way" (*see page 234*). For Daoists, the Way is the way of the natural world, constantly transforming and present in all things. A Daoist ruler would allow events to take their own course; leaving the people alone and not attempting to govern them.

Daoism emerged around the same time as Confucianism, perhaps even earlier, and has had almost as great an impact on Chinese society, although more in the realms of art, literature, and speculative thought than in government. Chinese scholar-officials would often be Confucian in their public lives, but Daoist in private life. Even though these two philosophies are fundamentally opposed in many ways, and were often rivals for imperial patronage, paradoxically it was possible to be both Confucian and Daoist at the same time. One of the most engaging aspects of Chinese culture is the degree to which different religions or philosophies are able to live in relative harmony, even taking on each other's characteristics. Nonetheless, there are basic differences between Daoism and Confucianism, particularly concerning civilization and government. To the Confucians, "the Way" means a moral code of behaviour, which people had to strive to preserve.

LAOZI AND THE DAODE JING

Laozi (the Old One) is considered the father of Daoism. Little is known about this shadowy figure, although many legends have developed, including the belief that he influenced Buddhism in India, as well as apocryphal tales of his encounters with Confucius. The poetic *Daode jing* (*The Way and its Power*), attributed to Laozi, is perhaps the most translated of all Chinese texts. Rich in metaphor and paradoxical statements, this text tells us that the "Way", central to the Daoist philosophy, is impossible to define. "The Way that can be spoken of is not the Way", it says.

ZHUANGZI

The text of the *Zhuangzi*, attributed to Zhuang Zhou, or Zhuangzi, is considered to be one of the masterpieces of Chinese literature and one of the earliest sources of fiction. It is believed that it was actually composed by a number of different writers over two centuries, but the seven "Inner" chapters give an unforgettable portrait of the Daoist master Zhuangzi. He expresses his ideas about the Way

∧ LAOZI
Opinion varies as to whether Laozi (also known as Lao Tzu), the father of Daoism, was a mythical figure or a philosopher from the 6th or 4th century BCE.

through a fascinating and humorous assault on reason and established (Confucian) values, using anecdotes, parables, stories, and jokes. The Daoist philosophy of noninterference is given voice in a parable by Zhuangzi (below). Like the Confucians at whom the parable is aimed, Shu and Hu had the best of intentions, but they defied nature and eventually destroyed their friend.

> The Emperor of the South Sea was called Shu (Brief) and the Emperor of the North Sea was called Hu (Sudden), and the Emperor of the Central region was called Hundun (Chaos). Shu and Hu from time to time came together for a meeting in Hundun's territory and he treated them very generously. Shu and Hu wished to repay his kindness. "All men", they said, "have seven openings so they can see, hear, eat, and breathe. But Hundun alone doesn't have any. Let's try boring some into him!" Every day they bored another hole, and on the seventh day Hundun died.
>
> A parable, Zhuangzi

The message given by Zhuangzi in this story is that nature is in ceaseless flux, and one should not try to fix or halt changes. Death is part of the transformation of all things, and in a parable designed to shock the Confucians with their reverence for rituals to honour the dead, Zhuangzi is depicted joyously drumming on a barrel after the death of his wife, saying that while he mourns her death, he also celebrates her latest natural transformation. All things must change, as the seasons continue to progress.

Like Laozi, Zhuangzi claims that it is impossible to quantify the Dao – it is not a set of rules for ordering the state, family, and the individual, as it is for the Confucians. Instead, the closest one can come to understanding the elusive Dao is through the kind of unthinking skill or knack that only develops over years of training and practice. Once you have acquired the skill, you can discard the tools that gave you that knowledge.

> The bait is the means to get the fish where you want it; catch the fish and you discard the bait. Words are the means to get the idea where you want it; catch on to the idea and you forget about the words.
>
> A parable, Zhuangzi

∧ THE HARMONY OF NATURE
For Daoists, mountain landscapes are considered meeting places between Heaven and Earth. Life should be lived in harmony with the natural world.

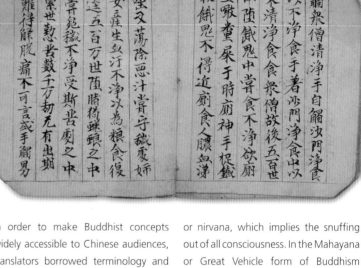

> **ANCIENT BUDDHIST TEXTS**
Buddhist manuscripts and scrolls, like this 1,000-year-old script, are highly revered by followers of the religion.

佛 buddhism

教 Buddhism is the most practised religion in China today, and is considered, with Confucianism and Daoism, as one of the "three ways". Buddhism came to China from India along the Silk Road around the 1st and 2nd centuries CE and swiftly became an established force in Chinese thought and society. In the early stages, scholars looked to Buddhism in their search for immortality through spiritual exercise and meditation. Later thinkers were fascinated by the philosophical concepts of

Buddhism, while many people found spiritual consolation in the Buddha's message of compassion and salvation.

CHINESE BUDDHISM
In the 4th century, the first great scholar-monks travelled to India to study Buddhism and returned with Buddhist texts translated for the first time into Chinese. Others studied with resident foreign monks, the most famous of whom was Kumarajiva (350–413), who headed a major translation project of nearly 40 texts. His translation of the *Lotus Sutra* became one of the most treasured of all Buddhist scriptures in China.

In order to make Buddhist concepts widely accessible to Chinese audiences, translators borrowed terminology and ideas from Daoism. This speeded up Buddhism's acceptance in Chinese society, but also meant that unique Chinese schools of Buddhism emerged that had no counterpart in India (where Buddhism had long been in decline). The best known of these in the West is the Chan (Zen) school, which appeared in the 7th century during the heyday of Buddhism in China, but there are others with broader followings, such as the Pure Land school that focuses on the Buddha Amitabha and the Boddhisattva Guanyin, who was male but transformed over time into a female goddess of mercy and compassion to whom people prayed for sons.

Common to all Buddhist schools are the central doctrines summed up in the Four Noble Truths preached by Gautama Buddha, who lived around 563–483 BCE (roughly contemporary with Confucius).

If an individual could cut off all worldly ties through meditation, prayer, performing good deeds, and disciplined resolve, he (women had to be reborn as men first) could achieve enlightenment

< **EFFIGIES OF BUDDHA**
Giant sculptures and statues, like this stunning gold Buddha from Hong Kong, are testament to the dramatic effect of Buddhism on religious art in China.

or nirvana, which implies the snuffing out of all consciousness. In the Mahayana or Great Vehicle form of Buddhism popular in China, people are given the promise of salvation and the possibility of an afterlife, rather than the complete extinction of being after death. This was more in keeping with the optimism of Confucianism and helped Buddhism to flourish, especially among ordinary people. The Buddhist concept of karma, or re-birth based on one's deeds in a former existence, found resonance in traditional Chinese belief in *bao*, or heavenly

> Gautama Buddha said that all life is suffering. People are caught on a wheel of endless life and rebirth, from which they cannot escape until they free themselves of the attachments and desires that cause suffering.

requital, whereby good deeds are rewarded and bad ones punished. This remains a central part of Chinese culture, especially in popular religious practices.

ENCOUNTERING RESISTANCE
There were many powerful people who embraced Buddhism, and in fact later on Confucianism adapted certain

Bodhisattva, such as Guanyin, reached enlightenment, but rejected Buddha-hood in order to remain in the world and work for the salvation of others.

Buddhist terms and concepts in a successful effort to reinvigorate a rather moribund philosophy. However, among the Confucian-educated elite in China there were many others who deeply resisted the new religion. The resistance to Buddhism was based in part on distrust of its foreign origins, but mainly because it contradicted central Chinese beliefs, especially the fundamental importance of family relationships.

To be celibate and cut off ties to the world (known in Chinese as *chujia*, literally "leaving the family") runs counter to Mencius's famous dictum that the most filial act of all is to have a son to carry on the family line. Shaving the head to become a monk or nun is also unfilial, because it disfigures the body given to you by your parents. However, Buddhists were able to argue that praying for the salvation of one's parents was a profoundly filial act, and one of the most famous Chinese Buddhist dramatic narratives, which is still performed today, is the story of Mulian (or "Turnip"), a devout monk who journeys through the Buddhist hells to rescue his greedy, selfish, and ungrateful mother and ensure her salvation.

THE BUDDHIST LEGACY

The impact of Buddhism on China has been profound, from the first encounter with a foreign civilization as great as their own, to the ways in which Buddhism has become entwined in all aspects of Chinese life. Buddhist art transformed Chinese culture and the landscape, especially through sculpture, architecture, and painting. Chinese mountains, which were traditionally regarded as sacred places, became home to innumerable Buddhist temples and monasteries, and major pilgrimage sites. Astonishing cave temples and massive Buddhist statues are proof of the wealth and devotion of Buddhist followers over the centuries. Chinese literature and language were also deeply affected by the introduction by Buddhist monks of semi-vernacular popular narratives printed for broad consumption, as well as a wealth of Buddhist motifs and stories. Over time, these saints, deities, guardians, and demons gradually entered the Chinese pantheon, and Buddhist hells were swiftly incorporated into indigenous beliefs about the underworld and judging the dead for their misdeeds and right conduct during their lifetime. The Buddhist belief in the importance of compassion has helped to shape Chinese philanthropy, which is still active today.

民间宗教 popular religion and folklore

Popular religion in China has always existed side by side with Confucian ideology, sometimes even sharing the same temples. These traditional belief systems suffered some temporary setbacks in the modern era, when popular religion was decried as superstitious by the modernizing communists, but these beliefs are now flourishing again today all over China and in Chinese communities around the world. While Chinese authorities over the centuries have suppressed some of the more powerful and charismatic of the popular religions, fearing peasant rebellions and uprisings, local and regional beliefs have been allowed, and even encouraged, to exist because they maintain community identity and a sense of public order. It is not unusual for local communities to worship a particular god or goddess associated with that region, or to build shrines to honour famous or virtuous individuals, including Confucius, whose temples can be found throughout China.

RELIGIOUS DAOISM

Around the same time that Buddhism entered China, there emerged a new form of Daoism that has come to be known as religious Daoism, to distinguish it from its more austere philosophical cousin. Religious Daoism has adopted many of the attributes of Buddhism, developing its own temples and shrines, liturgies, mystical rituals, and an otherworldly pantheon of immortals and

∧ **KITCHEN GODS**
This print depicting Zao Jun and his wife would have been placed above the stove. At New Year, the kitchen gods report the deeds of the household to the Jade Emperor in Heaven.

∨ **DOOR GUARDIANS**
Colourful posters such as these are
traditionally placed on the door of
a house to deter malevolent spirits
or destructive forces from entering.

deities living in remote sacred mountains. Daoist practitioners searched for the secrets of longevity and immortality, ingesting plants like chrysanthemum petals and poisonous substances like cinnabar (mercury), experimenting with alchemy, meditating, and engaging in sexual activities that increased their bodily yang component. Many became recluses, living high up in cloud-topped mountains, far from crowds. Those who achieved immortality were believed to become light enough to fly away on the

> Many Confucian scholar-officials were active public participants in local rituals and festivals, but they followed Buddhist or Daoist doctrines in their private lives.

back of a crane. Religious Daoism was at times a rival with Buddhism for imperial patronage, but over time the two religions took on many of each other's characteristics, and their priests, monks, and nuns would be present at the same major festivals or family rituals like weddings and funerals without incongruity, and were accepted by Confucian scholars as an inevitable, if rather distasteful, part of everyday life.

OTHER GODS AND DEITIES

The City God is found almost universally all over China and is revered for his role in maintaining underworld justice (in mirror image of the legal system above ground), meting out rewards and punishments to the local dead. His effigy is still taken on processions around different town limits to mark out his territory and to remind the local residents of his importance. Temples to the City God are decorated with terrifying scenes from the ten Hells, and ferocious door guardians loom, armed to the teeth, eyes bulging, ready to punish any wrongdoers.

Another popular figure is the ghost- and demon-queller, Zhong Kui. Having been stripped of his title as scholar, because of his deformed appearance, Zhong Kui committed suicide and became "king of the ghosts". He returned to the world to banish demons, and his image is still painted on doors of houses and businesses as a guardian spirit. It is said that if one should encounter a ghost in Zhong Kui's absence, spitting at the spirit should deter it.

Shrines can be found in many parts of China to Guan Yu, the god of war and one of the heroes of the novel *Romance of the Three Kingdoms* (*see page 268*), who was honoured by merchants and secret brotherhoods for his integrity and his sense of justice. The Eight Daoist Immortals, a motley crew of eccentric characters, are popular figures who are found in shrines and folklore throughout the country. In many parts of China, powerful female deities like Ma Zu, sometimes linked to Guanyin, are worshipped, and many regions have their own special gods and shrines. Families will usually have ancestor shrines and spirit tablets inside their homes or more formally set up inside lineage halls where solemn rituals take place in honour of deceased elders. Kitchen gods are placated with offerings to keep a household wealthy, healthy, and fertile, three attributes that are an important focus of many beliefs.

> **GODDESS OF MERCY TEMPLE**
Burning incense as an act of devotion is a common sight throughout Chinese culture. This temple is dedicated to the Goddess Guanyin.

∨ **SYMBOLIC ART**
This painting is packed with references to spring and good fortune, including spring flowers and incense. This suggests that the piece was used at New Year.

符号 symbols, signs, and fortune

Symbols and signs are central to traditional Chinese belief systems. In Chinese, many different words sound identical (known as homophones) although their meaning and written character are not the same. The homophonic nature of the Chinese language has led to a love of verbal puns, which when expressed visually, has helped to develop a rich and fascinating system of symbols and signs. These symbols usually denote good fortune and long life, and the desire for sons, and are to be found on everything from pottery, jewellery, and clothing, to papercuts and woodcuts, and even food.

Bats (*fu*) and fish (*yu*) – Chinese words that are homophones for wealth and abundance – are often used as auspicious images, as are seeds (*zi*), the name for which sounds similar to the word for sons. Bronze vessels and vases are considered symbols of good fortune and prosperity. The components of the word for bronze literally mean "gold-like", inferring wealth; meanwhile, the word for vase is a homophone for "peace".

Numbers also have different cultural connotations. Generally, even numbers are considered auspicious, as it is thought that good luck comes in pairs. For example, eight is traditionally a lucky number in both Buddhist and Daoist iconography, and is linked to the Eight Trigrams of the Confucian divination

classic, *The Yi Jing*, also known as the *I Ching* (Book of Changes). This number is considered lucky throughout China with everyone from gamblers to homeowners. In contrast, the number four, which sounds similar to the Chinese word for death, is to be avoided. Numerology, the auspiciousness of certain numbers or combinations of numbers, finds its way into many aspects of Chinese culture, particularly in relation to horoscopes and fortune-telling.

ASTROLOGY AND HOROSCOPES

The Chinese zodiac is based solely on the calendar: traditional Chinese astrologers do not consult the stars in

The wealth of decorative symbolism and colourful iconography gives extra layers of significance to visual Chinese culture, providing a sense of playfulness and vitality, as well as promising protection and good fortune in difficult times.

the same way as Western practitioners of astrology. A person's horoscope plays an important role in arranging marriages, business ventures, and other significant undertakings and life events. The 12 animals of the Chinese zodiac are: rat, ox, tiger, rabbit, dragon, snake, horse, sheep, monkey, rooster, dog, and pig. The cycle of the 12 zodiac animals, their associated colours, along with the hourly and yearly cycles, are said to determine an individual's fate and character. For example, according to tradition, a woman who was born in the Year of the Tiger was not thought to

< DIVINATION STICKS
These carved and decorated sticks are used to predict the future. A diviner interprets the patterns formed when the sticks are thrown to the ground.

be a good prospect as a wife. The notorious Pan Jinlian, villainess of the 16th-century novel *Water Margin* (*see page 270*), was one such individual. Born in the year of the White Tiger, her horoscope was considered doubly unlucky because of the associations of the colour white with death.

Almanacs and calendars are consulted in order to make decisions regarding many everyday events. Agricultural almanacs are used to plan the most favourable days to plant or harvest crops. Diviners and priests traditionally advise bereaved families regarding the best time and place for burials. Funerals have to be conducted in the most propitious way possible in order to avoid incurring the displeasure of the deceased (which could manifest itself as a possible return as a vengeful ghost), and subsequent bad luck for his or her descendants.

FENG SHUI

Feng shui, literally meaning "wind and water", or Chinese geomancy, is the art of siting buildings or graves in the most auspicious place based on divination and numerology. This traditional practice remains an important part of Chinese culture, particularly in the southern regions of the country, where it is regarded as less superstitious than in other parts of China. Essentially, feng shui is another example of the traditional quest for harmony between the cosmic triad of Heaven, Earth, and Mankind (*see pages 234–35*). Feng shui practitioners trace the flow of qi within an area in order to determine the placing and overall design of buildings, such as the positioning of doors and windows, and even how many floors a building should have. The dramatic high-rise skyline of Hong Kong has been heavily influenced by feng shui beliefs and practices. Earlier buildings, such as traditional pagodas, were also designed to maximize the flow of qi and therefore improve the general well-being of the inhabitants by harmonizing the yin and yang energies (*see page 240*). In accordance with the Chinese reverence for ancestors, these measures are carried out as much for the benefit of the dead as for the living.

< ASTROLOGICAL SYMBOLS
This papercut depicts the 12 animals of the Chinese zodiac. At its centre is an eight-sided trigram, which is placed around the yin yang symbol.

∧ PAGODA AT 10,000 BUDDHAS MONASTERY
The Chinese believe that pagodas bring good fortune to the surrounding area. The word "pagoda" means "eight-sided tower", and the number eight is particularly auspicious.

Calligraphy, poetry, and painting – known collectively as
书道 the "three perfections" – form an integral part of traditional
Chinese culture, and are considered throughout the East to
be the highest forms of art. Huizong, the last emperor of the
Northern Song dynasty (960–1126), was an avid painter, poet,
and calligrapher, and it was under his guidance that writing
became an art form in its own right. Since that time it has been
popular to combine these three disciplines within single pieces
of work. Exploring the three perfections provides an insight
into the unique grace and beauty of traditional Chinese art.

中 the written word

文 According to Chinese tradition, an ancient sage with four eyes and eight pupils named Cang Jie invented Chinese characters by observing the patterns present in the natural world. The official historian of the Yellow Emperor, he was charged with the task of creating characters for writing. With his double set of eyes, Cang Jie marked the movements of birds in the sky and the tracks of animals on Earth below, and then transmuted the signs into written words. Despite the existence of such popular myths, the real origins of Chinese writing have been lost in time.

A LITERARY ELITE
A complete writing system of Chinese characters was created during the Shang dynasty (1766–1122 BCE). This developed over time into the Simplified Chinese characters in use today. Each character corresponds to a single syllable, and the majority are "pictophonetic": part of the character is derived from a pictogram, and part from its sound. Most words in the Chinese language contain more than one syllable, and require two or more characters to write. The absence of a purely phonetic alphabet makes Chinese a difficult language to read and write and this meant that, historically, literacy was limited to a minority of educated elite, whose power and status were very closely tied to their abilities in reading and writing. The civil service examination system dating from the Tang dynasty onward, created a means of recruiting talented scholars based on their knowledge of the Confucian classics and their writing ability.

Chinese characters were unified throughout the country under the Qin dynasty in the 2nd century BCE, and over the following centuries the written language, and the classical texts that formed the basis of the education system, became a tangible link for the disparate population.

BRINGING THE COUNTRY TOGETHER
The invention of printing in the 11th century and the subsequent availability of cheap printed books – as well as the adoption of the vernacular as a written form – meant that the ability to read and write could be achieved by the majority of the population. Books printed on paper were much cheaper and more convenient to use than the

> The written word has remained the same over the centuries, ensuring that educated people could always communicate with each other through reading and writing.

earlier fragile scrolls on silk, or the unwieldy bamboo scrolls that were so heavy that carts were necessary to move them from place to place.

China is a very large country with many mutually incomprehensible local dialects, but for centuries (and still today) Chinese characters have been a means of communication for people throughout the whole country.

THE WAY OF THE BRUSH
CALLIGRAPHY, PAINTING, AND POETRY

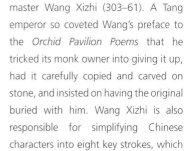

书 calligraphy

法

The written word is very highly prized in Chinese culture, and this can be seen most clearly in the esteem with which the art of calligraphy is regarded. Practised for millennia, this ancient art form is about more than just creating symbols in an attractive way. The calligraphy artist combines body, mind, and brush to create spontaneous but controlled strokes that reveal both the artist's inner integrity and harmony with nature's rhythms. The history and development of Chinese calligraphy is complex, but there is an inextricable link between the characters and the overall progression of Chinese culture as the various symbols and scripts have evolved over thousands of years. Attempts to modernize Chinese symbols and even Romanize them have never fully succeeded, partly because the characters are about far more than just words – they represent the history, art, and culture of the whole nation.

Early Chinese symbols have been found on Neolithic pots and Shang dynasty bronzes, but it is in the characters incised on Shang oracle bones that we first find a fully developed writing system that closely resembles the Chinese language of later times. Traditional calligraphic texts are often poems or Buddhist or Daoist scriptures, chosen with care by the calligrapher and their essence ideally embodied by the strokes of the brush. The practice of calligraphy is a traditional way to achieve a state of inner harmony, involving clearing the mind, assuming the correct posture, and breathing smoothly and deeply. The tools assume an almost sacred status, creating a spiritual state in which to create these works of art.

THE MASTER CALLIGRAPHERS

The great masters of Chinese calligraphy have traditionally been revered not just as great artists, but also as great thinkers. The most famous of all calligraphers is the Daoist master Wang Xizhi (303–61). A Tang emperor so coveted Wang's preface to the *Orchid Pavilion Poems* that he tricked its monk owner into giving it up, had it carefully copied and carved on stone, and insisted on having the original buried with him. Wang Xizhi is also responsible for simplifying Chinese characters into eight key strokes, which can all be found in the character for "eternity", *Yong*. Mastering these will allow the artist to form characters in any calligraphic style. The Eight Components of the Character Yong are: the dot (*Ce* or *Dian*), the horizontal (*Lei* or *Heng*), the vertical (*Nu* or *Shu*), the hook (*Ti* or *Gou*), the raise (*Ce* or *Tiao*), the aside (*Lue* or *Pie*), the downward raise (*Ce* or *Tiao*), and the right falling (*Zhe* or *Na*).

The Tang dynasty was a golden age for calligraphy when many script styles developed into the forms we know today, including the formal, archaic seal script, the clear clerical script, and the swift-flowing Grass or Running scripts.

Calligraphy brush and ink stone

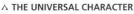

∧ **THE UNIVERSAL CHARACTER**
All Chinese characters can be created from eight basic strokes. The character for "eternity" (*above*) contains each of these strokes.

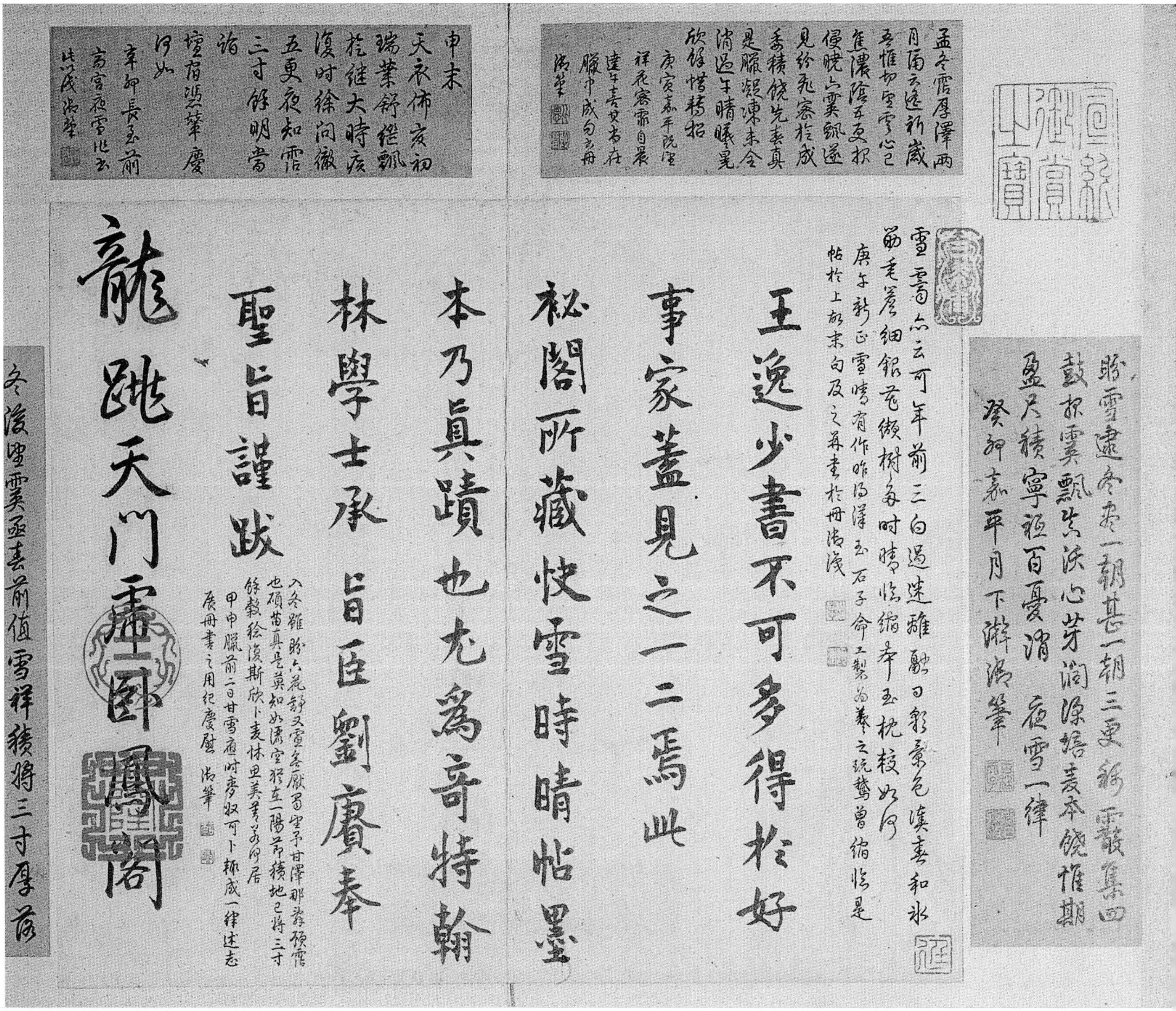
王逸少書不可多得於好
事家蓋見之一二焉此
秘閣所藏快雪時晴帖墨
本乃真蹟也尤為奇特翰
林學士承旨臣劉賡奉
聖旨謹跋
龍跳天門虎臥鳳閣

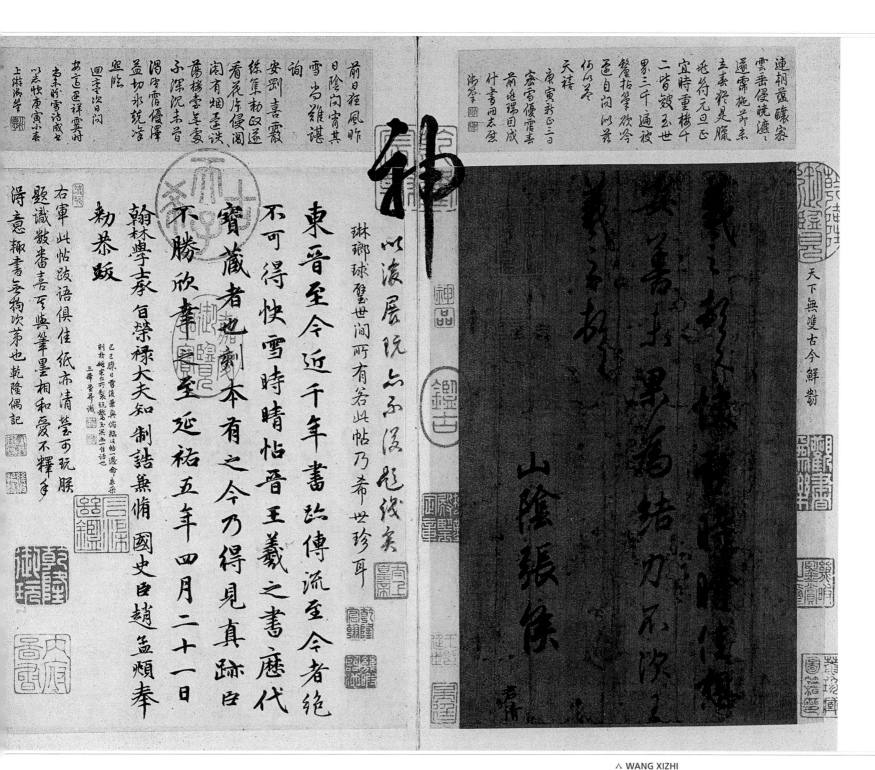

∧ **WANG XIZHI**

This piece is by Wang Xizhi, known as the "Sage Calligrapher". His varied work influences Chinese calligraphy to this day.

绘 painting

画 Closely allied to calligraphy in terms of its underlying philosophy, materials, and techniques is the art of Chinese painting. While murals and figure painting have a long and revered tradition in Chinese culture, it is landscape painting that is most highly regarded, perhaps because it is believed to embody the patterns found in the natural world.

Painted on silk or paper, using brush and ink and watercolour washes, landscape paintings could be created for long-hanging vertical scrolls or horizontal scrolls designed to be unrolled scene by scene. Chinese landscape paintings express the artist's desire for a world of cultivation and beauty.

Another popular genre comprises charming albums of landscape paintings in miniature, or scenes of birds, flowers, or bamboo painted in fan shapes or rounded squares.

SONG LANDSCAPES

Song dynasty landscape paintings are often seen as the pinnacle of the art. Natural order within the landscape was used as a metaphor for order within the political state. The monumental mountain scene, *Travellers Among Mountains and Streams* (*see right*), by the Daoist artist Fan Kuan (c.990–1020) is the prime example. In this vast

> PINNACLE OF THE ART
Fan Kuan's large-scale work is designed to make the individual viewer feel small in comparison to the natural landscape.

∨ NI ZAN
This 14th-century ink and brush painting
of a sparse landscape is embellished
with calligraphic inscriptions by the
acclaimed artist Ni Zan.

painting, which is more than 80 in
(2 m) in height, towering tree-topped
mountains with rounded peaks block
out the sky and a torrent falls from the
heights, emphasizing the vertical lines
of the painting. At mid level the vertical
is cut by a horizontal bank of mist or
cloud, suggesting a mysterious void
where mountain recluses or immortals
might dwell, connecting the lower
foreground to the mountainous background. Below can be seen rocky
outcrops, woods, travellers, and a small
temple: the human presence dwarfed
by the vastness of nature.

BRUSH AND INK PAINTINGS

The lush and detailed quality of Song
landscapes like Fan Kuan's provides a
stark contrast to the sparser, dry
monochrome brush and ink landscapes
of the Yuan dynasty, and particularly the
work of Ni Zan, an eccentric and great
artist. Ni Zan's work is often described as
non-representational, with variations on
the basic elements of rocks, water, and
trees or bamboo that are read as
statements about the artist's character.
Chinese landscape painting is about
more than reproducing the scenery;
either representing particular virtues or
qualities of the artist, or embodying the
patterns of the cosmos (or Way), or

The Chinese word for landscape is
Shanshui, literally "mountains and
water", and these are the central
elements that make up the majority
of landscape paintings.

offering a subtle and indirect critique of
political affairs through the style of the
brushwork and the application of ink.

TRADITIONAL SCROLLS

A different kind of landscape painting
is found in the extraordinarily detailed
long horizontal scroll depicting
urban Kaifeng life at the end of
the Song by an artist named
Zhang Zeduan (*see pages 258–
59*). Here are a wealth of
vignettes of life along the river
within the city walls: restaurants,
shops, offices, and boats, with a

great variety of people mingling on the
streets and bridges, including minor
officials, performers, entertainers,
soldiers, and boatmen. This scroll
provides a vivid picture of a bustling city
and its inhabitants over 900 years ago.

INSCRIPTIONS AND SEALS

Chinese paintings are rarely left to stand
alone by their artists or untouched by
their owners. It is the custom for artists
to write inscriptions giving the date of
composition and a few words about
the context in which a painting was
produced. They might also add a poem
that inspired, or was inspired by, the
painting. Successive owners
add their own personal seals
(sometimes lavishly in red) and
often their own inscriptions, so
that the written word and the
painted image become closely
entwined and add extra layers
of meaning to the work of art.

CHINESE FIGURE PAINTING

While landscape painting has always
been held in the highest regard in the
canons of Chinese art, there has also
been a long and very fine tradition of
figure painting, with lively and beautifully
executed images of both humans and
animals. Western-style realism and
perspective influenced Chinese painting
very late, but the lifelike sculptures
of terracotta warriors found in pits
near the First Emperor's tomb in
Xi'an (*see pages 84–85*), and
the Greek-influenced Buddhas
throughout Northern China suggest
that ancient Chinese artists were not

unfamiliar with such concepts and
employed them to a greater or lesser
degree in their work. It is the lines or
outlines made by brushstrokes that
have shaped the development of
Chinese art, rather than the mass,
shadow, and light that so fascinated
Western artists. Chinese artists rarely
painted from life and early work found
on tomb and temple frescoes and tiles

> FLORAL ALBUM ART
This ink and colour
painting of willow
and peach blossoms
is by the 18th-century
artist Li Shan.

CITY LIFE

> SCROLL BY ZHANG ZEDUAN
The famous 12th-century scroll, *Along the River During Ching Ming Festival*, is 211in (528cm) long, and is held at the Palace Museum in Beijing.

> CITY LIFE
Chinese scrolls are designed to be read from right to left, and the end of the scroll shows the seals of ownership.

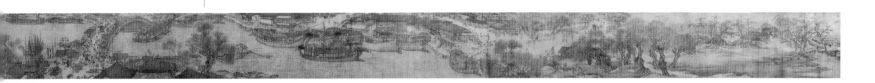

< THE WATERFRONT
Zhang's scroll painting offers
a tantalizing glimpse into the
clothing and architecture of
the Song dynasty, and reveals
the differing lifestyles of all
levels of Chinese society.

> BADA SHANREN
This 20th-century painting is a tribute to a painter and calligrapher of the early Qing period, Bada Shanren, who was a great exponent of the brush and ink style.

is often highly stylized, yet filled with suggestions of movement created by sweeping brushstrokes and splashes of flat colour washes.

Buddhist art imported from India along the Silk Road played a central role in influencing the iconography, colours, and style of Chinese painting, including portraiture, which tended toward the generic rather than the individualistic representation. Buddhist, Daoist, and folk art provide a wealth of images, particularly of gods, demons, and temple guardians, which are once again highly stylized. Nonetheless, increasingly individualized portraits emerged of monks, scholars, and philosophers, as well as wonderfully rendered pictures of birds and animals.

There are many examples over the centuries of charming images of palace women or women in their boudoirs, and children and servants involved in a variety of activities from horseback riding to weaving, or playing games. Detailed crowd scenes of ordinary people, soldiers, actors, and traders can be seen in a number of paintings from the Song dynasty onward. Cheap woodblock printing in the Ming dynasty led to the production of some finely illustrated pictures of popular characters in fiction and drama.

During the Qing dynasty, under Jesuit influence, came the development of grand imperial portraits using Western perspective, popular with the Manchu emperors in particular. Perhaps the most powerful examples of these can be seen in paintings of the Qianlong emperor and in the theatrically playful but self-conscious expressions of empire embodied in the series of portraits of the Yongzheng emperor wearing the religious garb and ethnically diverse costumes of his far-flung imperium (*see below*). The highly individual and dramatic self-portraits of Ren Bonian in the late Qing represent a remarkably effective blending of Chinese and Western aesthetics in portraiture, the strong outlines of his brushwork augmented by the three-dimensional nature of his figures.

∧ THE YONGZHENG EMPEROR
These portraits of the Yongzheng emperor in a variety of costumes are typical of the Western-influenced paintings popular in late-imperial China.

诗 poetry

歌 With the exception of the Confucian and other philosophical and religious classics, poetry is the most highly esteemed form of writing in Chinese culture. Poetry is believed to embody the integrity and moral character of the individual poet, and is also deemed to be the supreme channnel for emotional, philosophical, and intellectual expression. Poets write for a like-minded reader who understands them, and hope that their aspirations and qualities will receive proper recognition by later generations.

It is generally held that Chinese poetry has its source in two ancient streams: the earthbound, realistic folk songs and hymns of the Confucian *Classic of Poetry* and the fantastic landscapes and spirit journeys of the *Songs of Chu*, linked to the shamanistic poet Qu Yuan (c.340–278 BCE).

The tonal and homophonic nature of the Chinese language has had a profound influence on the writing of poetry. Several classical genres insist on particularly complex rhyme and tonal patterns, which add to the challenge of composition. Poetry was written to be chanted aloud, rather than read silently, and children still learn to recite large numbers of poems, often without fully understanding their meaning. Poetry has always been a central part of Chinese life, particularly for the educated elite, who were expected to be able to compose poetry at the drop of a hat at social gatherings of all kinds, from drinking parties to saying farewell to a friend leaving for a distant posting. At certain times the composition of poetry was part of the imperial examination system, since it was believed that an individual's character was revealed through his work. Most poets were men, but a few Chinese women poets have achieved fame as well. Vast quantities of occasional poetry have been written over the centuries, much of it negligible, but there are many extraordinary poets whose work more than stands the test of time.

TAO YUANMING

During the Six Dynasties period (265–589), the number of writers creating poetry in a literary style increased. Tao Yuanming (365–427), also known as Tao Qian, is one of the best loved of the poets from this era. Tao's poetry was strongly Daoist in theme and imagery, but he was also an idealist Confucian, nostalgic for a lost, simpler, and better time. He is famous for his self-portrait as a hermit-farmer living a peaceful life in poverty: farming, drinking, and being at one with nature. Alcohol figures heavily in his poetry, offering an escape from daily drudgery, but also acting as a channel for closer communion with the natural world. His language is deceptively simple, and his themes philosophical. He is also known for his influential *Account of Peach Blossom Spring*, a brief story in which a fisherman discovers a lost, ideal Daoist community but never finds it again after leaving. This tale and the accompanying poem influenced later fiction and poetry as an allusion to lost utopias and Daoist ideals.

I built a cottage right in the realm of men,

Yet there was no noise from wagon and horse.

I ask you, how can that be so? –

When mind is far, its place becomes remote.

I picked a chrysanthemum by the eastern hedge,

off in the distance gazed on south mountain.

Mountain vapours glow lovely in twilight sun,

Where birds in flight join in return.

There is some true significance here:

I want to expound it but have lost the words.

Drinking Wine V, Tao Yuanming

∧ **MISTY MOUNTAINS**
The peaceful solitude of the Wolong Valley in the Himalayas is typical of the idealized landscape conjured up in the imagery of much Daoist poetry.

THE GOLDEN AGE OF POETRY

It was during the cosmopolitan and confident Tang dynasty (618–907) that Chinese poetry reached its peak, with some of the greatest poets writing in what has become known as the "High Tang" era, coinciding with the long and glorious reign of the Emperor Xuanzong (or Minghuang) (r.712–56), which ended tragically with the upheavals of the An Lushan rebellion. The golden age of Chinese poetry is best represented by the work of three poets: Wang Wei, Li Bai, and Du Fu, each very different in terms of their poetry and philosophy, but united in their extraordinary gift to give voice to their feelings in words that speak across time and space.

WANG WEI

Wang Wei (701–61) was a devout Buddhist and active Confucian official whose poetry often draws on Daoist themes and imagery. A famous artist (whose work, unfortunately, is no longer in existence), musician, scholar, and filial son, Wang Wei is one of the greatest of Chinese poets. His poems, many of which were composed at his family estate, are often tiny literary vignettes of landscapes featuring woods, streams, mountain temples, the moon (which is a symbol of enlightenment), and bamboo stirred by the breeze.

Buddhist and Daoist images of quiet contemplation, emptiness, and selflessness imbue his poetry, which is often described as having a transparent, calm simplicity like a deep pool. His poems frequently refer to a quest for true understanding through a oneness with nature. This is symbolized by the wise fishermen and woodcutters who the poet encounters in the course of his wanderings or as he sits quietly strumming his lute in a bamboo grove.

No one is seen in deserted hills,

Only the echoes of speech are heard.

Sunlight cast back comes deep in the woods

And shines once again upon the deep moss.

Deer Fence, Wang Wei

I sit alone in the bamboo that hides me,

plucking the harp and whistling long.

It is deep in the woods and no one knows –

The bright moon comes to shine on me.

Lodge in the Bamboo, Wang Wei

∧ **THE NATURAL WORLD**
Bamboo groves and forests are popular images in Tang dynasty poetry, reflecting the Daoist love of the natural world and quest for harmony in nature.

LI BAI

The poet Li Bai, who is also known as Li Bo (702–62), has acquired the title "The Banished Immortal" as a result of his fantastic Daoist flights of fancy and on account of his carefree persona. Approximately 1,100 of his poems are still enjoyed today.

Possibly of Central Asian origin, Li Bai is perhaps the most popular of all Chinese poets. He is famous for his grand, sweeping lines and stunning vistas, but most of all for his playful spontaneity. As befits a Daoist acolyte, Li Bai loved mountains and communing with nature, but he was equally at home in the taverns and court of the cosmopolitan Tang capital. There are many stories that tell of his outrageous behaviour, and he seems to have delighted in creating myths about his life and personality.

Li Bai came from an affluent family and was an incessant, restless traveller at a time when the Tang empire was threatened with collapse. However, his poetry is rarely unhappy or anguished, unlike that of his distinguished younger contemporary, Du Fu, and instead rings with his sheer, unadulterated pleasure in life. Legend has it he drowned in the Yangtze River when drunk, leaning out of his boat in an attempt to admire the reflection of the moon.

Here among flowers one flask of wine,

With no close friends, I pour it alone.

I lift cup to bright moon, beg its company,

Then facing my shadow, we become three.

The moon has never known how to drink;

My shadow does nothing but follow me.

But with moon and shadow as companions the while,

This joy I find must catch spring while it's here.

I sing, and the moon just lingers on;

I dance, and my shadow flails wildly.

When still sober we share friendship and pleasure,

Then, utterly drunk, each goes his own way –

Let us join to roam beyond human cares

And plan to meet far in the river of stars.

Drinking Alone by Moonlight, Li Bai

DU FU

Du Fu (712–70) is known as the poet-historian or Sage of Poetry. If Li Bai was Daoist and Wang Wei Buddhist, then Du Fu can be characterized as a profoundly Confucian poet, a man of great integrity and compassion who cared deeply for his country and its people.

Du Fu is a very complex and deeply personal poet who used the background of the strife-ridden Tang dynasty to write powerful and profound poems on the ways in which current events and historical calamities affect human beings. His poems are often about himself and his family, separated from him by the tides of war. Where Li Bai travelled through choice, Du Fu had to move around through circumstance. Forced to flee his home on several occasions in his later years, Du Fu rarely enjoyed the carefree life Li Bai describes, and the poetry of these two great Tang poets reflects their very different personalities and life experiences.

Du Fu's poetry is perhaps more challenging for the modern reader than Li Bai's, being densely packed with layers of historical allusions and often highly formal in structure, but it is deeply moving and politically engaged. His poetry links the workings of the cosmos and nature with the human world, swooping down low or flying up high to encompass a view that is at once grand and intimate. Du Fu is considered to be China's greatest poet, and it is the personal and humanistic concerns of this often anguished, sometimes self-mocking man that continue to speak to us across the centuries.

A kingdom smashed, its hills and rivers still here,

Spring in the city, plants and trees grow deep.

Moved by the moment, flowers splash with tears,

Alarmed at parting, birds startle the heart.

War's beacon fires have gone on three months,

Letters from home are worth thousands in gold.

Fingers run through white hair until it thins,

Cap-pins will almost no longer hold.

The View in Spring, Du Fu

A single bird of prey beyond the sky,

a pair of white gulls between the riverbanks.

Hovering wind-tossed, ready to strike;

the pair, at their ease, roaming to and fro.

And the dew is also full on the grasses,

spiders' filaments still not drawn in.

Instigations in nature approach men's affairs –

I stand alone in thousands of sources of worry.

I Stand Alone, Du Fu

< TRIBUTE TO DU FU
This landscape painting, one of
a set of 12, was created by the
16th-century artist Wang Shimin
in response to the poems of Du Fu.

BO JUYI

Bo Juyi, or Bai Juyi, (772–846) lived in a more subdued time in the Tang dynasty than Li Bai and Du Fu, but his poetry is equally popular. He is highly regarded in modern China for his satirical critiques of the inequalities that cause ordinary people hardship. His life was full of ups and downs, as his controversial opinions got him into trouble at court. His poetry is highly accessible because he deliberately chose to use simple language and imagery. He was able to boast that his poems were written on city and inn walls by ordinary readers anxious to share their pleasure in them. Perhaps his most famous poems are two long narratives, one about the doomed affair between Emperor Xuanzong and his consort, Yang Guifei, and one about a lute-player fallen on hard times.

Bo Juyi often uses the playful persona of a forgetful old man living in retirement and "madly singing in the mountains" for the sheer pleasure of being at one with nature. One of his most moving poems describes the death of his little daughter, Golden Bells. The content of this poem is unusually personal for the times (*see below*).

Ruined and ill – a man of two score;

Pretty and guileless – a girl of three.

Not a boy – but still better than nothing:

To soothe one's feeling – from time to time a kiss!

There came a day – they suddenly took her from me;

Her soul's shadow wandered I know not where.

And when I remember how just at the time she died

She lisped strange sounds, beginning to learn to talk,

Then I know that the ties of flesh and blood

Only bind us to a load of grief and sorrow.

At last, by thinking of the time before she was born,

By thought and reason I drove the pain away.

Since my heart forgot her, many days have passed

And three times winter has changed to spring.

This morning, for a little, the old grief came back,

Because, on the road, I met her foster-nurse.

Golden Bells, Bo Juyi

> BO JUYI
The poet Bo Juyi was born to a
poor but scholarly family. He is
famous for his uncomplicated
use of language.

While poetry was always a part of elite private and official

古典文学

life in China, traditionally fiction had a less prestigious role and at times was even despised as "petty talk" (a literal translation of the Chinese word for fiction: *xiaoshuo*). Chinese poets were happy to claim authorship of their poems, but fiction writers were often obscure or anonymous figures about whom little is known. Nonetheless, despite its often less-than-respectable status, fiction in China has always enjoyed enormous popularity. The great novels in particular have become major cultural artifacts, read and reread, and reproduced in many forms over the centuries, from drama and television series to comic books and even video games.

小说之源 the origins of fiction

The origins of Chinese prose fiction have been traced back to the playful and profound parables and stories of the Daoist *Zhuangzi* (*see page 244*). However, perhaps the most influential source of Chinese fiction has been the dynastic histories such as the 4th century BCE *Zuozhuan* (Zuo Tradition), which provides vivid details of court intrigues and rivals to power. The most important examples of this genre are the wonderful biographies of emperors, empresses, generals, officials, warring kings, court jesters, and hired assassins written by the Han dynasty court historian Sima Qian (c.145–85 BCE). Sima Qian's biographies have long been valued for their compelling and moving stories, and his narrative format and use of direct speech, as well as his historical characters, became the model for much later fiction as well as official histories.

RECORDS OF THE STRANGE
A new fictional genre of brief classical supernatural tales began to emerge from the 4th century CE onward. Known as *Zhiguai* or *Records of the Strange*, these anecdotes and short

stories were written by devotees of the Buddhist and Daoist religions who were anxious to spread the message of their respective beliefs. Using the format of historical biographies, the stories of the *Zhiguai* were collected either as ethnographic records of bizarre events and strange creatures, or as belief tales that described various miracles performed by saints and sages.

TALES OF THE MARVELLOUS
By the time of the Tang dynasty (618–907), a more refined version of these earlier tales had begun to appear,

> At this Ren turned her eyes to him...
> "The only reason my kind is despised and loathed by human beings is because we are thought to harm people. I'm not like that. If you don't despise me, I would want to serve you all my days as your wife."
> *Ren's Story*, Shen Jiji

called the *Chuanqi* or *Tales of the Marvellous*. These were often written by aspiring young scholars who were anxious to be recognized for their literary accomplishments. Elegant and lyrical in style, these tales frequently featured unhappy romances between beautiful young ladies, or courtesans, and young scholars having a fling before

CLASSICAL LITERATURE
THE GREAT NOVELS OF CHINA

settling down to a respectable life as a government official and husband. Perhaps the most famous of these stories is the ultimately doomed romance between the unconventionally passionate and enigmatic Yingying and Zhang, a rather staid scholar. Zhang chooses to abandon Yingying after deciding that her unconventionality poses a threat to both his career and his moral reputation. Today, the pros and cons of this story are still the subject of heated debate, with people tending to sympathize strongly with the character of either Yingying or Zhang.

MISS REN

Another well-known story of the genre is that of Miss Ren. This beautiful fox-fairy remains loyal to her rather unappealing human lover, and uses a series of schemes and magical tricks to help him and his friend prosper and come up in the world. Despite her magical abilities, Miss Ren has few practical skills – the narrator notes that she cannot even sew her own clothes. Ultimately she is powerless to prevent her own death when she is chased down by hunting dogs, even though she had foreseen what was going to happen. Miss Ren reverts to the form of a fox after her death, and her human clothes are simply abandoned on the ground like the shed skin of a cicada.

Such *Tales of the Marvellous* and other stories gradually became woven into the fabric of Chinese culture, being retold again and again in other genres such as opera or vernacular fiction, or used as motifs in poetry or art.

the six classic novels

During the Ming dynasty (1368–1644), a new genre of lengthy narrative fiction, written in the vernacular rather than the classical style, emerged with the appearance of four great masterworks: *Romance of the Three Kingdoms* (*Sanguo yanyi*), attributed to Luo Guanzhong (c.1330–1400); *Water Margin* or *Outlaws of the Marsh* (*Shuihu zhuan*), attributed to Luo Guanzhong and/or Shi Nai'an; *Golden Lotus* (*Jin Ping Mei*), anonymous; and *Journey to the West* or *Monkey* (*Xi You ji*), by Wu Cheng'en (c.1506–82).

These four novels were joined in the Qing dynasty (1644–1911) by two other masterpieces: *The Scholars* (*Rulin Waishi*) by Wu Jingzi (d.1754) and *The Story of the Stone* or *Dream of the Red Chamber* (*Shitou ji* or *Hong lou meng*) by Cao Xueqin (1715–63 or 1724–64). Although myriad other Chinese novels have been published, these six books are still considered to be the finest flowering of Chinese fiction.

> OMENS OF DEFEAT
The antihero, Cao Cao, stands in a boat on the night before his greatest battle. He hears the call of crows, birds of ill omen, and loses the battle.

三国演义 romance of the three kingdoms

Based on historical events and real characters, *Romance of the Three Kingdoms* is set in the turbulent years of disunion and civil war following the fall of the great Han dynasty in 220 CE.

Three rival kingdoms, the Shu-Han, the Wei, and the Wu, are competing to win the empire. The novel follows the fortunes of the three rival houses and their successors, but the narrative focuses mainly on the career of Liu Bei, the ruler of the Shu-Han, and his

> The world under Heaven, after a long period of division, tends to unite; after a long period of union, tends to divide. This has been so since antiquity.
>
> Opening of *Romance of the Three Kingdoms*, Luo Guanzhong

two sworn brothers, the proud Guan Yu (Lord Guan) and a wild, rash warrior called Zhang Fei.

Liu Bei is a poor and distant relation of the Han royal house who parlays his way into power with the help of the wizardly Zhuge Liang (or Kongming), whom he woos out of seclusion to become his main advisor and strategist. After Liu Bei's death, the loyal Zhuge Liang strives to realize his master's dream to reunite China under the banner of the Shu-Han.

Liu Bei is portrayed as a righteous, benevolent, but flawed ruler, whose main failing is his misplaced urge to avenge the deaths of his sworn brothers at the cost of the great enterprise to rule China. His followers, Guan Yu (also called Beautiful Beard, for his long and lustrous beard) and Zhang Fei, are famous in the popular imagination as great warriors, but their heroic stature is diminished gradually in the course of the novel.

Liu Bei's rival is Cao Cao, ruler of the Wei. The historical Cao Cao was an administrator and poet whose charisma won him many followers. Like Richard III of England, he has been portrayed on stage and in literature as a symbol of disloyalty and villainy. In the novel, Cao Cao is a ruthless but attractive figure: his ability to laugh in the face of danger contrasts with Liu Bei's habit of weeping. Such ambivalent characterization adds to the power of this great novel.

Many argue that Zhuge Liang is the true hero of the novel, for it is his cunning schemes (such as

"stealing" the enemy's arrows; setting ships on fire with the aid of a magic wind; and tricking another enemy into an ambush with his "empty city" ruse) that have long captured readers' imaginations. Zhuge Liang is depicted as having a marvellously persuasive tongue and magic ability, but even his deep loyalty to his master's cause is undermined by his overconfidence.

The narrative ends, more than 300 years after it began, with China finally truly united again, first under the Sui and then the glorious Tang. Perhaps the greatest achievement of *Romance of the Three Kingdoms* is the complexity of the storytelling, with the main narrative

being cleverly interwoven with many subsidiary plots that could make fascinating novels in their own right.

Romance of the Three Kingdoms is written in a simple, rousing semi-classical style. This long novel of 120 chapters and a rich cast of hundreds of wonderfully drawn characters has been a central cultural document in Chinese and East Asian societies for centuries. The novel's main characters and events have found their way into comic books, business strategy texts, and many other genres throughout the region. In fact, the Koreans have embraced the book so deeply that many now consider it to be a Korean national novel.

< A MUCH MALIGNED FIGURE
History records that Cao Cao, the antihero of *Romance of the Three Kingdoms*, was a brilliant ruler, but his fictional character is cunning and deceitful.

> We three, though of separate ancestry, join in brotherhood here, combining strength and purpose, to relieve the present crisis. We will perform our duty to the Emperor and protect the common folk of the land. We dare not hope to be together always, but hereby vow to die the selfsame day.

Oath of the Peach Garden from *Romance of the Three Kingdoms*

∧ MODERN ADAPTATIONS
The action-packed nature of the story, with its many battles, has made *Romance of the Three Kingdoms* a popular subject for film and television adaptations.

< BAND OF OUTLAWS
The colourful characters of
Water Margin, including 108
bandits, are enduring favourites
in Chinese literature.

水 water margin
许
传

Conservative Confucian officials believed very strongly in the power of the written word to influence readers, for good or for ill, and *Water Margin* was banned on several occasions because of its subject matter. The fact that it was one of Mao Zedong's favourite books suggests that its detractors were correct to fear its revolutionary potential.

This very popular novel, believed to have been written around the 16th century, describes the establishment of a band of rebels and outlaws who are unjustly forced into the world of the "greenwoods" or "rivers and lakes" by corrupt officials. Written in ten-chapter cycles, this episodic novel tells the story of each bandit hero as he makes his way to join the band. The novel's narrative revolves around the heroes' journeys and the roadside inns, country manors, and bustling market towns they encounter along the way.

The most famous of the novel's outlaws include the comic wild fighter Lu Zhishen, who has to disguise himself as a Buddhist monk but disgraces himself by getting drunk, eating vast quantities of meat (thus shocking the vegetarian monks), and creating havoc in the temple. The bandit leader is the petty official Song Jiang, a generous, if rather weak, individual. Song Jiang is always accompanied by Li Kui, his violent sidekick. Nicknamed "The Black Whirlwind," Li Kui's battle cry is, "Kill one, kill them all!"

One of the best-known and popular episodes of the novel deals with the story of the heroic Wu Song. He kills a tiger with his bare hands when drunk, and then avenges the murder of his dwarflike older brother at the hands of his sister-in-law, Pan Jinlian, or Golden Lotus, and her accomplices. Once Wu Song and the other heroes join the group of outlaws, they fight rival bands

for power and finally are given amnesty by the ruler in order to battle a larger rebel group.

Water Margin ends on a rather gloomy note, with the band of 108 outlaws finally dispersing. Most of the novel's main characters either die or decide to become monks, including the erstwhile false monk Lu Zhishen, who is now truly enlightened.

> There is a saying in Chinese that the old should not read *Romance of the Three Kingdoms* because it will transform them into schemers and plotters, while the young should avoid *Water Margin* because it will incite them to rebellion.

Water Margin's heroes are flawed and misogynous, and they are not exactly Robin Hood types, but their exploits are famous and they are the prototypes of the popular martial arts tradition found in novels, movies, and comic books. The bestselling martial arts novels of the Hong Kong writer Jin Yong, which are read by Chinese (and others) everywhere, owe much to the patterns set out in *Water Margin*.

金 golden lotus
瓶
梅

The notorious pornographic novel *Golden Lotus* takes as its starting point the story of Pan Jinlian and her lover, Ximen Qing. The novel focuses on Ximen Qing's household and his various affairs. He is a wealthy and corrupt merchant with six wives and innumerable hangers-on and servants.

The novel is studded with descriptions of luxury goods, dubious deals, sexual shenanigans, and details of everyday life in the Ming dynasty. It ends on a moral note, with Ximen Qing and most of the other negative characters encountering a horrible comeuppance. Wu Song (from *Water Margin*) avenges his brother's death by killing the cruel, selfish, and voracious Pan Jinlian.

No one knows who wrote *Golden Lotus*, although there are several theories, including the unlikely but popular belief that a famous poet penned it and infused the manuscript with poison before presenting it to the official responsible for his father's unjust death. The official, in his eagerness to race through the novel, licked his fingers to turn the pages more easily and died after ingesting the poison.

< MARTIAL ARTS INSPIRATION
The kung fu and other martial arts scenes featured in *Water Margin* inspired a wealth of martial arts novels and, later, movies and television programmes.

西 journey to
游 the west
记

This famous comic fantasy novel features some of the most well-known characters in Chinese fiction, and is set in the Tang dynasty (7th century). The novel is a fictionalized account of the legendary Chinese Buddhist monk, Xuanzang, who made a pilgrimage to India in order to bring the Buddhist scriptures to China.

In *Journey to the West*, the holy, but helpless and rather peevish, Tripitaka (who is the novel's version of the monk Xuanzang) sets off on a pilgrimage with a motley group of helpers found for him by the Bodhisattva, Guanyin (*see page 247*), in order to protect Tripitaka on his journey. These disciples include the mischievous Monkey King, Sun Wukong, who was thrown out of Heaven for stealing the peaches of immortality belonging to the Queen Mother of the West (*see page 238*). Also in Tripitaka's band of helpers are two former celestial generals, called Pigsy and Sandy, who must redeem themselves for their past misdemeanours. Pigsy, a creature of huge appetites, was once an immortal but was banished to Earth as punishment for his drunken behaviour during a celebration with the gods. Sandy, too, was exiled to the mortal world, being changed into a river monster after smashing a crystal goblet belonging to the Queen Mother of Heaven.

Along the way the intrepid travellers are beset, time and time again, by a variety of monsters and mythical

∧ **MONKEY MISCHIEF**
The mischievous Monkey King is shown here creating his usual havoc among a garden of women.

> In ancient times there was a magic rock on the Mountain of Flowers and Fruit... The rock had been favoured by the elements of nature for millions of years. One day, it suddenly burst open, giving birth to a stone egg from which a stone monkey emerged.
>
> *Journey to the West*, Wu Cheng'en

creatures, who believe that if they consume the saintly Tripitaka they will achieve immortality. Each time, Tripitaka is rescued from his peril by his band of disciples, especially the Monkey King, who has the ability to transform his shape and size, becoming a fish, a bird, or a dragonfly at will, while wielding his magic cudgel. The journey takes 14 years, at the end of which the disciples are rewarded with places in Heaven.

BUDDHIST INFLUENCES

The philosophical core of this novel is the Buddhist *Heart Sutra* with its message that "Emptiness is Form, and Form is Emptiness". This promotes the Buddhist belief that everything is an illusion (Emptiness) and in order to achieve enlightenment one must reject all worldly attachments (Form), including even apparently positive feelings of love and compassion. It is the Monkey King – whose name, Sun Wukong, translates as "Understanding Emptiness" – who truly takes the message to heart, rather than his monk-master Tripitaka. At the end of the novel, both Monkey and Tripitaka attain Buddhahood.

POPULAR CULTURE

Episodes from this novel are extremely well known throughout China and beyond, in particular the exploits of the irrepressible Monkey, whose famous and distinctive features can be found adorning everything from postage stamps to Olympic logos.

The novel has been adapted many times, and is the subject of myriad movies and television programmes in Asia and around the world, as well as theatrical productions and even computer games.

> Together, the Monkey King and Master Tripitaka started toward the Western Paradise on their new adventure, the Pilgrimage for the Buddhist Scriptures.
>
> *Journey to the West*, Wu Cheng'en

∧ **THE BAND OF PILGRIMS**
The main characters from *Journey to the West* – Monkey, Pigsy, Sandy, and Tripitaka – are brought to life by these donkey-skin puppets.

儒 the scholars
林外史

The 18th-century (Qing dynasty) novel *The Scholars* by Wu Jingzi is the shortest of the classic Chinese novels, totalling 55 loosely connected chapters. It is also the least well known to modern readers. Set in the Ming dynasty (1368–1644), Wu Jingzi's masterpiece is a novel of satiric realism, in contrast to the supernatural fiction of writers such as Pu Songling (*see page 275*). The novel is written in a pure, smoothly crafted vernacular style and tells the story of the lives of a group of Confucian scholars living in the wealthy southeastern coastal region of the country.

Wu Jingzi mercilessly lampoons the decadence of the literary classes of the time, the injustice of the feudal examination system, and the social inequalities that the system created. Using paired and contrasting characters, and with a semiautobiographical base, the novel provides a series of realistic vignettes of a bustling world in which a number of scholars choose to avoid their expected roles as government officials in order to pursue more satisfying artistic and cultural lives.

< **MOUNTAIN HERMITS**
The Scholars begins with the story of Wang Mien, a popular painter who rejects the attention of the influential and eventually takes up the life of a hermit.

石头记 the story of the stone

Also known as *The Dream of the Red Chamber*, and often regarded as the pinnacle of traditional Chinese fiction, *The Story of the Stone* is perhaps the most popular of the six classic novels of Chinese fiction.

Written over many years and heavily revised, this vast novel was left incomplete by its author, Cao Xueqin, until a later editor added 40 chapters. A debate still rages as to the success or failure of these additional chapters. *The Story of the Stone* is a complex mixture of myth, allegory, and realistic events, including multiple beginnings and messages. Written and set in the 18th century, the core of the book focuses on the life of the eccentric hero Jia Baoyu, the nonconformist son of Jia Zheng, an important and wealthy man, and Jia Baoyu's female cousins, maidservants, and others. Baoyu's fate is linked symbolically and emotionally to his two girl cousins, the delicate and sensitive Lin Daiyu, and the more

> The whole garden had become a shimmering sea of nodding blossoms and fluttering coloured streamers.
>
> *The Story of the Stone*, Cao Xueqin

conventional, but highly intelligent, Xue Baochai. Baoyu and his cousins live an initially idyllic existence in Prospect Garden, within the walls of the Jia mansion, but over time their innocent pleasures are threatened by the corrupt encroachments of the outside, adult world. After the death of his beloved Daiyu, Baoyu renounces the world in order to become a Buddhist monk.

Filled with detailed descriptions of objects, architecture, cultural pursuits, and medical lore, and with character vignettes, the novel presents a vision of a great household in decline. Partly autobiographical, it was the first Chinese novel to truly explore psychological and emotional ties, and its complexity and richness ensure that it continues to retain its hold on readers today.

There is an entire cottage industry devoted to *The Story of the Stone*, with products ranging from reconstructions of the Jia mansion and other knick-knacks to operas and television series, as well as libraries of studies on the novel, equivalent in number to those relating to Shakespeare in the West.

∧ **ARISTOCRATIC LADIES IN A GARDEN**
Unusually, female characters are at the centre of *The Story of the Stone*. They are often shown to be more capable than their male counterparts.

> **FLYING CELESTIAL BEING**
Supernatural women feature strongly
in the tales of Pu Songling. This painting
of a celestial nymph was found at the
Mogao Caves in Dunhuang.

短篇小说 shorter chinese fiction

The 17th century saw a flourishing of short fiction written and edited in vernacular Chinese that dealt with the lives of ordinary people such as merchants, shopkeepers, minor officials, and servants. These lively and often comic stories were usually written as if told by a storyteller in a marketplace. They have the immediacy and vividness of oral tales, plus a requisite moral ending that ties up all the loose ends. The genre fell into decline after the Qing conquest in 1644, but there is a renewed interest in such tales today.

One 17th-century writer whose short fiction has enjoyed enduring popularity is Pu Songling (1640–1715). Pu's famous *Strange Tales from a Chinese Studio* (*Liaozhai zhiyi*) is a collection of brief classical language tales of the supernatural, based on the model of the ancient *Zhiguai* or *Records of the Strange* (*see page 266*).

Pu was an impoverished scholar who lived in famine- and war-ravaged Shandong Province, the home of Confucius and a region notorious for its otherworldly links, including the presence of Mount Tai, seat of King Yama, ruler and judge of the underworld. Legend has it that Pu set up a table on a main thoroughfare and plied travellers with tea in exchange for stories, which he then crafted into elegantly written and often playful pieces.

All of Pu's tales deal with strange events, but he is perhaps best known for his stories about hapless bookworms who become the target of beautiful female ghosts or fox-women. In many of the *Strange Tales* the supernatural beauties undergo a rebirth or transformation to become fully human, and the fortunate scholar-hero ends up with two wives living happily ever after. Pu's ghost tales, despite their often compressed and difficult classical language, are exceptionally popular, and have become the source for many supernatural films and other genres.

> "There are so many beautiful women in this world", complained his mother. "Why pick a ghost and a fox?"
>
> *Silkworm*, Pu Songling

∧ **FESTIVAL BY A LAKE**
The vernacular short story tradition, which began in the 17th century, gives a vibrant picture of everyday Chinese life, from work and business to festivals and leisure.

Visually stunning and musically dramatic, traditional Chinese

戏
曲 opera has been woven into the fabric of Chinese life in
innumerable ways, with performances at temple fairs, village
festivals, market towns, in private theatres in elite households,
at court, and, in modern times, on radio, television, and in film.
Theatre, and particularly opera, has a long history in China,
with roots in ritual dance, acrobatic performances, and street
entertainment. For many visitors to the country, the sights and
sounds of Chinese opera are phenomena not to be missed,
bringing a taste of the China of the past to the modern world.

戏
曲 the history of
历 chinese opera
史

Music, dance, and acrobatics have always been essential elements of Chinese drama, and singing is very much the core. In contrast to Western forms of opera, there tends to be a rather limited repertoire of songs and musical instruments (drums, gongs, two-stringed Chinese violins, and clappers). Rhythm is stressed over harmony, and the focus is on the singing itself, which is usually solo, with the emphasis firmly on the performance of familiar and highly poetic arias.

Audiences are extremely loud in their appreciation of virtuoso performers, and there is none of the respectful hush that is typical of opera-going in the West. Performances are loud and exhilarating: there is nothing more exciting than hearing the gongs and cymbals that signal the entrance of the performers. Props and scenery are minimal and gestures are highly stylized.

SYMBOLISM OF COLOUR

Chinese opera costumes and head-dresses are elaborate, even gaudy, and complex painted faces indicate the characters' personality traits. Yellow and white represent cunning, red indicates straightforwardness and loyalty, black means valour and wisdom, blue and green indicate rebellious heroes, and gold and silver represent mystic or supernatural powers. Experienced audiences can therefore "read" a character as soon as they make their entrance without actually hearing them sing or seeing them dance.

THE PERFORMERS

Actors and actresses are trained from a very young age and tend to specialize in particular roles: young scholar, brave general, righteous official, beautiful young lady, mischievous maidservant, or clown. The social status of actors and actresses was traditionally very low, and for centuries women were not allowed to act, which meant that men played all the female roles. This changed in the early 20th century, although the popularity of female impersonators ensured that female roles continued to be played by male performers until much later.

During the Tang dynasty, an opera school was established called *Liyuan*, which literally means "the pear garden". As a result, from then on opera performers in China have been known, rather poetically, as "disciples of the pear garden".

Arguably the most famous female impersonator was Mei Lanfang, who travelled to Europe and North America in the mid-20th century and proved to be a great success, bringing Chinese opera to the rest of the world. Born into a family of opera singers, his performances during his 50-year career have become legendary. He was particularly well known for his portrayal of the heroine of *The Peony Pavilion*, Du Liniang.

乙
酉
二
月
梅
蘭
芳

TRADITIONAL OPERA
THE HEART OF CHINESE THEATRE

< MEI LANFANG
Mei Lanfang (1894–1961), Chinese opera's famous female impersonator, performs the lead role of the concubine Yang in *The Drunken Concubine*.

DIVERSE STYLES

There are many different types of regional operas and styles, but their stories tend to be familiar to all because they come from the vast storehouse of Chinese myths, legends, and history. In this way, Chinese opera, appealing to audiences of all kinds, gives Chinese people throughout the country, and the world, the opportunity to understand and be proud of their wonderfully rich and diverse cultural heritage.

The most dominant form of opera in the Ming and early Qing dynasties (16th–18th century) was *Kunqu*. This elitist style of drama was highly influential on later forms, such as Peking (later Beijing) opera. Works are often very long, and feature romantic love stories. Some of the most popular dramatic works in Chinese culture have evolved from, or been adapted for, the *Kunqu* stage, including *The Peony Pavilion* (see page 279), *The White Snake*, and *The Peach Blossom Fan*.

Peking opera, or Beijing opera, began in 1790, and by the mid-19th-century it had become a great favourite at the court of the Qing dynasty, as well as at temple fairs and markets. Beijing opera pieces tend to be very long. They feature love stories and combine solo singing, duets, and choruses.

The Northern *Yuan zaju* operas, such as *The Injustice Done to Dou E* (see page 278), date from the Yuan dynasty (1279–1368), and the stories deal with social issues. Generally comprising four acts and a prologue, each act features one singer. These variety plays are relatively short, and are characterized by the use of fast-paced drums and cymbals.

Shaoxing opera originates from the 800-year-old *Yue* opera, which is a type of "story-singing". *Shaoxing* is a popular form of opera, and is often performed today by all-female troupes.

During the Cultural Revolution (1966–76), Mao's fourth wife, Jiang Qing, a former actress, used the medium of opera to deliver communist messages to the masses. The official versions of the "eight model plays" were Beijing operas, although they were also adapted to other, provincial operas.

∧ TRADITIONAL COSTUMES
Magnificent costumes and face masks are a hallmark of Chinese opera, like this one from the Beijing opera.

> "Heaven and earth both bully the weak and fear the strong, not daring to go against the flow. Earth, you make no distinction between right and wrong; and Heaven, you mistake the wise for the foolish."
>
> *The Injustice Done to Dou E* by Guan Hanqing

∧ **THE GHOST OF DOU E**
The role of Dou E is one of the most
famous in the opera repertoire, and one
that many performers aspire to play.

窦娥冤 the injustice done to dou e

This Yuan dynasty (13th-century) tale, also known as *Snow in Midsummer*, is arguably the most popular work of Guan Hanqing, one of China's favourite playwrights, who is sometimes referred to as "China's Shakespeare". He used this story, based on the Han dynasty folk tale, *A Filial Woman of Donghai*, to highlight the injustices he saw in contemporary Chinese society, and the opera based on his play remains one of the most popular in the repertoire of Northern *Yuan zaju* operas.

The Injustice Done to Dou E is the tragic story of a young woman (Dou E), from Chouzhou, who is widowed very early in her marriage. After her husband's death, this filial daughter-in-law tries to protect her mother-in-law from Donkey Zhang, a local bully, and unwittingly attracts his attentions. When Dou E refuses to become his wife, Donkey Zhang falsely accuses her of the murder of his father (who Zhang has in fact unintentionally killed himself). The local officials listen to Zhang's accusations. Dou E is unable to prove her innocence, and she is condemned to death.

At her execution, Doe E foretells that her innocence will be proven by three dramatic events: when she is killed her blood will spurt high enough to stain the white silk streamer overhead; snow will fall in summer; and Chouzhou will be blighted by a terrible drought for three consecutive years. In due course, all three predictions come true exactly as Dou E foretells, proving her innocence, and the scene in which snow falls in the summer is one of the most dramatic and well-known in all of Chinese opera.

Three years later, Dou E's father returns to Chouzhou after a long absence, and unwittingly presides over a retrial of the case, prompted by the bidding of Dou E's ghost. Finally, Dou E is exonerated and Donkey Zhang and all the corrupt officials who wronged her ultimately face the justice they deserve.

> "I want to say three things, officer. If you let me, I shall die content. I want a clean mat and a white streamer twelve feet long to hang on the flagpole. When the sword strikes off my head, not a drop will stain the ground. It will all fly up instead to the white streamer. This is the hottest time of summer, sir. If injustice has indeed been done, three feet of snow will cover my dead body. Then this district will suffer from drought for three whole years".
>
> *The Injustice Done to Dou E* by Guan Hanqing

牡丹亭 the peony pavilion

Tang Xianzu's romantic tale, written during the Ming dynasty (1368–1644), is one of China's best-loved operas. It tells of a governor's daughter, Du Liniang, who falls asleep in a garden and in a dream meets Liu Mengmei, who becomes her lover in a pavilion of peonies. Woken by falling petals, she searches in vain for her lost love. Unable to recreate the bliss of her dream, she paints her portrait and inscribes it with a love poem, then dies of a broken heart. The portrait is buried next to her grave in the garden, beneath a plum tree.

After her death, the judge of hell releases Du Liniang on the grounds that her marriage to Liu Mengmei is predestined, and sends her back to the garden as a ghost. Meanwhile, the real Liu Mengmei stops at Du Liniang's shrine on his way to take his civil-service exams. He discovers her portrait, and recognizing her as the girl of his dreams, he opens her grave, and her soul is reunited with her body.

At Du Liniang's request, Liu Mengmei goes to tell her father that his daughter has returned from the grave, but when he reveals his story Liu Mengmei is accused of being a grave robber and is condemned to death. At the last moment the results of the imperial exams are announced, and as Liu Mengmei tops the list he is pardoned by the emperor, who convinces Du Liniang's father to let love conquer all.

THE LEGACY OF THE TALE

Traditionally, the plot of *The Peony Pavilion* is considered to be rather scandalous because of its erotic overtones, although the sexual relationship between the two young lovers is generally tolerated because the events take place as part of Du Liniang's dream, and later when she returns as a ghost.

During the Ming and Qing era, the tragic yet romantic nature of Du Liniang's plight created a disturbing trend among some young girls of styling themselves on the waiflike, broken-hearted heroine of *The Peony Pavilion* and effectively starving themselves to death.

"Has the world ever seen a woman's love to rival that of Du Liniang? Dreaming of a lover she fell sick; once sick she became ever worse; and finally, after painting her own portrait as a legacy to the world, she died... To be as Du Liniang is truly to.have known love".

The Peony Pavilion by Tang Xianzu

∧ **DU LINIANG AND LIU MENGMEI**
Two actors perform a scene from *The Peony Pavillion* in a modern production of this *Kunqu* opera masterpiece.

ARCHITECTURE

建筑 BUILDING A NATION

The beauty and complexity of the spaces in which Chinese people live, work, and worship is astounding. From modest dwellings, specially adapted to the local environment, to imperial palaces and modern office blocks, Chinese builders have always been true craftsmen. Since earliest times, construction in China has centred on wood. The timber frame, with its unparalleled flexibility, versatility, and ability to withstand earthquakes, is the country's major contribution to world architecture. China has a 7,000-year history of interlocking wooden frames, and today "the four layers" (foundation platform, columns, brackets, and a roof frame) still identify a Chinese-style building anywhere in the world. The silent, symbolic language of Chinese architecture is such that the structure of a palace might be indistinguishable from that of a temple, even though one contains a throne and the other an altar. This chapter features visual tours of 16 important Chinese buildings – both public and private, traditional and modern – from around the country.

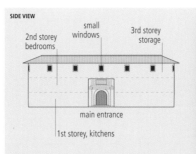

SIDE VIEW

2nd storey bedrooms · small windows · 3rd storey storage

main entrance

1st storey, kitchens

< CIRCULAR CONSTRUCTION
With only a few small windows cut out of the upper walls, Shengwu Lou looks like a circular fortress from the outside.

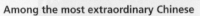

AERIAL VIEW

single-storey inner ring

portico

courtyard

well

residence

three-storey outer ring

doorway

main entrance

Among the most extraordinary Chinese

绳武楼

buildings are the massive, multistorey structures known as *tulou* (earthen dwellings) – residential complexes built of earth and timber principally by a Chinese subethnic group called the Hakka. Resembling vast fortresses, they are found in the rugged mountains of southwestern Fujian Province, with variant forms in neighbouring Jiangxi and Guangdong. It is likely that there are still many undiscovered *tulou* in the deep hills. Structures of this type were largely unknown until the last half of the 20th century, but today many are accessible via modern roads to travellers willing to digress from the well-trodden tourist routes.

Around 1,000 Hakka dwellings are still standing from China's pre-20th-century imperial past, and a handful have survived for more than 500 years. Large *tulou* were still being built even at the end of the 20th century in villages in Yongding and Nanjing counties, the core region for this type of building. Many of the very old *tulou* still stand as partially abandoned structures in the more rugged areas of neighbouring counties. Constructed in various distinctive

shapes – square, oblong, pentagonal, octagonal, and rhomboid – the most striking *tulou* are the circular ones.

Shengwu Lou (Exercise Restraint Building) in Jiaolu village, Pinghe county, is a typical, smaller *tulou*, built some time during the Qing dynasty (1644–1912). The single-storey inner ring and three-storey outer ring are divided into 15 vertical "apartments" that surround a courtyard with a well in the centre. Now somewhat run-down, these were all once grand residences. Cooking and eating facilities are at ground level and bedrooms and storage areas are spread over the second and third storeys.

Chinese architects have calculated that a circular wall is able to wrap more interior space than a square wall of the same length, thus economizing on scarce building materials. Furthermore, the interior space can be divided more equally as pie-shaped apartments in round structures than in square ones – an important principle in the egalitarian organization of Hakka society. Some authorities also suggest that round buildings are better suited to resisting earthquakes and deflecting the strong winds of seasonal typhoons.

∧ RESIDENCE NAME
All Hakka dwellings have a three-character name, derived from a literary allusion, carved above the main entrance.

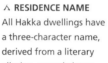
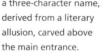

> MAIN ENTRANCE
Shengwu Lou's main entrance, which leads to the central courtyard, is made of stone blockwork topped by refined and elegant carving.

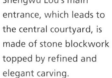

> NARROW PORTICO
This area is usually occupied throughout the day by women, children, and elderly men, who prepare food, husk rice, and embroider cloth.

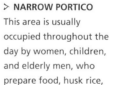

> PILLAR ORNAMENTATION
While much of the building is necessarily plain and functional, wherever possible it is enlivened by decorative details, such as this finely carved woodwork on the facade of a wooden roof support.

SHENGWU LOU
QING DYNASTY HAKKA DWELLING, FUJIAN

> VIEW ACROSS THE ROOF TOPS
Sections of the roof intersect at a variety of angles and are capped with clay tiles sealed with mortar.

∨ MULTI-LAYERED RESIDENCE
Arranged in concentric circles around a central courtyard, the single-storey inner ring stands in front of the three-storey outer ring.

< CORNER DETAIL OF ROOF
A flourish of decorative tiling on the roof ends reflects the former status of Shengwu Lou as a residence of some grandeur and wealth.

∨ CARVED SUPPORTS
Atop the brick columns on the second level are stone carvings supporting the timbers that hold up the joists.

< CENTRAL WELL
A deep well set in the centre of the paved courtyard is a hub of daily life in the *tulou*. The kitchens of the apartments are all at ground level, so that they open out onto the courtyard for easy access to water.

∧ > DECORATIVE DOORWAYS
The wooden posts of the pivoting "saloon"-style doors slot into ornamented stone sockets that extend out from the brick walls. New Year's greetings hang on this kitchen door.

∧ CENTRAL COURTYARD
The entrance to each apartment opens out
onto the communal courtyard that functions
as a social gathering spot, a roaming area for
domestic animals, and a storage space for grain.

> **NEW YEAR'S DECORATIONS**
At New Year, each doorway in
the building is brightened with
red strips of paper bearing a
propitious phrase.

> **VENTILATION PORTS**
Carved and slatted wooden
panels draw air and light
into the rooms of the
upper storeys.

∧ **BRICK CARVING**
Besides wood and stone
carving, fired bricks
were also carved into
ornamental patterns.

∧ ▷ **BALCONY WOODWORK**
Elaborately carved wooden
elements add elegance to the
exteriors of bedrooms on the
second and third levels.

< ROOF SUPPORT
With interlocking mortised and tenoned timber members, this eaves projection supports the overhanging roof.

∨ EATING AREA
At ground level in the *tulou*'s outer ring, each apartment has an informal family room for eating and relaxing.

> AT THE HEAD OF THE STAIRS
The compacted earth of the outer wall is clearly visible at the top of the staircase. The wooden frames of the houses are set into this wall.

∧ INFORMAL RITUAL CORNER
Clustered in a corner are clay vessels and a metal dish on fired bricks, which is used for burning paper money offerings to the ancestors.

< ALCOVE BED
A veritable room-within-a-room, an alcove bed is usually heavily ornamented with auspicious and instructional imagery.

∧ TOWELS DRYING
Laundry is air-dried on a wire strung beneath photos of ancestors. Mementos of ancestors have a prominent place within many Chinese homes.

SIDE VIEW
three storey
two storey
single storey
bedroom
front hall
front door
bedroom
skywell
skywell

AERIAL VIEW
bedroom
skywell
skywell
kitchen
front hall
front hall
skywell
front hall
front door
house 1 house 2 house 3 house 4 house 5

∨ SIDE VIEW
Ming dynasty building regulations governed the external appearance of Huizhou dwellings, leading to a lack of ostentation. The windows are small, and generally in the upper storeys.

∨ WINDOW
The small windows in the upper wall capture little air and light, which are instead provided by the skywells.

五房厅

Among the oldest surviving dwellings in China are those built by prosperous merchants in the Huizhou region of Anhui and Jiangxi provinces during the Ming dynasty (1368–1644). These magnificent residences and ancestral halls remained relatively unknown until recent times. From the outside, these plastered houses with their black-tiled roofs look modest, even austere, but within they are expansive and heavily ornamented. Although three storeys high, most have the appearance of squat boxes. Some are arranged horizontally as a series of connected adjacent housing units for an extended family.

One of the finest examples is Wu Fang Ting (Five Branches' Halls) in Chengkan Village, Shexian County, Anhui Province. The structure seen today was once a linked series of five residences built by five brothers in the late Ming dynasty (16th century). One of the residences deteriorated beyond repair in the 1970s, but the other four have recently been restored.

Nothing distinguishes Huizhou dwellings more than their *tianjing*, or skywells. These mini-courtyards are open to the skies above, and sunken below

floor level to collect rain and drain excess water. They also draw light and air into what, from the outside, appears to be a dense and solid structure.

The first skywell, at the front of each house, creates a narrow entrance forecourt. Behind this is an open hall, followed by a middle skywell, and a formal reception hall. Flanking each of these spaces is a pair of bedrooms, which would have been used by servants and visitors. At the rear are the kitchens, two of which have adjacent skywells, and bedrooms where the elderly women of the family spent their days. Steep stairs lead to the living space for the rest of the family on the upper floors, where the bedrooms, halls, and storage rooms are better ventilated and much less humid. At least one room of the cool, dry upper storey was a grain store.

The interiors have carved wood, brick, and stone panels, balustrades, roof members, brackets, pillars, and doors, as well as couplets written on hanging scrolls, paintings, and poetic calligraphy. The upper storeys have galleries lined with hinged lattice panels that allow air and light into the rooms, few of which have exterior windows.

∧ ENTRANCE TO FIRST RESIDENCE
A narrow paved alleyway leads to each of the main entrances of the five Wu Fang Ting houses.

> STONE PANEL DOOR
The double-leaf entrance to the first residence is made of square stone panels set into a heavy metal frame. Large metal pins secure each panel.

WU FANG TING
A MING DYNASTY RESIDENCE IN CHENGKAN, ANHUI

> GRANITE BASE
This ornate granite base alongside the entrance to the second residence reveals great attention to detail in its carving.

∨ ENTRANCE TO SECOND RESIDENCE
Entry to this residence is through a massive double-leaf gateway topped by a lavishly decorated brick-and-stone canopy known as a *menzhao*.

> THIRD RESIDENCE DOORWAY
The third dwelling's entry is less ornate. High above the gate, the canopy offers little protection from the elements. The gate of the fourth house is next door.

∨ GABLE PROJECTION
At the end of the uppermost part of the step-like gable walls are ornamented projections.

∧ ROOF TILES AND EAVES TILES
The alternating concave and convex roof tiles are made of fired clay. *Wadang*, or eaves tiles, are placed at the ends of rows, where they serve both practical and ornamental functions. The eaves tiles are decorated with the character *wan* (longevity) and the face of a tiger.

> **VIEW UPWARDS TO THE SKY**
The rectangular opening of the skywell admits light and rainwater, while allowing heat and smoke to pass out of the house.

> **FADED WALLPAPER**
Fragments of colourful wallpaper with a plum-blossom motif, probably from early in the 20th century, are still visible in an upstairs bedroom of the first house.

V **SUNKEN FLOOR**
The ground level is abundantly lit by the narrow opening of the skywell, which is two storeys higher up. The sunken floor helps to drain rainwater.

Λ **VENTILATION PORT**
Stone apertures draw air underneath the wood floors to keep them dry.

Λ **EXPOSED BEAMS**
Wooden columns and beams are rarely hidden and become important visual elements of the interior walls.

< SKYWELL OF THIRD RESIDENCE
All five houses have a skywell
immediately inside the main gate,
forming a small entrance courtyard.

∨ DOORWAY OF FOURTH HOUSE
The doorway to the fourth residence
is shorter in height than the other
houses, as the house itself is lower,
and more modest in ornamentation.

∨ KITCHEN COURTYARD
This low and relatively open area to
the rear of the third residence is next
to the kitchen and allows smoke from
cooking to escape through the opening.

< ORNATE GALLERY
Wooden lattice
panels surround
the third-floor galleries
of the houses. They
epitomize simple,
elegant Ming-dynasty
decorative styles.

∧ FIFTH RESIDENCE
This simple shuttered
doorway once led to
the fifth residence,
which has deteriorated
beyond repair and
is now an open space
overgrown with weeds.

291

> **ENTRY GATE**
The red-painted entrance faces directly onto the narrow alleyways or *hutong*. High grey walls enclose the courtyard.

∨ **ADDRESS PLATE**
After 1949, *siheyuan* came to be occupied by many unrelated families. As the former residence of Cheng Yanqiu, number 39 Beidajie Third hutong was spared this fate.

AERIAL VIEW

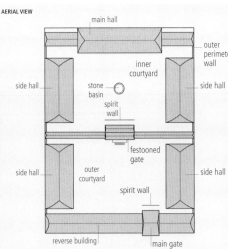

main hall

outer perimeter wall

inner courtyard

side hall

side hall

stone basin

spirit wall

festooned gate

side hall

outer courtyard

side hall

spirit wall

reverse building

main gate

The uncovered open space of a courtyard

四合院 is a vital area within any well-developed Chinese dwelling. The classic form of courtyard residence is found in northern China, centring on Beijing, the capital. Called *siheyuan*, dwellings of this type comprise a quadrangle of low buildings enclosing a nearly square courtyard, with subsidiary courtyards framed by buildings to the front, rear, or sides.

Before the modern transformation of Beijing, these rectangular courtyard houses were arranged closely together along narrow lanes known as *hutong* within well-defined checkerboard-like neighbourhoods. Following half a century of degradation and destruction, less than a thousand *siheyuan* still survive in Beijing. A small number have been saved because they once served as residences for prominent people, such as political figures, writers, or artists, and have been transformed into museums. Still others are now hotels for tourists. An even smaller number of *siheyuan* continue to be occupied by descendants of their original owners.

The courtyard house featured here was once the residence of the Beijing Opera singer Cheng Yanqiu

(1904–58), a Manchu who lived in this modest two-courtyard house from 1937 until his death. Since then, his three sons have maintained the structure in a form that echoes life more than a half-century ago. With an area of 390 sq m (4,200 sq ft), the house embodies the full range of classical features.

The key elements of any Beijing *siheyuan* are enclosure, symmetry, and hierarchy: high grey walls enclose the residence; side-to-side symmetry frames the dwelling; a single off-centre entry gate affords seclusion; and there is a hierarchical organization of open and enclosed spaces along a clear axis. All the buildings face inwards towards the courtyards so that the open spaces become integrated parts of the whole and can also be regarded as "rooms" within the home. The main structure of a *siheyuan* usually faces south or southeast, an orientation that exposes the courtyard to the maximum amount of sunlight during winter.

The protection of *siheyuan*, one of China's essential domestic architectural types, remains a key challenge to those who struggle to preserve the historical character of the nation's capital.

∧ **FESTOONED GATE**
The red "festooned gate" leading to the inner courtyard is emblazoned with old auspicious hangings for the New Year.

> **GATE PIER**
Carved with floral patterns in bas-relief, this oblong stone block, one of a pair, serves as an ornament outside the recessed entrance.

COURTYARD HOUSE
CLASSIC WALLED DWELLING, BEIJING

∨ BRASS DOOR PULLS
The double-leaf red gate at the external entrance features brass rings as door pulls. Traditionally, these might be chained together to lock the entrance.

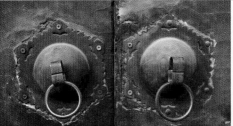

< ∨ INTERIOR VIEW OF GATE
A spirit wall blocks the view into the courtyard from outside and prevents entry by evil spirits, who cannot turn corners. Ornamented gables overhang the gate.

∨ INNER COURTYARD
The main inner courtyard is enclosed by a quadrangle of single-storey buildings: the main hall on the north side, smaller side buildings (the main image shows the hall to the east), and the interior entrance gate to the south. The *siheyuan's* courtyards cover almost half the total residential area.

∧ GATE DECORATION
These carved wooden decorations protrude from the lintel above the gate. They have symbolic pictorial or calligraphic carvings.

˅ SIDE HALL RESIDENCE
Smaller side buildings flank the main hall along either side of the courtyard. Traditionally, these housed the younger or less important family members.

< WOODEN FRAMEWORK
The entire dwelling is constructed from wood and brick within a graceful, carved wooden framework.

> PRIVATE RETREAT
As the outside walls of each hall have only small, high windows, the house has a level of seclusion from the busy streets outside.

> CARVED STONE BASIN
The central courtyard is simple, open, and uncluttered. A carved stone basin of this sort was probably once in a temple or palace courtyard.

˅ SIDE PASSAGEWAY
Due to an absence of storage space, outside passageways and corners tend to accumulate old building materials and defunct household items.

> STORAGE ON PORCH
Wooden eaves overhanging the buildings provide protection from the elements for items that have been stored outside.

> DINING ROOM
This *siheyuan* is still a busy family home. The dining room features contemporary furniture and modern glass windows.

∨ LATTICE PANELS
Wooden lattice window panels frame the view from the kitchen, providing a glimpse across the half-obscured courtyard to the facing hall beyond.

∧ SUNNY CORNERS
All the buildings around the courtyard have large windows facing the centre of the compound to make the most of the year-round sunlight that is provided by the large open space.

∧ WORKING QUARTERS
In many *siheyuan*, the main hall is divided in three, with a communal area in the centre and smaller rooms, such as this study, at either end.

> LIVING QUARTERS
A hanging scroll, showing the character for longevity (*wan*), adds a harmonious touch to the living area. The seating faces the courtyard.

< **RESIDENCE ADDRESS PLATE**
This wall sign at the top of the external stairs gives the address of the house: # 26 Ma'an Hamlet, Pingyan Village, Linxi Township.

AERIAL VIEW OF FIRST FLOOR

stairs to outside area

outside area

stairs to 2nd floor

rear room

fire pit

hallway

living room

stilts

kitchen

stairs to front door

∧ **SUMMER KITCHEN**
Tucked beneath an overhang beside one of the timber "stilts" is an outside kitchen for use during the summer.

∧ **UTILITY AREA**
A washing machine is stored underneath the house. The clothes are dried under the eaves, like rice sheaves.

Of China's 55 minority nationalities, no

侗
族
吊
脚
楼

group has a more distinctive architecture than the Dong. Numbering around 2.5 million people, the Dong live in villages in a region that straddles the borders of Guangxi, Guizhou, and Hunan provinces. While village gates, drum towers, opera stages, and "wind-and-rain bridges" are all structures associated with Dong villages, the sophisticated and unusual structural carpentry of their timber-framed, stilt- or pile-supported dwellings is particularly noteworthy.

Ma'an hamlet, in Sanjiang, northern Guangxi, is surrounded by undulating hills and rests snugly within the loop of the Linxi River, which embraces the hamlet's meticulously tended paddy fields and fishponds. It is regarded as one of the country's most beautiful villages because of its spectacular location and impressive architecture. Dwellings throughout the hamlet are spacious, even though families rarely exceed two generations.

The wooden framework of a Dong house is strikingly adaptable to uneven terrain. A typical dwelling is three storeys high and divided into three lateral bays. Tall supporting

timber pillars, or "stilts", form a kind of skeletal structure that is independent of the internal room partitions.

The main body of the house is raised about 2m (6ft) above the ground, with the space beneath being used to keep domestic animals and provide storage. The first level above ground is partitioned into two or three large rooms. In many homes, the first room is a combination of kitchen and living room, with ample electronic equipment, desks, tables, chairs, and sofas, plus a gas stove and a refrigerator. It is in this airy and generally bright room that women weave textiles or embroider, and also carry out myriad household chores in the company of other family members. The adjacent room usually contains an open fire pit sunk into the floor. The top floor of the house consists of numerous small rooms for sleeping and storage.

With limited numbers of window openings, the walls of a stilt house are not built very tight. This allows air to flow readily between the timbers in order to reduce humidity, dissipate heat from outside, and let out heat and smoke from the fire pit inside.

STILT HOUSE
DONG MINORITY DWELLING, GUANGXI

侗 族 吊 脚 楼

∨ THE FACADE

The exterior walls are sided with unpainted sawn lumber that is allowed to weather to develop a dark hue.

> WATCHING THE WORLD

From an upstairs window this girl gets a clear view of the rest of the house and all the comings and goings in the village square.

∧ DRYING GRAIN

Sheaves of newly harvested rice are hung beneath the eaves to dry before being winnowed and threshed.

< PROTRUDING CABINET

The house's timber-frame construction makes it simple to incorporate a storage cabinet into the exterior wall.

< HOME FOR LIVESTOCK

Pigs, as well as ducks and chickens, are kept at ground level in the storage space beneath the dwelling.

> TIMBER-FRAME JOINERY

The timbers are secured with thin wooden pegs, knitted together to create the structure of the stilt house.

∧ ENTRY STAIRS

The upper floors are accessed via a steeply pitched wooden staircase, which leads to the main entrance of the house on the first floor.

ᐯ HALLWAY

Just inside the front doorway at the top of the steep staircase is a rectangular hallway – a place to remove shoes and hats when entering the house.

ᐯ THE FIRE PIT

In the rear room on the first floor is an open fire pit, where water is kept boiling year-round. The fire pit represents family solidarity and continuity.

ᐱ ENTERTAINMENT CENTRE

In a colourful corner of the living room is a bank of electronic equipment that today forms a part of family life in many Dong homes.

> THRESHING GRAIN

Outside, at the back of the house, dried rice sheaves are threshed using a machine powered by a foot pedal.

> KITCHEN AREA

In addition to a fire pit, many Dong stilt houses today have electric rice cookers and gas burners in a separate kitchen area.

∨ HERB BASKET

Bamboo baskets woven by the Dong women are used to collect herbs, fruit, and vegetables.

∧ WOODEN WEAVING LOOM

The slats of the windows allow plenty of light to stream into the living room where a woman weaves a traditional textile panel.

∧ TIME FOR A CHAT

Elderly neighbours gather in front of the drum tower in the square, an important place in the village where people meet and celebrate.

< NEW YEAR'S POSTER

More than a year later, this colourful poster celebrating the Year of the Cockerel still hangs on the wall of the living room as decoration.

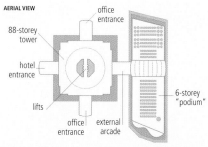

AERIAL VIEW

office entrance
88-storey tower
hotel entrance
lifts
office entrance
external arcade
6-storey "podium"

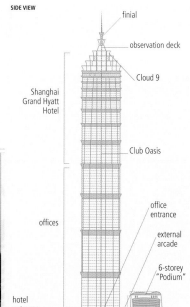

SIDE VIEW

finial
observation deck
Cloud 9
Shanghai Grand Hyatt Hotel
Club Oasis
offices
office entrance
external arcade
6-storey "Podium"
hotel entrance

∨ PAGODA-LIKE STRUCTURE
The tower is divided into 16 articulated segments, the rhythmic setback pattern of which evokes the form of a traditional wooden Chinese pagoda.

∨ SCULPTURAL FINIAL
Rising above the 88th-floor observation deck is a flower-like finial, which is brightly illuminated at night.

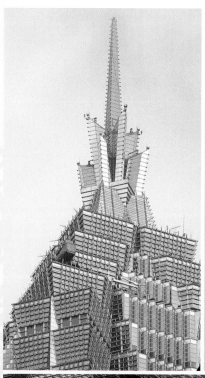

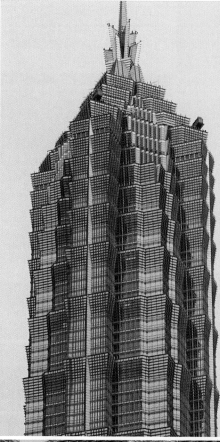

Until it is eclipsed in 2008 by the much-

金
茂
大
厦

delayed, 101-storey Shanghai World Financial Center, the 88-storey Jin Mao Tower in Shanghai's Pudong district remains China's tallest building. In less than 20 years, these two landmarks, together with the Oriental Pearl Tower and myriad other high-rise buildings, have transformed Shanghai's skyline. What was in 1990 an expanse of farmland, shabby villages, old docks, and warehouses is now a futuristic landscape of banks, hotels, shops, cinemas, gyms, office complexes, green spaces, and a modern transportation network – a monument to China's fast-growing prosperity.

Designed by a Chinese and American team led by the Chicago office of Skidmore, Owings, & Merrill, the Jin Mao Tower, with a height of 420.5m (1,380ft), was completed in 1998, just as China's mania for the super-tall was taking off. Promotional literature claims that the slim tower's design exemplifies "traditional Chinese style" and symbolizes Shanghai's entry into the 21st century. Literally "Golden Luxuriance Building", the name Jin Mao invokes prosperity by word

association, which is customary in the naming of palaces, gardens, and palatial residences in China.

Unlike sleek, modern skyscrapers, with their regular planes of metal and glass, the tiered Jin Mao Tower mimics the form of the ancient wooden Chinese pagodas that once loomed above towns across the country. With its tapered profile and octagonal concrete core, the tower climbs in a telescoping succession of 16 tiers, or segments, that terminate with a dramatic sculptural finial at the summit.

The overall design incorporates talismans relating to the number eight. In Chinese, eight (*ba*), is regarded as auspicious because of its similarity in sound to the word *fa*, meaning "to acquire wealth". As well as being 88 storeys high, the tower's height-to-width ratio is 8:1. The building was sited and given form by modern feng shui masters to harmonize a complex environment. According to feng shui, Jin Mao's architecture is designed to bring in wealth and repel misfortune. The tower also helps satisfy the hunger for the modern and the high-rise in China's most international city.

∧ STEPPED EXTERIOR
The exterior walls of the skyscraper are made from angled glass, stainless steel, and aluminium.

JIN MAO TOWER
88-STOREY HOTEL AND OFFICE BUILDING, SHANGHAI

> SHANGHAI GRAND HYATT HOTEL
This 555-room, five-star hotel occupies floors 53 to 87, and is approached via a canopied ground-level entry.

∨ EXTERNAL ARCADE
Offices occupy the floors below the hotel. They are accessed by two entrances, one of which is this arched glass arcade with a view of the tower.

< PORTAL TO THE GRAND HYATT
This key-shaped portal offers entry into the hotel's ground-floor lobby. The Grand Hyatt has the highest hotel rooms in the world.

< PROPORTIONAL SEGMENTS
The tower's measurements are linked to the auspicious number eight. It tapers in 16 stepped segments, each one of which is one-eighth shorter than the one below.

> STRUCTURAL PIPES
The glass entrance arcade shown above is supported by a simple but elegant latticework of tubular structural supports made from stainless steel.

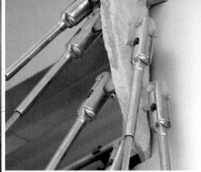

∧ EARTHQUAKE-PROOF STRUCTURE
The tower employs an advanced structural engineering system which fortifies it against typhoons and earthquakes.

∨ PODIUM ESCALATORS

Escalators hug the exterior wall in the "Podium" – a six-storey building set at the base of the Jin Mao Tower, which is used for entertainment and leisure facilities.

∧ STRUCTURE ON DISPLAY

Internally, no attempt has been made to hide the supporting structure of the Podium, and this dictates the building's inner character, which is modern, metallic, and functional.

< **INSIDE THE PODIUM**
All gleaming stainless steel and glass, the
Podium houses the Hyatt's conference and
banqueting facilities, the Jin Mao Concert
Hall, and shops, restaurants, and nightclubs.

> **TRANSLUCENT FLOORS**
Light enters through the
glass floor panels of this
suspended walkway in the
Podium's shopping mall.

∧ **SPIRALLING STAIRWAYS**
In addition to the escalators, the six
floors of the Podium are linked by
shiny spiral stairways wrapped around
vertical internal supports.

∧ **OFFICE LIFTS**
These lifts in the main entrance
lobby take workers to the tower's
offices, which occupy the 3rd to the
50th floors of the building.

∧ THE GRAND HYATT'S ATRIUM
Ascending 115m (377ft) upwards from the 54th
to the 87th floors, the Grand Hyatt's spiralling
atrium is lined with corridors and staircases. It is
one of the tallest atriums in the world.

> **THE ATRIUM FROM ABOVE**
Looking down from a higher floor, the 27m (89ft) diameter cylindrical atrium – lined with 28 spiral corridors and staircases – is breathtaking in its sheer scale.

∨ **PATIO LOUNGE**
Located at the base of the 33-storey atrium is the patio lounge, with its grand piano and elegant ambience.

∧ **GRAND HYATT LOBBY**
With its warm Art Deco styling, the hotel's upper lobby is wrapped around the building's central core, providing a panoramic view of the city.

< ∨ LIFT LOBBY

The floor and ceiling designs at each bank of lifts use a contrasting pattern of tiles – the black and white elements are reversed on either side of the hallway.

< INVITING LIFT

A feeling of opulence infuses every detail of the hotel's decor, including the lifts, which are sheathed in accents of shimmering gold.

∨ CLOUD 9

One of the hotel's many bars, Cloud 9 is located on the 87th floor. From here, the highest point of the Grand Hyatt, there is a 360-degree view of the city.

∧ GRAND ROOM

Each of the spacious rooms has a magnificent view of the Shanghai skyline through floor-to-ceiling windows.

> SKY POOL

The 57th-floor swimming pool, or "sky pool", the world's highest swimming pool, is part of the Club Oasis gym and spa.

∨ **XIAOXIN BRIDGE LANE**

The Garden is surrounded on three sides by canals, and entry into the gardens is through an unassuming gate on a quiet canalside lane.

> **COVERED ACCESS**

This narrow corridor alongside the Hall for Drink Setting Out provides sheltered space as well as access to the Eastern Garden.

AERIAL VIEW Old House for Curtain Weaving | Hall for Drink Setting Out | Huang-shi Rockery | bridge | pond

He-shou Pavilion

CANAL

gateway

entrance | footpath

Hall for Sedan Chairs **CANAL** | Pavilion to My Love Hall for Group Virtuous

> **LATTICE PANEL DOORS**

Large hardwood lattice doors open onto narrow courtyards. Panels are hinged so that they open easily and wide, connecting interior and exterior spaces when required.

∨ **COURTYARD AREA**

A part of the built-up portion of the Western Garden, this section includes a courtyard and a well. It is separated from other spaces by buildings and whitewashed walls.

However large or small, whether formal 藕 园 or informal, Chinese gardens are scripted landscapes that reflect simplicity and elegance, as well as an aesthetic shared with poetry and painting. Among the most renowned are the privately-owned gardens of Suzhou, Hangzhou, and Yangzhou in the fertile Jiangnan region of the lower Yangzi River. Such gardens are usually walled and self-contained, with elements of both purposeful symmetry and seeming disorder. Each one bears a name, just as a painting has a title, and each part of the garden has an epithet drawn from textual allusions.

While space is laid out according to a set of conventions, the individual site and the owner's tastes encourage idiosyncratic elements to emerge. The garden must look "natural" even though it is essentially artifice in which water and rocks are manipulated to create "scenes". Rocks are sometimes placed individually, but more often piled up as rockeries. Halls, corridors, and pavilions are strategically located for maximum effect. Latticed windows made of wood and brick, as well as moon gates and other geometric openings, lure visitors from enclosed to open spaces and back

again. Literary inscriptions are integral components: scenes and poetry are employed to complement each other.

The Ou or "Couple's" Garden on Xiaoxin Bridge Lane in Suzhou embodies all the elements of the classic garden retreat. First designed in the late 17th century, Couple's Garden acquired its current form during the 19th century. Here, behind high walls, a house separates the garden into two distinct parts. The Western Garden is itself subdivided by the Old House for Curtain Weaving into two courtyards. Inside the entrance to the Eastern Garden is a small courtyard that leads to an open space bounded by a white wall with several open-cut ornamental windows and a moon gate that entices one to move on. Covered walkways wind their way through the garden, protecting visitors from the elements and leading them to hidden spaces and buildings within the complex. Beyond the garden and accessible via a doorway is one of Suzhou's many canals.

Here, in relative miniature, is a sanctuary and a scholar's oasis where visitors can both indulge their senses and pursue artistic enrichment.

COUPLE'S GARDEN RETREAT
QING DYNASTY PRIVATE GARDEN, JIANGSU

> HE-SHOU PAVILION
Light pours into this pavilion through the open lattice doorways and illuminates calligraphy hung on the walls and porcelain pieces set on long tables.

∧ ORNAMENTED DOORWAY
Imposing doorways, each with an evocatively poetic name, lead from courtyard to courtyard, luring visitors onwards to the next area.

< COVERED CORRIDOR
This narrow covered corridor with wooden lattice balustrade on one side and lattice doorways on the other, provides a sheltered route to the Western Garden.

∧ HALL FOR SEDAN CHAIRS
With calligraphy and paintings on the walls and heavy furniture in set patterns around the room, this hall serves as a formal room to welcome guests.

⌄ COURTYARD
Immediately outside the Hall for Sedan Chairs is a small courtyard paved with pebbles arranged into patterns, small trees and shrubs, and large rock formations.

⟨ ZIGZAG BRIDGE
Angled sections of short stone plank lengthen the passage across the water while changing the field of vision of the person crossing it.

⟩ BOULDERED PASSAGEWAY
Large boulders inscribed with the characters "Deep Ravine" create a sense of constraint that contrasts with the open spaces beyond.

⋀ LATTICED MOON GATE
This circular opening, framed with a wooden lattice pattern, provides an inviting entry into a small study, which is furnished with a desk and an ornamented wooden bench with a marble inlay.

⋀ RECLINING BENCH
Often used to overhang water, reclining wooden back supports, like this one, provide comfortable sitting areas along the narrow corridor walls around the garden.

∨ **WINDING CORRIDOR**
The winding, covered corridor runs next to an open, pebbled walkway, allowing visitors to choose the most appropriate route around the garden according to the weather.

∨ **FRAMED TRACERY WINDOWS**
Geometric patterns and designs rooted in nature perforate this wall, linking nearby spaces and providing contrast between solids and voids, and darkness and brightness as the light changes.

∧ **MOON GATE**
A circular gate leading into another area of the garden frames the natural composition of the rocks and vegetation.

> **STONE SPIRES**
Needle-shaped stone spires, resembling young bamboo shoots, complement clumps of gently swaying bamboo.

< **LATTICE WINDOWS**
The cracked-ice pattern on the wooden lattice window panels maintains harmony with the natural setting behind them.

∧ **BALANCED COMPOSITION**
The zigzag bridge links together elements of the garden – water, land, buildings, vegetation, and rocks – into a single composition.

> **RISING LIKE A CENTIPEDE**
Soaring above the river beneath, the Beijian
Bridge resembles a crawling centipede, and
locals call it the "centipede bridge".

∨ **TIMBER ARCH-BEAM**
Viewed from beneath, the interlinking
timbers that create a unique arch-beam
substructure are visible. The bridge is in
fact level with gentle steps at either end.

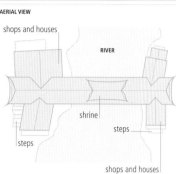
AERIAL VIEW
shops and houses
RIVER
shrine
steps
steps
shops and houses

Beijian Bridge is a fine example of a
北润桥 covered "rainbow bridge", a type of
bridge previously known only from a
12th-century silk scroll painting. Until
recently it was thought that true rainbow
bridges had disappeared some 900
years ago. However, in the last decade,
around 100 of these bridges have been
documented throughout China. The
majority are found in the mountains of
southern Zhejiang and northern Fujian
provinces, where they cross steep
chasms, rearing up dramatically over
the waters. Bridges of this type are
truly unique and have not been built
anywhere else in the world. Their
rediscovery makes clear the originality
and resourcefulness of Chinese
carpentry and engineering.

Beijian Bridge crosses a river in
Taishun county, Zhejiang Province. Just
over 50m (164ft) long and 5m (16ft)
wide, the bridge was first built in 1674.
Reconstructed in 1987, it survived
serious floods in 2005 when rushing
torrents inflicted substantial damage
but failed to destroy it.

Due to the presence of "skirts"
that disguise the underlying structure,
the Beijian Bridge appears from a

distance to be arched. In fact, it is an
illusionary shape that emerges from sets
of interwoven logs, ingeniously formed
to create a soaring rainbow shape. The
"arch" is formed from inclined timbers
set into abutments at either end of the
bridge. The gap is bridged by horizontal
timbers that slot into these inclines and
are also tied with rattan ropes. Buildings
above create a covered bridge and act
as additional pressure to compress all
the components together into a tight
and stable structure. Timber columns,
beams, and roof tiles add a substantial
weight that enhances the bridge's ability
to withstand flash floods and typhoons.

The internal timber framework of
the long covered gallery is composed
of pillars and beams cleverly mortised
together without the use of nails.
Projecting beams create overhanging
eaves that protect the timbers beneath.

Wooden structures at both ends
of the bridge serve as shops on the
ground floor and homes above. At the
bridge's centre is an elaborate alcove
containing images of local deities. As
well as a river crossing, the bridge serves
as a meeting place for the community
where local people gather to chat.

∧ **COMMEMORATIVE BOARD**
These four Chinese characters proclaim
"Old Architectural Cultural Heritage". The
Beijian Bridge is more than 300 years old.

> **COVERED GALLERY**
With its 88 wooden columns and a countless
number of carved wooden beams, the
gallery of the bridge has a timber frame
construction similar to that found in
traditional Chinese houses and temples.

> **ORNAMENTAL COLUMN BASE**
This stone column base is carved with a
lingzhi, the "fungus of immortality", an
auspicious wish-granting motif.

BEIJIAN BRIDGE
COVERED RAINBOW BRIDGE, ZHEJIANG

> PHOENIX
Usually paired with the dragon, this auspicious creature symbolizes the South and the sun.

< SINUOUS DRAGON
One of four divine animals, the dragon is associated with the East and is said to ensure rain. It also symbolizes fertility.

> BRIDGE CORRIDOR
Although today they are nearly empty, the three recessed niches once held images of gods and goddesses, which would have been used in rituals.

∧ STATUE OF A DEITY
The porcelain image of a deity and offerings of flowers merely suggest what ritualistic objects might once have been housed in this shrine.

< TEMPLE-LIKE PORTAL
With its soaring roofline, the western approach to the bridge gives the appearance of entering a temple.

< COMMEMORATIVE STELAE
Looking out of the western entrance, commemorative stone stelae are visible. These record the bridge's original construction and later rebuilding.

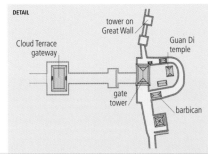

DETAIL

tower on Great Wall

Cloud Terrace gateway

Guan Di temple

gate tower

barbican

AERIAL VIEW

modern road

tower on Great Wall

reconstructed fortified structure

old road

Cloud Terrace gateway

side road

reconstructed loop of Great Wall

towers on Great Wall

< RECONSTRUCTED FORTIFICATIONS
The restored complex includes multiple gates surmounted by towers, and a U-shaped structure called a barbican.

∨ CLOUD TERRACE
The white marble archway originally had three pagoda-like structures on top, but these collapsed during an earthquake in the 15th century.

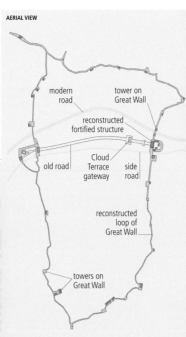

China's greatest construction feat is the 2,500-km- (1,550-mile-) long wall that was built to stretch from end to end of its northern border. The earliest existing piece is believed to date from the 7th century BCE. Over the next few centuries, warring states constructed their own defensive barriers, often joining together disparate parts of walls left over from earlier times. When the First Emperor, Qin Shihuang, unified China in 221 BCE, he ordered that the walls of states he had conquered along the country's northern border should be linked and strengthened, with the aim of creating a continuous barrier along the northern frontier. However, more than 1,500 years were to pass before China would again engage in serious efforts to build the Great Wall.

The goal of construction during the Ming dynasty (1368–1644) was a northern wall approximately 6,300km (3,900 miles) long. The wall was divided into nine regions, each with its own fortresses, watchtowers, and strategic passes. Today, about a dozen of the passes are well-preserved. The most famous are: Shanhaiguan, at the wall's eastern end; Jiayuguan, in western

China; and Juyongguan, about 60km (35 miles) north of Beijing. The white marble archway at Juyongguan, known as the Cloud Terrace (Yuntai), came into being just before the Ming dynasty, near the end of the period of Mongol rule.

In principle, the Mongols were opposed to a barrier between their homeland in the north and China. In 1213, Genghis Khan's troops had been unable to penetrate Juyongguan, which is located in an 18 km- (11-mile) valley, and they were forced to regroup and attack from a different direction. However, between 1343 and 1345, in the reign of the last Mongol emperor, a Tibetan-style pagoda (now destroyed) was erected there. The 9.5-m- (31-ft-) high Cloud Terrace archway was built at the same time, and three towers stood on it until the early 15th century. On the underside of the archway are relief sculptures of Tantric Buddhist deities, passages from Buddhist *sutras*, and an inscription in the six most common languages of the Mongolian Empire. One of these is Tangut, the language of the Xi Xia kingdom, which ruled North Asia from 1028 until the Mongol conquest.

∧ CROSSED THUNDERBOLTS
This carving on the archway's outside wall symbolizes the Five Esoteric Buddhas, important figures in Tantric Buddhism.

> GUARDIAN DEITY
Stone carvings within the arched gateway represent the Celestial Kings of the Four Directions, one of which is depicted here.

JUYONGGUAN
YUAN DYNASTY PASS, GREAT WALL, BEIJING

< CARVED FRIEZE OVER ARCH
Above the Cloud Terrace arch is a carving of the king of the birds surrounded by figures and beasts.

∨ TANTRIC CARVINGS
Along the walls of the passageway through the archway are bas-relief sculptures depicting a range of Tantric Buddhist deities.

∨ BARBICAN TEMPLE
Set within the barbican – the projecting U-shaped structure that forms part of the Juyongguan complex – is a small temple to Guan Di, the God of War.

∧ MULTILINGUAL INCANTATIONS
The Cloud Terrace archway bears finely carved Buddhist writings in six common scripts of the Mongol Empire: Chinese, Tibetan, Sanskrit, Mongolian, Uighur, and Tangut.

∧ GATE TOWER
The reconstructed, multitiered gate tower is known as "The First Great Pass Under Heaven" and is protected by gray walls studded with small portals.

< ARCHED PASSAGEWAY
With beautiful glazed tiles on the roof and below to match those on the gate tower, this small arched passageway leads down into the barbican.

⟨ ARCHED PASSAGEWAY

Arched stairways and passages throughout the Juyongguan complex allow access from one level to another, as well as from one room to another inside buildings.

⋁ BRICK AND WOOD

Rising above the brick battlements of the Juyongguan gate towers, wooden structures such as this one provided accommodation for on-duty troops.

⋁ INTERIOR OF SIGNAL TOWER

Troops were billeted in the signal towers, where the thick, fired-brick walls offered the soldiers excellent protection against both attackers and the elements.

∧ LOOPED PORTALS

All along the wall, small looped portals opened outwards, giving soldiers a safe viewing point to scan the surrounding countryside.

∧ SMALL STOREROOM

Juyongguan provided barracks for troops and needed storage for supplies. Storerooms such as this, used for keeping weapons and food, are found throughout the complex.

∧ BATTLEMENT WALKWAY

The walkway along the wall's battlements runs through the signal towers, which are often approached by steep steps.

⟩ TOWERS FOR SIGNALLING

Usually built near the top of a ridge for visibility, the signal towers could be used to send smoke signals along the wall.

> **THE GREAT WALL**
Tapering from about 7.5m (25ft) at the base to about 4.5m (15ft) at the top, the wall is made of earth, stone, and brick.

∨ **CLIMBING WALL**
The Great Wall snakes upwards and then away from the signal tower in the narrow valley at the strategically important pass of Juyongguan.

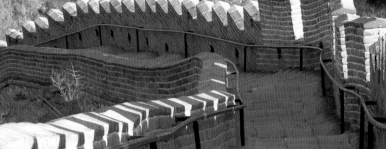

< **FOLLOWING THE RUGGED TERRAIN**
Rising and falling with the uneven and rocky terrain, the Great Wall secured the mountainside against intruders.

∧ **SAFETY RAILS**
Today, iron railings assist visitors climbing the steeper portions of the sinuous wall as it ascends the mountain slopes.

> SERPENT GUARDIANS
Nagas are believed to protect stairs, doors, and other temple features. This one guards the way to a huge golden statue of the Buddha.

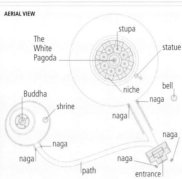

AERIAL VIEW

The White Pagoda — stupa — statue
Buddha — niche — bell — naga
shrine — naga
naga
naga
naga — naga
path — entrance

> WALL PAINTING
Stencilled on the vermilion wall near the monastery entrance (far left) are depictions of the Buddha and Buddhist structures.

∨ NAGA FIGURE
A naga is a representation of the mystical serpent king who is said to have sheltered the Buddha while he was meditating.

Jinghong County, in the Xishuang Banna 曼飞龙塔 autonomous region in the south of Yunnan Province, is located on the banks of the Mekong River near China's border with Myanmar. This tropical region is home to the monasteries of the Dai, a Sino-Burmese ethnic group who practice Theravada Buddhism.

Dai monasteries are built in the centre of villages or on high ground outside them. The centrepiece of every Dai monastery is a Buddha hall, and almost all have a pagoda. Gates, *sutra* libraries (which hold scriptures said to record Buddha's teachings), and monks' residences are also typical structures.

The monastery that stands on elevated ground just to the south of Manfeilong Village is named after its central feature – the White Pagoda. In reality, the White Pagoda is not a single structure but a cluster of nine white-painted pagodas, or stupas, set on a roughly circular platform raised 3m (12ft) above ground level. The whole ensemble forms a fusion of Southeast Asian Buddhist style with typical Dai architecture. The nine stupas each have a solid, gourd-shaped structure that rises into a spire ringed with decorative

masonry. The largest stupa – the three-story structure in the centre of the cluster – rises to a height of 16.29m (53½ft). The eight smaller, single-story stupas are arranged in an octagon around this central tower. Each of the smaller stupas is 9m (28ft) high, with a portico-like niche at the base that contains a statue of the Buddha. The niches are painted red, yellow, and green, and decorated with wooden carvings. At the summit of all nine pagodas is a bronze spire from which bells are suspended. There is an image of Shakyamuni, the only Buddha worshipped by the Dai, below the main platform. An imprint in the rock nearby is said to be Shakyamuni's footprint. Locals have nicknamed the Manfeilong stupa complex the "Bamboo Shoot Pagoda", because from afar it is said to resemble a clump of sprouting bamboo.

The White Pagoda was first built in 1203, allegedly to a design by Indian monks under the sponsorship of a local tribal chieftain. The current structure is believed to date from the 19th century. Nearby in Damenglong is the White Pagoda's sister structure, the 18-m- (59-ft-) high Black Pagoda, built in 1204.

THE WHITE PAGODA
DAI BUDDHIST MONASTERY, MANFEILONG, YUNNAN

< NAGA DETAIL
Some nagas resemble dragons more than snakes. They often flank temple stairways, run along roofs, or coil around outer walls.

> GOLDEN BELL
The sound of bells is central to Buddhist practices. This large bell is struck by the piece of wood that lies on top of it.

< SHRINE DETAIL
From the top of the carved shrine, decorative finger-like projections rise skywards, some carved to resemble foliage, others into serpentine shapes.

∧ STANDING BUDDHA AND SHRINE
Beyond the carved stone shrine in the foreground, the Buddha raises his hand in a gesture of reassurance and blessing to visitors. The "parasol" over his head indicates the supremacy of Buddhism.

∧ PAGODA CLUSTER
Viewed from the pathway leading from the monastery entrance, the cluster of stupas that form the White Pagoda is an impressive sight.

∧ THE WHITE PAGODA
Overlooked by a naga head, the eight smaller
stupas encircle a taller spire. With various niches
holding Buddha images along the shared base,
this is the principal holy structure at Manfeilong.

< WHITE PAGODA SPIRES
The spires all employ the same geometrical and symbolic shapes, such as the lotus flower (far left).

> SPIRE ADORNMENTS
At the top of each spire are a weather vane, bells, and a "sky flute", which whistles in the wind.

< ∧ DETAIL OF NICHE FRIEZE
Carved mythical figures, both in low relief and fully sculpted, decorate the painted wooden bargeboards on the front of the niches' pitched roofs.

< BUDDHA IN A NICHE
Set within an ornate carved niche at the base of each of the smaller stupas is a Buddha figure painted in gold. Here, the faithful have left flowers as an offering.

∧ PAINTED STATUE
Standing guard over a model structure that mimics the shape of the niches at the foot of the smaller stupas is this brightly painted statue of a woman.

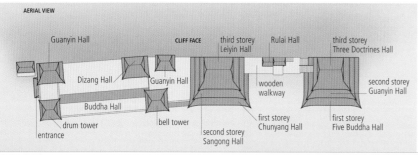

AERIAL VIEW

Guanyin Hall
Dizang Hall
Buddha Hall
drum tower
entrance
Guanyin Hall
bell tower
CLIFF FACE
third storey
Leiyin Hall
second storey
Sangong Hall
Rulai Hall
wooden
walkway
first storey
Chunyang Hall
third storey
Three Doctrines Hall
second storey
Guanyin Hall
first storey
Five Buddha Hall

∨ TIERED ROOFTOPS
Golden hip-gabled roofs top the uppermost two storeys of the temple's halls, which seem literally to "hang" from the mountainside.

> BUILT INTO THE ROCK FACE
External wooden facades and roofs protect the rooms that have been carved into the sheer cliff face. The halls are linked by narrow walkways of planks.

Xuankong Si, literally Suspended in the
悬
空
寺
Air Monastery, is a universally recognized marvel of Chinese architecture. It is located halfway up a dangerous precipice of Mount Heng, close to the city of Datong in northern Shanxi Province. First built in the early decades of the 6th century, today there are more than 40 structures, all connected by walkways, or corridors, spread north to south across the face of the cliff. Its many halls of worship are hewn from natural hollows and caves in the cliff and covered with ornate wooden facades. Supported by horizontal beams and vertical posts, the monastery appears to cling precariously to the side of the cliff.

The two dominant buildings have three storeys with hip-gabled roofs. Entry into a rock-carved place of worship is possible on each storey. By necessity, every structure is as narrow as physically possible in depth. Even so, more than 80 bronze, iron, clay, and stone images of various deities are found within them. The many images reflect the fact that worship at Xuankong Si was syncretic, a place where aspects of China's three main faiths, Buddhism, Daoism, and Confucianism, merged.

Traversing the wooden walkways, the stability of Xuankong Si is perhaps as impressive as the view down into the deep ravine below. The monastery has survived its fair share of wind and rainstorms, and the cliff has even suffered earthquakes, yet the buildings have never collapsed. The Northern Wei (386–535) were the first to build here, but the buildings have, of course, been repaired through the ages, specifically in the Jin (1115–1234), Yuan (1279–1368), and Ming (1368–1644) dynasties.

An undated stele at the site relates that upon seeing the mountain, many of the builders held back, but one of them, a craftsman called Zhang, was determined to succeed. Taking charge, he organized the transportation of lumber for the buildings to the foot of the mountain, where it was cut and sized. Then, the workers lifted the components, each individual tool, and themselves up to the site on ropes, winding their way through the natural features of the cliff. This description only begins to capture the challenges that would have been faced, in any time period, to construct something so remote, and spectacularly sited.

∧ SUPPORTING PILLARS
Slender wooden pillars of varying lengths are sunk into the cliff face to prop up the walkways and halls.

XUANKONG SI
SUSPENDED IN THE AIR MONASTERY

∨ GLAZED CHIWEN
The seams along the main roof ridges are capped with protective *chiwen*, mythological dragons that are said to conjure up rain should a fire break out.

> ORNAMENTED EAVES
The halls' double-tiered projecting eaves, also known as "flying eaves", are highly characteristic of traditional Chinese storeyed buildings (*lou*).

∧ DRUM TOWER AND WALKWAY
Narrow wooden walkways hug the cliff face, here connecting the two-storey drum tower (left) and the Buddha Hall (right).

> SUPPORTING BRACKETS
Where a pillar meets a roof beam, sets of interlocking, carved wooden brackets provide additional support.

∧ PROTECTIVE ROOF TILES
Glazed blue and gold tiles, decorated with the face of a protective lion and a phoenix, fringe the end of the roof surface.

∨ **PAINTED ROOF DETAIL**
No part of the monastery is left untouched by decoration and every surface is beautifully painted, including the roof beams, door frames, pillars, and supporting brackets.

> **DECORATIVE EAVES TILES**
Set above a painted beam, moulded clay *wadang* – round and triangular roof-tile caps – serve as drip tiles to channel water from the roof.

< **WOODEN WALKWAY**
Running along the outside of a hall, this cliff-side walkway also serves as an entrance into another hall.

∧ **INTERIOR ROOF STRUCTURE**
Stacked wooden beams support the roof of a hall. They recede as they rise, giving shape to the pointed roof.

∧ **ALTAR CENTERPIECE**
Within Three Doctrines Hall, a golden Buddha and a pair of monks are framed by an intricately carved wooden frame.

< STATUE OF A SAGE
Within Leiyin Hall, on the third storey of the monastery complex, a large, carved, and painted wooden sage is the focal point of the altar.

> NICHE OF DEITIES
Chunyang Hall, on the first storey below Sangong Hall, contains within it a collection of wood-framed niches housing groups of small deities.

∧ ZOOMORPHIC FIGURE
The face of a demon-like figure with animal features sits atop a pillar in Three Doctrines Hall.

< BUDDHA STATUES
These images of Buddha are set within concave niches, carved into the cliff face along the temple walls.

> **ROOF ORNAMENTATION**
The seams of the temple's sloping roofs are topped with polychrome ceramic shapes and plaster mouldings of traditional patterns and figurines.

AERIAL VIEW

main altar

side room

side room

altar

entry portico

steps

∨ **ROOF-TOP MOTIF**
Richly coloured ceramic figurines depicting the story of Tin Hau are towered over by a radiant sunlike pearl, set with mosaic tiles.

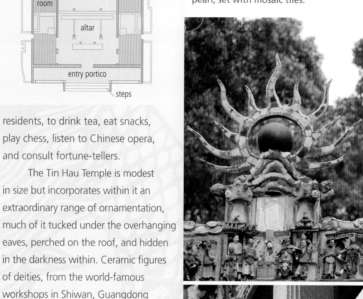

Tin Hau (Heavenly Empress) is among the most important deities found in southeastern China. In Hong Kong alone, some 60 temples are dedicated to Tin Hau, who is also widely known as the compassionate motherly figure, Goddess Mazu. As the patroness and protector of fishermen, Tin Hau has traditionally been worshipped in temples situated along China's coastlines, with boats clustered at the door.

However, this Tin Hau Temple is found in one of Hong Kong's most densely populated urban areas, in Causeway Bay on the northern shore of Hong Kong island. In fact, when the temple was built in the early 18th century by a wealthy local family, the land on which it sits was along the harbour. Over time, reclamation efforts gradually created large swaths of much-needed land by filling in the coastline. As a result, this waterfront temple was swallowed up within an urban landscape of skyscrapers.

The public square in front of the temple is a communal meeting point in Causeway Bay, a pulsating node of social life. During the day, it is a popular place for locals, particularly retired

residents, to drink tea, eat snacks, play chess, listen to Chinese opera, and consult fortune-tellers.

The Tin Hau Temple is modest in size but incorporates within it an extraordinary range of ornamentation, much of it tucked under the overhanging eaves, perched on the roof, and hidden in the darkness within. Ceramic figures of deities, from the world-famous workshops in Shiwan, Guangdong Province – where it is said that 60 per cent of the world's pottery products are made – are outstanding features. Entering across a courtyard, a visitor catches a darkened glimpse of the red-cloaked statue of Tin Hau inside, and the eye is drawn to brightly coloured narrative tales painted on the eaves.

While many surfaces of the temple are made of wood, pillars, protruding beams, and doorways are all made from cut stone. Almost all visible structural parts are carved or painted. Auspicious images and motifs echo those found in other Chinese buildings, with most there to serve as invocations of the "five good fortunes": longevity, wealth, health, love of virtue, and to die a natural death in old age.

∧ **SUPPORTING BRACKETS**
Where a stone pillar intersects with a stone beam, carved brackets are placed to provide additional stability.

TIN HAU TEMPLE
SHRINE TO THE HEAVENLY EMPRESS, HONG KONG

∧ **BAT MOTIF**
The Chinese word for bat (*fu*) sounds the same as the word for luck, and bats are therefore widely used as emblems of good fortune, like on this stone carving.

< EAVES TILES
Alternating circular- and triangular-end decorative tiles lead water from the roof to the ground below.

> ENTRANCE DECORATION
Several small carved lions sit above the entrance. Behind them are painted scenes, many featuring fishermen, whom Tin Hau protects.

∨ MINIATURE FIGURES
Tiny carved and painted figures depicting the legend of the goddess Tin Hau are tucked under the overhanging eaves.

∧ LUCKY LANTERN
Paper lanterns, like this one, with bamboo frames, adorn many temples in Hong Kong.

∧ ENTRY PORTICO
Quiet and still in the early morning, the courtyard outside the portico becomes a bustling area for worship later on.

> VOTIVE NICHE
Several small altar-like niches, with small incense holders, are set around the temple for individual worship.

< INCENSE HOLDER
The carved motifs on the handles and legs of this iron incense holder serve protective purposes, and the colours red and gold are said to be auspicious.

∧ CARVED LIONS
This is one of several lions, each carved in stone, that are situated around the temple. They serve a protective purpose.

∨ DOOR GUARDIANS

A central focus of the entrance to the temple are two brightly painted door guardians, dressed in martial regalia.

∨ SHRINE TO TIN HAU

A vast collection of porcelain images of the Heavenly Empress is set in front of red embroidered panels in the main chamber of the temple.

∨ THE MAIN CHAMBER

Bathed with the aura of auspicious red hues, the main chamber houses offering tables, tiered cases of votive candles, incense coils, brass vessels, and symbolic embroidery.

∧ FORTUNE STICKS

Bamboo cups containing numbered bamboo sticks are found within the temple. Each stick, selected by shaking the cup, corresponds to a fortune.

＜ PROTECTOR

Looking stern and alert, this carved, wooden demon-like figure is one of numerous "protectors" whose purpose is to keep safe the deities in the temple.

< FIGURE OF TIN HAU
At the head of the shrine in pride of place is the illuminated and bedecked Heavenly Empress.

< INCENSE COILS
These large coils of incense burn very slowly over days, and are said to represent the burning away of material attachments.

∨ HANGING LANTERN
With auspicious coins suspended from the mouth of a dragon and delicate women painted on gauze, this lantern is symbolic as well as a source of light.

< BRONZE INCENSE HOLDER
Bundles of aromatic incense sticks are placed in this decorative brass vessel. Lit as an offering to Tin Hau, ash collects in the pot beneath.

> GUAN YU
Traditionally shown as a red-faced warrior, Guan Yu is a figure from the Han dynasty worshipped by both Buddhists and Daoists.

AERIAL VIEW

Hall of Prayer for
a Prosperous Year

corridor

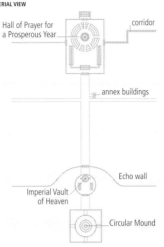

annex buildings

Echo wall

Imperial Vault
of Heaven

Circular Mound

The Temple of Heaven is a complex of

天坛

buildings enclosed by a horseshoe-shaped wall nearly 6.5km (4 miles) long. Here, the emperor performed the two most sacred ceremonies of imperial China, one at the winter solstice and the second during the first moon of the year. The three main ceremonial "halls" incorporate the two ideal Chinese shapes: the circle, representing Heaven, and the square, symbolizing Earth.

Since the first millennium BCE, ritual texts had prescribed that the worship of Heaven should take place south of the Chinese capital. When first built under the Ming emperor Yongle (r.1403–24), the Temple of Heaven was to the south of Beijing's city wall. However, after the addition of the outer city in 1553, the Temple of Heaven lay north of the new perimeter wall.

Unusually, the emperor entered the complex from the west, rather than from the south, which was the norm with most planned imperial space. In this western section of the Temple of Heaven, ritual instruments were stored and animals were sacrificed. Here, too, the emperor fasted and abstained from activities that might distract him from

his task: for several days prior to the rituals he had vegetarian meals and no female companionship or recreation. At the winter solstice he went to the first of three halls, the Circular Mound, where he reported to Heaven on the events of the year. For the second ceremony, during the first moon, the emperor entered the third hall, the Hall of Prayer for a Prosperous Year, where he made obeisance to Heaven.

The Circular Mound consists of three round, white marble terraces. The rings of flagstones that comprise them are arranged in multiples of nine – a symbol of the Chinese emperor. When the emperor knelt on the centre stone and spoke, even softly, his voice echoed and was amplified. Acoustic effects were also built into the second hall, the Imperial Vault of Heaven. A whisper anywhere into the outer wall (the Echo Wall) of the Imperial Vault can be heard at a point 180 degrees opposite it. The third hall is the Hall of Prayer for a Prosperous Year. Of its 28 internal pillars, the four largest symbolize the seasons; the other 24 represent the 12 moons of the Chinese lunar calendar and the 12 hours of the Chinese day.

∧ CIRCULAR MOUND
This ceremonial "hall" has three round, balustraded terraces of white marble, which are accessed by four stairways.

> BALUSTRADE PILLARS
Sweeping in a controlled arc, the pillars along the three balustrades are found in multiples of nine: 72, 108, and 180.

∨ DRAGON-HEAD WATER DRAIN
The carved dragon heads that protrude from the marble terraces drain water away from the structure.

> PILLAR CAPS
Each of the elevated portions of the marble pillars around the Circular Mound is ornamented with intricately carved, writhing dragon motifs.

TEMPLE OF HEAVEN

MING DYNASTY TEMPLE COMPLEX, BEIJING

∨ VIEW NORTH FROM UPPER TERRACE
The four marble staircases of the Circular Mound are oriented to the points of the compass. This is the view north, toward the Imperial Vault of Heaven.

< GILT-EDGED SIGNBOARD
The Vault of Heaven's three-character name, Huang Qiong Yu, is emblazoned on the signboard above the entrance.

> IMPERIAL VAULT OF HEAVEN
Set on a single marble terrace with circular lattice-panel walls, the Vault of Heaven is covered by a conical roof of blue tiles capped by a golden knob.

∧ PAINTED CEILING OF ANNEXE BUILDING
Ritual paraphernalia and tablets representing various gods were stored in ornate annexe buildings near the Hall of Prayer.

∧ FLAGSTONES OF UPPER TERRACE
Around the centre stone of the upper terrace are rings of flagstones, starting with nine stones, followed by 18, and then outward in multiples of nine to 81.

> INTERIOR OF VAULT OF HEAVEN
The richly decorated roof of the Imperial Vault of Heaven is supported by eight large columns. Tablets used in imperial ceremonies line the walls.

∨ HALL FOR PRAYER

The three-tiered Hall of Prayer for a Prosperous Year sits at the centre of three concentric terraces.

< HALL OF PRAYER SIGNBOARD

Every key Chinese building has a sign displaying its three-character name. This reads "Qi Nian Dian".

> STONE POST ON BALUSTRADE

A circular balustrade with carved features surrounds both the Hall of Prayer for a Prosperous Year and the Imperial Vault of Heaven.

∧ LATTICE WINDOWS

Perforated lattice windows, set between a blue-brick base and painted beams above, allow light and air into the Hall of Prayer.

> CARVED MARBLE RAMP

The emperor was carried up this marble ramp, past clouds and dragons symbolizing the route to Heaven, to enter the Hall of Prayer.

∨ HALL OF PRAYER CEILING
The multicoloured painted ceiling of the Hall of Prayer is supported by 18-m- (60-ft-) high lacquered columns.

> LACQUERED COLUMNS
Wooden columns are covered with multiple layers of lacquer, polished and carved into brilliant red and gold patterns.

∧ POLYCHROME TIERS ABOVE HALL
The three-tiered round roof of the Hall of Prayer for a Prosperous Year is vividly painted in primary colours. It is the only triple-eaved circular structure in China.

< ∧ ALTAR IN HALL OF PRAYER
Inside the Hall of Prayer there are serene altars. One holds tablets representing former emperors, another the paraphernalia for offering obeisance to Heaven itself.

AERIAL VIEW

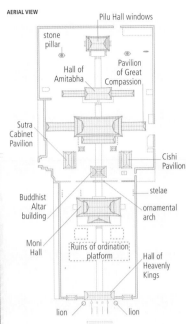

Pilu Hall windows
stone pillar
Hall of Amitabha
Pavilion of Great Compassion
Sutra Cabinet Pavilion
Cishi Pavilion
stelae
Buddhist Altar building
ornamental arch
Moni Hall
Ruins of ordination platform
Hall of Heavenly Kings
lion   lion

> **GLAZED TILE WALL ORNAMENTATION**
Composed of five glazed green tiles, this floral pattern is emblazoned on a wall beside the Hall of Heavenly Kings (far left).

∨ **ORNAMENTED ARCHWAYS**
The facade of the Hall of Heavenly Kings, which marks the entry into the monastery precinct, is adorned with carved stone arches and doorways.

Longxing Monastery in Zhengding,

隆
兴
寺

Hebei Province, is the main surviving Buddhist monastery from the Song dynasty (960–1279). The monastery was founded in 586, and four exquisite Song buildings, built in the 10th and 11th centuries, still stand today.

The entry to Longxing Monastery, right on the street in Zhengding, is a marble gate that probably looks much the same as it did a millennium ago. Some 5m (16ft) behind it was a hall for the Sixth Patriarch of the Buddhist faith, now destroyed. Nearby is Moni Hall, the only cross-shaped building known from early China. It was constructed as a six-by-six-pillar frame with a portico projecting from the middle of each side.

In the Song dynasty, an ordination platform lay behind Moni Hall. To either side beyond the platform's ruins are a pair of pavilions: the Cishi Pavilion is dedicated to the Bodhisattva Maitreya; the second pavilion houses a unique rotating cabinet of sutras (scriptures that hold the teachings of Buddha). Although the two are identical on the exterior, the Pavilion of the Revolving Sutra Cabinet has a more complex timber frame than the Cishi Pavilion. The cabinet itself is a

masterpiece of woodworking. The pavilion's roof is supported by a form of bracketing that was reserved for elite Chinese buildings, like those of the Song imperial palaces. That scripture would be housed in such an eminent structure attests to the importance of the written word in Buddhism.

The final Song building is the Pavilion of Great Compassion. This massive building was constructed in 971 by order of the first Song emperor, Taizu (r.960–75). The lecture hall that once stood behind it has since been pulled down. The pavilion's grandeur befits both imperial patronage and the monumental bronze image, originally 24m (79ft) tall, of the Bodhisattva of Mercy, Guanyin, around which the building was erected.

The sculpture and other interior decoration of all the Song buildings at the monastery has been added to or restored through the centuries. The superb relief sculpture of the sacred Buddhist mountain Sumeru and its deities was added to the interior walls of Moni Hall during the Ming dynasty. Every part of the monastery has been extensively repaired in the last decade.

∧ **LION SENTRIES**
This male lion, with one foot resting on an ornamental ball, guards the entry to the monastery with a nearby female lion.

> **MONI HALL**
Often judged to be the most elegant structure of the Song era, Moni Hall is dedicated to the Buddha Sakyamuni.

LONGXING SI 寺
SONG DYNASTY BUDDHIST MONASTERY, HEBEI

< HALL OF THE HEAVENLY KINGS
These three characters declare the Tian Wang Dian (Hall of the Heavenly Kings) – the first building encountered in the monastery.

ᵛ > CELESTIAL GUARDIANS
The four Heavenly Kings, or Celestial Guardians, protect the Buddha and his realm. They stand in pairs on either side of the hall.

∧ ROOFTOP CREATURES AND BELLS
Along the roofline of Moni Hall's extended lower eaves is a procession of four creatures ahead of a dragon. Bells hang down below the eaves.

< PORTION OF TABLEAU
Inside Moni Hall are highly colourful clay tableaux that represent scenes from the life of Buddha Sakyamuni.

> ORNAMENTAL ARCH
Looking north from Moni Hall is an ornamental arch called a *paifang*, with the tiered roofs of other buildings rising behind.

˅ TIERED GATEWAY
With its massive roof structure supported by large brackets and capped with glazed tiles and figurines, this imposing gateway is stabilized with inclined timbers on both sides.

< FRONT VIEW OF BUDDHIST ALTAR
Called Jietan, or Buddhist Altar, the monks once used this building as a lecture hall. It now houses a double-faced statue of the Healing Buddha.

> PRAYER FLAGS OUTSIDE ALTAR
The faithful hang flags bearing mantras, invocations, and symbols. The wind is said to carry their messages to heaven.

∧ SIDE VIEW OF BUDDHIST ALTAR
The triple-tiered projecting eaves of the Buddhist Altar are supported by an extended arcade which lines the perimeter of the building.

< BUDDHA ON LOTUS THRONE
With two faces and four arms, this statue of Bhaishjyaguru (Yaoshi), the Healing Buddha, sits in the Ordination Altar, facing both its front and rear.

∧ INSCRIBED STELAE
Mounted on top of carved tortoises, each of these stelae – upright, inscribed stone slabs – records some aspect of the early history of the Longxing Monastery.

< ROTATING SUTRA CABINET
This revolving wooden bookcase, which can easily be turned by two people, was used to store holy texts. Its central shaft is reinforced with iron at the base.

> PAVILION OF GREAT COMPASSION
The large Foxiang (Great Compassion) Pavilion has an extensive open space in front for performing ceremonies.

> SUTRA CABINET PAVILION
This square, two-storey structure of the Northern Song dynasty (960–1127) has a distinctive frame, with a curved beam, intricate brackets, and diagonal struts.

ʌ CISHI PAVILION
This building, which stands opposite the Sutra Cabinet Pavilion, houses a statue of Bodhisattva Maitreya.

> STELA AND PAVILION OF KINDNESS
The multistorey Cishi Pavilion (also called the Pavilion of Kindness) and its associated stelae stand on a raised base accessed by four flights of steps.

< MAITREYA
This 7.4-m (24¼-ft) statue, carved from a single piece of wood, shows Bodhisattva Maitreya (the Buddha of the Future) in a kindly, sympathetic pose.

∨ PAVILION OF GREAT COMPASSION
This huge, three-storey building has five tiers of projecting eaves. Inside is a statue of Guanyin, the Bodhisattva of Mercy.

∨ MARTIAL FIGURINE
Made entirely of green ceramic, this martial figurine sits on top of a tiled eaves overhang on the Pavilion of Great Compassion.

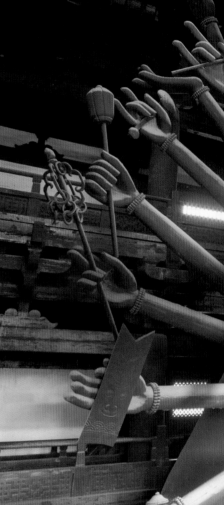

> BRIDGE CONNECTING HALLS
Constructed with curved beams, this bridge provides a passageway between two halls of the Pavilion of Great Compassion.

< FULL VIEW OF GUANYIN
With long legs swathed in a gown, the multi-armed Guanyin reaches nearly to the rafters of the pavilion.

> GUANYIN FROM THE REAR
Looking up towards the red-painted rafters from behind the towering statue, the breadth of the Guanyin sculpture is truly impressive.

∧ GUANYIN'S ATTENDANT
Dwarfed by the sheer height of the Guanyin statue that dominates the Pavilion of Great Compassion, this human-scale figure serves as an attendant at the feet of the Buddha.

< CLOTH HUNG FROM THE RAFTERS
From many of the beams high up in the pavilion, long swaths of red cloth drape down to surround the bronze statue of Guanyin.

∨ BRONZE STATUE OF GUANYIN
The 22-m- (72-ft-) tall statue of Guanyin has 42 arms that hold the Sun, Moon, a sword, a cane, and various musical instruments.

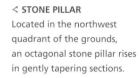

∧ GUANYIN GALLERY
A wooden staircase leads to an upper gallery supported by large wooden brackets from which visitors can view the higher portions of the Guanyin statue more closely.

< STONE PILLAR
Located in the northwest quadrant of the grounds, an octagonal stone pillar rises in gently tapering sections.

∨ PILU HALL
Originally the main hall of Chongyin Temple, Zhengding, this Ming dynasty building was moved to Longxing in 1959. It holds a statue of the Vairocana Buddha, the personification of wisdom and teaching.

> MUDRA GESTURE
One of Guanyin's hands, which is not carrying an object, is positioned into a symbolic gesture called *mudra*.

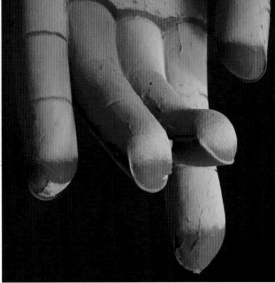

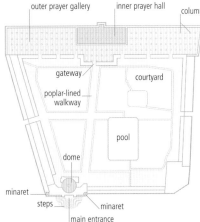

AERIAL VIEW

outer prayer gallery — inner prayer hall — columns

gateway — courtyard

poplar-lined walkway

pool

dome

minaret

steps — minaret

main entrance

Two asymmetrically placed minarets flank the main entrance. Each has a lantern-like crown and ribbed small dome, topped by a crescent moon.

The mosque faces onto a large public square. The building's elegant facade is constructed of yellow bricks pointed with gypsum.

China has in excess of 34,000 mosques.

清
真
寺

More than 10,000 of them provide worship space for the Hui people, a designated minority of the population who are spread throughout China's provinces. Most of the rest of the mosques are located in or near Xinjiang Autonomous Region – the territory formerly known as Chinese Central Asia or Chinese Turkestan – and over 100 of those are in the city of Kashgar. Close to the borders with Kyrgyzstan, Uzbekistan, Tajikistan, Afghanistan, and Pakistan, Kashgar has a population that comprises mainly people of the Uighur ethnic group, and its mosques and worshippers have strong links with West Asia and its Muslim population.

Built in a yellow brick that echoes the arid landscape, Id Kah (or Aidika'er) is the largest mosque both in Kashgar and in Xinjiang as a whole. It is also one of the best examples of Uighur architecture in China. The name Id Kah combines both Arabic and Persian words to give the meaning "place of worship on a festival day". Muslim worship at the site can be traced back to the Ming dynasty (1368–1644), but the structure seen today was begun in 1798 and

enlarged in 1838. The mosque's central courtyard is entered via a massive 8-m- (26-ft-) high gateway, which is linked to two 18m (60ft) corner minarets by a low wall that continues around the mosque. Although the minarets are the same height, they are not identical. The thicker minaret joins a shorter, plain wall, while the more slender structure is built into the corner of a facade that bears two pointed-arch recesses.

Inside the main gateway, the large, garden-style courtyard is divided into quadrants by tree-lined pathways. Surrounding the courtyard are ablution areas, lecture halls, and residences for the imam and students, as well as the enormous 38-bay *masjid* (main worship area). The *masjid* is divided into an outer prayer gallery and inner prayer hall, each with its own *mihrab* (prayer niche) oriented westward to Mecca.

The inner courtyard of the Id Kah mosque can accommodate several thousand worshippers. In addition, the huge public square in front of the main gate is a gathering place for Kashgar's Muslims and street vendors. Shops along the base of the exterior walls help to pay for the mosque's upkeep.

∧ MINARET DETAIL
The richly ornamented minarets are ringed with decorative brickwork, tiles, and carved stone reliefs.

ID KAH MOSQUE
PLACE OF ISLAMIC WORSHIP, XINJIANG

< ORNAMENTAL PANEL
Arabic script and geometric designs shape the composition of this wooden panel over the main entrance.

∨ SCULPTED BRICKWORK
The arched entryway is framed by a series of 15 window-like niches. These are topped by decorative brickwork.

< ∧ DOUBLE-LEAF DOOR
The mosque's main doorway is wide enough to allow the entrance and exit of large numbers of worshippers. The double-leaf door has heavy metal pulls and riveted metal panels.

< FLORAL ORNAMENTATION
Exquisitely sculpted floral patterns in both plain and painted stonework surround the doorway.

< SHADY AVENUE
The shady courtyard has a pool and tree-lined paths. This path leads from the main entrance to the worship area.

∨ GATEWAY TO PRAYER HALL AND GALLERY
The raised *masjid* (main worship area) runs along the entire length of the western side of the courtyard. The *masjid* is accessed by a short flight of steps.

∨ OUTER PRAYER GALLERY
The vast *masjid* – the widest individual building in China – has a colonnaded outer gallery with a *mihrab* (prayer niche), and an enclosed inner prayer hall.

∧ WEATHERED GATE
The parched climate of southwestern Xinjiang has contributed to the deterioration of paint and wood on this gateway, which opens out onto the courtyard garden to the *masjid*.

> COLUMN BASE
The outer prayer gallery's flat roof is supported by 140 slender octagonal timber columns. Carved details decorate the base of each green-painted column.

DECORATED ARCHES
Repeating, yet varied, geometric and floral patterns decorate the arched recesses and *mihrab* of the gallery's otherwise plain wall.

DOOR DETAIL
The door pulls and bosses of the heavy wooden doors are among the few obviously Chinese details in the Id Kah mosque, which is overwhelmingly West Asian in character and architectural style.

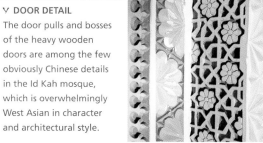
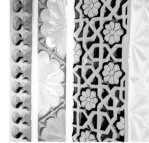

GREEN DOOR
This double-leaf wooden door separates the outer prayer gallery from the inner prayer hall of the *masjid*.

PRAYER GALLERY CEILING
The relatively unadorned white ceiling of the prayer gallery has one highly ornate panel above the *mihrab*.

INNER PRAYER HALL
The imam's *minbar* (pulpit) sits beside the *mihrab* (prayer niche) in the inner prayer hall.

345

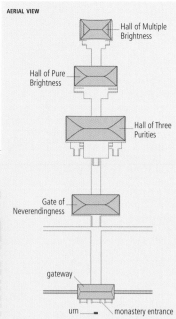

AERIAL VIEW

Hall of Multiple Brightness

Hall of Pure Brightness

Hall of Three Purities

Gate of Neverendingness

gateway

urn   monastery entrance

The Daoist Monastery of Eternal Joy,
永
乐
宫
Yongle Gong, at the southern tip of
Shanxi province, is unique: it has four
Yuan-period (1279–1368) buildings,
more than at any other architectural
complex. These buildings represent the
highest point of Chinese architecture
between the 9th and 14th centuries.
Yongle Gong was considered so
important that rather than destroy it to
construct the Sanmenxia Dam Project, it
was dismantled piece by piece between
1959 and 1963 and moved southeast
from its original location in Yongji
county to the present site in Ruicheng.

The monastery is entered via a
simple gateway (above) that resembles
the facade of a modest house. The four
Yuan buildings lie in a straight south–
north line from the main gate. First is the
Gate of Neverendingness, built in 1294.
Directly behind this is the crowning glory
of Yuan architecture, the Hall of Three
Purities. Built between 1247 and 1362,
and painted in 1324–25, its slim altar is
covered by the only ceiling with three
individual caissons (sunken panels)
known from this period. Except for the
altar and the front and back doors, the
hall, which measures about 28m (90ft)

by 15m (50ft), is empty. This allows
maximum space to view the murals of
Daoist deities that cover the walls.

The deities in the Hall of Three
Purities are of the Quanzhen Daoist sect,
founded in Shanxi province in the Jin
dynasty (1115–1234), but with legendary
ties to the Tang period (618–907). The
life of Lü Dongbin, one of the eight
Daoist immortals, is narrated in 52
scenes on the walls of the second,
smaller hall, the Hall of Pure Brightness.
These were painted in 1358.

Last in the line of Yuan buildings
is the Hall of Multiple Brightness, whose
murals recount the legendary life of the
historical founder of Quanzhen Daoism,
Wang Zhe, of the Jin dynasty. The
architecture of the second and third
halls is not as grand as that of the
Three Purities hall, but all the buildings
have huge front platforms, believed to
have been used for Daoist ceremonies.

Yongle Gong is one of several
hundred temple complexes in Shanxi
that possess pre-14th-century buildings.
Architecturally, Yongle Gong's structures
are spectacular; in combination with
their 500 sq m (5,380 sq ft) of murals,
they are unequalled in China.

ᐯ VIEW FROM THE URN
The monastery buildings are
set in parklike surroundings,
with trees and pavements
lining the straight pathway.

> DECORATIVE BRACKETS
Under the eaves of the Gate of
Neverendingness are ornate
brackets, some of which are
purely decorative in function.

ᐱ STELAE SUPPORTS
The inner pillars of this arcade at the
rear of the Gate of Neverendingness are
raised above the floor on stone supports
carved into the shape of turtles.

> EXTERIOR WALL BRICKWORK
Adding texture to the exterior wall of
the monastery complex is this inscribed
hexagonal pattern above a tiered set
of three triangular indentations.

YONGLE GONG
DAOIST MONASTERY OF ETERNAL JOY, SHANXI

< ROOF ORNAMENT
This green-glazed dragon is one of a pair on the roof of the Gate of Neverendingness.

> SIGNBOARD CHARACTERS
Above the entry is a four-character signboard declaring Wuji zhi Men, meaning "Gate of Neverendingness".

∧ SIMPLE WOODEN BRACKETS
The doorway of the Gate of Neverendingness is of a simple construction despite the grandeur of the surrounding gate.

< GATE OF NEVERENDINGNESS
The five-bay-wide Gate of Neverendingness has a hipped, glazed-tile roof that sweeps out in elegant arcs, rising upward at the tips.

∨ LINKING PATHWAY
The precise alignment of the four buildings can clearly be seen in this view of the path from the Gate of Neverendingness to the Hall of Three Purities.

∧ DOORWAY LIONS
As one leaves by the rear doorway of the Gate of Neverendingness, there is a pair of carved lions, each depicted in a curled, crouching pose and positioned on top of a stone block.

∨ RECESSED CEILING

With a colourful, writhing dragon at its centre, this is one of three of circular caissons (sunken panels) that grace the ceiling of the Hall of Three Purities.

∨ EXTERIOR BRACKETS

On the pillars at the exterior corners of the Hall of Three Purities are multiple-beaked wooden brackets that support the raised structure of the eaves.

∨ CARVED STONE CYLINDER

Rich decoration adorns the most functional of elements in the Hall of Three Purities. This stone cylinder, which fits over the top end of a wooden column, supports a roof beam.

∧ LION SENTRIES

Guardian lions carved from stone are found throughout the monastery, in a variety of poses but almost always in pairs. This one is a male with a curly mane.

∧ HALL OF THREE PURITIES

Raised on a stone platform, this magnificent hall is seven bays wide and four deep. The lattice-panel doors that line its facade allow light and air to enter the structure.

∨ CEILING BRACKETS
These highly ornamented, colourful brackets between the columns help to support the ceiling structure of the Hall of Three Purities.

< OCTAGONAL CAISSON
This painted caisson built into the ceiling of the Hall of Pure Brightness is surrounded by beautiful murals depicting the life of Wang Zhe.

< HALL OF PURE BRIGHTNESS
The hall is dedicated to the Daoist immortal Lü Dongbin. Like the Hall of Multiple Brightness (bottom), it is five bays wide and four bays deep.

∨ THE SEVEN PERFECT ONES
These small effigies of the Seven Perfect Ones are displayed in the Hall of Multiple Brightness.

< ALTAR STATUE
This is one of three statues of Daoist purities on an altar at the centre of the Hall of Three Purities, which also has murals of the Daoist pantheon.

< LÜ DONGBIN
This statue of Lü Dongbin in the Hall of Pure Brightness is surrounded by scenes narrating his cultivation of the Dao (Way).

∧ HALL OF MULTIPLE BRIGHTNESS
Also called the Hall of the Seven Perfect Ones, this hall is dedicated to the spiritual leader Wang Zhe, the founder of Quanzhen Daoism.

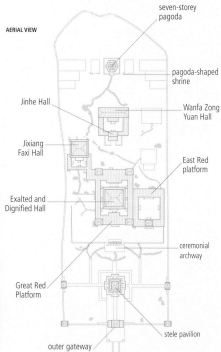

AERIAL VIEW

seven-storey pagoda

pagoda-shaped shrine

Jinhe Hall

Wanfa Zong Yuan Hall

Jixiang Faxi Hall

East Red platform

Exalted and Dignified Hall

ceremonial archway

Great Red Platform

outer gateway

stele pavilion

> **OUTER GATEWAY**
The modest ground-level gateway and approach provides little clue of the magnificent temples that lie beyond.

∨ **GUARDIAN LION**
A pair of stone lions, one male and one female, guard the entrance to the temple. The male lion has his paw on a ball.

The city of Chengde, earlier known as

须弥福寿庙

Rehe, nestles amid beautiful scenery about 250km (150 miles) northeast of Beijing. In 1703, Kangxi (r.1660–1722), second emperor of the Manchu dynasty known as Qing (1644–1911), began the construction of a resort palace, gardens, and temples. The site came to be known as Bishushanzhuang (Hill Station for Escaping the Heat). Construction was completed under Kangxi's grandson Qianlong (r.1736–1795) in 1792.

At Bishushanzhuang, the Qing emperors symbolically proclaimed the unity of the peoples under their rule. The eight outlying temples were built to imitate the architectural styles of the different ethnic nationalities. Puren Temple, the first temple to be built in 1713, followed the style of a Mongolian Buddhist temple, signifying the loyalty of the Mongolian nobles to the Qing throne. Puyou Temple was constructed in Chinese and Tibetan styles and Anyuan Temple was modelled after a temple in Yili, in western Xinjiang. Pule Temple was built in Han and Lamaist styles to receive homage from the Kazaks and Kyrgyz, and Putuozongcheng Temple was a replica of the Potola Palace in Lhasa.

Xumifushou, the last of the outlying temples to be built, was completed in 1760 in honour of Qianlong's 70th birthday. It was constructed for use by the Sixth Panchen Lama (the second-highest-ranking lama after the Dalai Lama), who came to Chengde for the great occasion, and was based on the Panchen Lama's own monastery at Trashi Lhumpo in Tibet.

Xumifushou's main structures lie along a sharp axial line, beginning with the front gateway. Behind it are a stele pavilion and a tall triple-entry archway covered in glazed ceramic tiles and flanked by elephants. After this lies the Great Red Platform, three storeys elevated on a high base with four corner towers. Concealed within is the Exalted and Dignified Hall where the Panchen Lama expounded the doctrine to the emperor. Its two roof eaves are made of gilded tiles with fish-scale ridges. The emperor sat on the adjoining East Red Platform when he listened to sermons.

The last building is the spectacular seven-storey, glazed octagonal pagoda, the most typically Chinese structure here. The construction of the buildings on the sloping terrain is a Tibetan feature.

< **STELE PAVILION**
Viewed though the outer gateway, the stele pavilion houses engraved stone tablets commemorating the construction of the temple.

> **BRASS CENSER**
An imposing brass censer dominates the pavilion entrance. Sticks of burning incense would be placed in the censer according to a strict ritual schedule.

XUMIFUSHOU MIAO
TRADITIONAL TIBETAN TEMPLE, HEBEI

< **GLAZED TILES**
Green and gold glazed tiles at the top of the ceremonial archway contrast with the vermillion colours on the base.

∨ **CEREMONIAL ARCHWAY**
This majestic three-portal ceremonial archway provides a fitting entrance to the Great Red Platform and the main temple complex.

< **ROOFTOP DRAGONS**
Dragons were historically a sign of imperial power and featured on the national flag in the Qing dynasty. They are also an auspicious creature.

< **GUARDIAN ELEPHANTS**
Two large stone elephants – a symbol of mental strength, and perhaps a reminder of Buddhism's origins in southern Asia – guard the entrance.

> **STONE CARVINGS**
Ornamental carved floral patterns and motifs adorn each of the sweeping stone archways leading into the main temple complex beyond.

∧ GREAT RED PLATFORM
From the gates of the ceremonial archway,
visitors can catch a glimpse of the magnificence
beyond: the three-storey tall Great Red Platform,
sitting high on its great stone base.

> **EXALTED AND DIGNIFIED HALL**
Entered from the Great Red Platform,
the Exalted and Dignified Hall contains
images of Shakyamuni Buddha and the
founder of the Yellow Sect of Buddhism.

∧ **CORNER TOWER ON GREAT RED PLATFORM**
With their red painted columns and multicoloured beams, the four corner towers add
greater height to an already imposing building.

∨ > **ENTRANCE**
The doorway into the Great
Red Platform is framed by
ceramic pillars with carved
stone bases and tiled,
ornamented beams. Glazed,
floral-patterned lozenges
decorate each of the pillars.

∧ **THE GREAT RED PLATFORM**
The extensive scale of the interior of the
platform is hidden behind high walls.
Only the gold glazed-tile roof of the
Exalted and Dignified Hall is visible.

> **INSIDE THE GREAT RED PLATFORM**
Concealed within the Great Red
Platform, the passageways around the
Exalted and Dignified Hall offer a place
for retreat and quiet contemplation.

< FIVE-CLAWED DRAGONS
Eight gilded dragons sit astride the roof ridges of the Exalted and Dignified Hall. Each dragon weighs over 1,000kg (2,200lb).

∨ PAGODA AND HALLS
Seen from the heavens, the octagonal stone base and hall are said to give the pagoda the shape of a huge geometric mandala – a symbol of the cosmos.

<∧ BUDDHA IMAGES
Images of the Buddha are set within carved and painted niches all around the inner periphery of the structure at the base of the pagoda.

< PAGODA
In the upslope portion of the temple complex, an octagonal glazed-tile pagoda rises high above a red-columned hall.

∧ PAGODA-SHAPED SHRINE
Carved buddhas, faded prayer flags, and piles of mani stones painted with Buddhist mantras adorn this small stone shrine.

INDEX

Page numbers in **bold** indicate
main references.

1911 revolution 117
10,000 Buddhas Monastery 251

A

A Hua 146–8
Abahai 108
Abaoji 98
actors and actresses 276
acupuncture 198, 200, 240
agriculture
   equal field system 91
   gods 237
   Han dynasty 86
   loess valley farmer **132–9**
   Mosuo ethnic minority **162–9**
   ploughs 89
   Song improvements 99
   tea **146–53**
   "well-field" system 83
Aguda 100
Ahmad 103
alchemy 86
almanacs 251
An Lushan rebellion (755–63) 94,
   96, 262
Anyang 81
arches, widow 112
architecture **280–355**
   Beijian Bridge **312–13**
   Couple's Garden Retreat,
      Suzhou **308–11**
   courtyard house, Beijing **292–5**
   Hakka dwellings **282–7**
   Id Kah Mosque, Xinjiang **342–5**
   Jin Mao Tower **300–307**
   Longxing monastery **336–41**
   Shanghai 128–9
   stilt houses **296–9**
   Temple of Heaven, Beijing **332–5**
   Tin Hau Temple, Hong Kong
      328–31
   White Pagoda **318–23**
   Wu Fang Ting, Chengkan **288–91**
   Xuankong Si **324–7**
   Xumifushou Miao temple,
      Chengde **350–55**
   Yongle Gong monastery **346–9**
Arrow War (1856–60) 113

art
   calligraphy **140–45**, 252, **253–5**
   painting 96, **256–60**
astrology **250–51**
Atsokh monastery, Qinghai **184–91**
Australia, Chinese workers in 114, 115
avian flu 129

B

Bada Shanren 260
bamboo 62–3, 262
Ban Chao 87, 89
Ban Zhao 88
Banpo 80
Bao Zhao 57, 76
Batuo 91
Bayan 102
Beijian Bridge **312–13**
Beijing **106–7**
   courtyard house **292–5**
   Temple of Heaven **332–5**
Beijing Film Academy 125
Beijing Olympics (2008) **126–7**
Beijing Opera 111, 226, 277
Beijing Young Artists Association 124
Bi Sheng 99
birds 34–5, 204
birth control 124
Bishushanzhuang 350
Black Dragon Pool 50–51
Bo Juyi 62, **265**
boats 92
Book of Changes (*Yi Jing*) 97, 235,
   250
Book of History 97
Book of Odes 97
books 97, 108, 252
Boxer uprising (1900) 116
Bridge, Beijian **312–13**
Britain
   Opium Wars 112, 113
   trade with China 111
Brocade Guard 104
Bronze Age **80–81**
bubonic plague 102
Buddha 20, 246
Buddhism **246–7**
   art 260
   calligraphy 253
   dissolution of monasteries 97
   festivals **208–15**

history 90
Leshan Giant Buddha 46–7
literature 266, 272
Longxing Si **336–41**
monasteries **16–19**, **184–91**
pilgrimages 20–21
poetry 262
and religious Daoism 248–9
in Tibet 94
White Pagoda **318–23**
Xuankong Si **324–7**
Burqin 40–41

C

Cai Lun 89
calendars 82, 250, 251
California, Chinese workers in 114
calligraphy **140–45**, 252, **253–5**
Canadian Pacific Railroad 114
canals 74–5, 84, **92–3**, 98
Cang Jie 252
Canton 111
Cao Xueqin 267, 273
Castiglione, Giuseppe 110
cave houses **132–5**, 138–9
Central Asia 95
ceramics
   Han 88–9
   Ju porcelain 98
   Ming 108, 109
   Neolithic 80–81
   Qing 113
   Shiwan 328
   Tang 95, 96
   terracotta army 84–5, 257
   Yixing ware 152
   Yuan 102, 103
Chan (Zen) Buddhism 246
Chang Hanlin 132–9
Chang'an (Xi'an) 86, 87, 94, 95
Changning 62–3
Changqu 132
Chao Yi 25
chariots 82
Chen Duxiu 117
Chen Kaige 125
Chen Yihe **192–9**
Cheng Yanqiu 292
Chengde, Xumifushou Miao temple
   350–55
Chengkan **288–91**
chess 222, 224–5
Chiang Kai-Shek (Jiang Jieshi) 117,
   118, 119
Chinatowns 114
Chongqing 119

Christianity
   Jesuits 108, 110
   missionaries 102
   Nestorians 94–5
   Tianjin massacre 113
Chu culture 239
Chuanqi (*Tales of the Marvellous*)
   266–7
cinema 125, 231
cities
   Beijing **106–7**
   Hong Kong 64–5
   migration to 137
   Shanghai 76–7
   young people in 128
civil service 104, 105, 252
Civil War (1946–49) 118
Cixi, Empress Dowager 113, 116
clocks 99
Cohong 111, 112
coins 83, 84
colour, symbolism 276
Communist Party 79
   China under Mao **120–23**
   civil war 118
   foundation of 116, 117
   Long March 118
   Red Army 118
   at Yan'an 118
compasses 99
concubines 88, 108
confectionery **182–3**
Confucianism **242–3**
   and the arts 252
   and Buddhism 246–7
   and Daoism 244
   in Han empire 86
   Nine Classics 97
   poetry 264
Confucius (Kong Fuzi) 82, **242**,
   248
   Analects 31, 49, **242–3**
   Kangxi emperor and 110
   temples 248
   and the three mythical
      "demigods" 237
corn, milling 136
Couple's Garden retreat, Suzhou
   308–11
courtesans 108
courtyard houses 32–3
   Beijing **292–5**
craftsmen
   jewellery **216–17**
   musical instruments **154–9**
creation myths 234–5
crickets **202–7**

Cultural Revolution 120, **121**, 122,
   124, 125, 277
culture **232–79**
Curse of the Golden Flower 125

D

Dai, Countess of 86
Dai monasteries **318–23**
Dalai Lama 19, 111
Dao 234, 240, 242, 244–5
Daode jing 82, **244**
Daoism (Taoism) **244–5**
   alchemy 90
   calligraphy 253
   festivals 210
   literature 266
   poetry 262, 263
   principles 82
   religious Daoism **248–9**
   Yongle Gong monastery **346–9**
Daowu, Emperor 90
demigods 237
Deng Xiaoping 79, 120
   and the Cultural Revolution 121,
      124
   fishing reforms 220
   Shanghai becomes financial
      centre 170
   and Taiwan 129
deserts 26–7, 129
Diamond Sutra 97
Diaspora, Chinese **114–15**
dictionaries 89
Ding Ling 118
Ding ware 96
diseases 102, 129
divination 144, **239**, 251
doctors, herbalism **192–9**
Dong minority architecture **296–9**
Dong Zhu **184–91**
Douglas, R K 107
drama, Yuan dynasty 102
drugs, opium 111, 112
Du Fu 96, 262, **264**, 265
Duan Chengshi 97
Dun Xunhe 17
Dunhuang caves 99

E

East India Companies 109, 111
economy, future of China 128
education 179, 252
   primary school **174–81**
Eight Trigrams 235, 250

elements, Five Phases **241**
emigration **114–15**
Empress Dowager (Cixi) 113, 116
entertainment 231
entrepreneurs 128, **216–19**
environment, future of China 129
Esen 104
ethnic minorities 158
eunuchs 88, 108
examinations 98, 104, 105, 252

F

families 234
   one-child families 124
Fan Kuan 100, 256–7
Fan Shenzhi 33
Farewell My Concubine 125
farming *see agriculture*
Feng Guifen 113
feng shui 104, 241, **251**, 300
festivals **208–15**
feudalism 82
fiction **266–75**
figure painting **257–60**
films **125**, 231
fireworks 99
First Emperor (Qin Shihuang) **84–5**,
   257, 314
fishing
   fisheries 72–3
   sea fisherman **220–23**
Five Phases **241**
Five-Year Plans 120, 122
Flaming Mountains 40–41, 43
floods 103, 237
folklore **248–9**
food and drink 169
   confectionery **182–3**
foot-binding 101
Forbidden City **106–7**
Forest of Stelae, Xi'an 97
forests 60–63
fortune **250–51**
Foster, Norman 126
Fotudeng 90
France 113
Fu Hao, Princess 81
Fu Xi **235**
funerals 251
future of China **128–9**

G

games 222, 223, **224–5**
"Gang of Four" 120
Gangga, Mount 14–15

Gao Qi 71
Gao Shi 72
Gaozong emperor 94, 100
Gaozu emperor 86
gardens 105
   Couple's Garden retreat,
      Suzhou **308–11**
Genghis Khan **101**, 102, 103, 314
geomancy **251**
Goachang 42–3
gods and goddesses 248–9
   creation myths **234–5**
   divination 239
   three "demigods" **237**
   Tin Hau 328
Golden Lotus 267, **270**
Gong Li 125
Grand Canal 74–5, **92–3**, 98, 103,
   106
Grand Historian (Sima Qian) 82, 88,
   266
"Great Green Wall" 129
Great Leap Forward (1958) 120, 122
Great Wall 44–5
   construction of 84, 105
   Juyongguan **314–17**
Great Yü **237**
Gu Kaizhi 90
Guan Hanqing 278
Guan Yin 246, 247, 271, 331, 336
Guan Zhong 83
Guangzhou 111, 112
Guanyuan Market, Beijing 202–5
Gui'de 33
Guilin Hills 68–9
gunpowder 99
Guo Shuojing 101
Guomindang (Nationalist Party) 116,
   117, 118

H

hair, queue (Manchu style) 110
Hakka architecture **282–7**
Han dynasty 79, **86–9**
Han Fei 83, 85
Han Gan 96
Han Shan 23
Han Yu 61, 97
Hangzhou 100, 108
Heart Sutra 272
Heilongjiang 60–61
Heng, Mount 324
herbalism **192–201**
Herzog and De Meuron 126
Heshen 112
history **78–129**

Hmong (Miao) people 111
Hong Kong 64–5
   cession to Britain 112, 114
   feng shui influences on
      architecture 251
   returned to China 124
   Tin Hau Temple **328–31**
Hong Xiuquan 113
Hongwu, Emperor 104, 108
horoscopes **250–51**
House of Flying Daggers 125
houses
   cave houses 132–5, 138–9
   courtyard houses 32–3, **292–5**
   Hakka dwellings **282–7**
   Neolithic 80
   stilt houses **296–9**
   Wu Fang Ting, Chengkan **288–91**
Hu Jintao 125
Hu Shi 117
Hu Weiyong 104
Hu Yaobang 124
Hua Guofeng 120
Huai Su 253
Huang Chao 94
Huang He (Yellow River) 32–3, 81,
   103, 132–3
Huangdi (Yellow Emperor) 80, **236**
Huangshan (Yellow Mountains) 66–7
Hui people 158, 342
Huizong emperor 100, 252
Hunan 122

I

I Ching (*Yi Jing*) 97, 235, 250
Ibn Battuta 102
Id Kah Mosque, Xinjiang **342–5**
Imperial Academy 87
industrialization 220
The Injustice Done to Dou E (opera)
   277, **278**
ink and brush paintings 257
inscriptions 257
iron technology 83
Islam 159
   first Muslim envoy 94
   Id Kah Mosque, Xinjiang **342–5**
   invasions 95

J

jade 80
Japan 105, 118, 119
Jesuits 108, 110, 260
jewellery **216–17**
Ji Shan Island **220–23**

Jiang Jieshi (Chiang Kai-Shek) 117,
   118, 119
Jiang Qing 120, 121, 277
Jiang Zemin 124
Jiangxi Soviet Republic 118
Jiangyin 110
Jiaohe 87
Jin dynasty 98, 100, 101, 108
Jin Mao Tower, Shanghai **300–307**
Jin Yong 270
Jingdezhen 98, 103, 108, 109
Jiuzhaigou 30–31
John of Montecorvino 102
Journey to the West 238, 267, **271–2**
Ju Dou 125
Ju ware 98
Junggar Basin 56–7
Jurchen 98, 100, 101, 108
Juyongguan, Great Wall **314–17**

K

Kaifeng 100
   Grand Canal 92
   paintings of 257
   siege of (1232–33) 101
   Song dynasty 98
Kaihuang Code 91
Kaiping (Shangdu) 103
Kangxi emperor 110, 350
Kashgar 154, 159, 342
Kham region 12–13
Khampa Dzong 22–3
Khubilai Khan 101, 102, **103**
Kissinger, Henry 120
Kong Fuzi (Confucius) 82
Korea 87, 116
Korean War (1950–53) 120
Kowloon Peninsula 65
Koxinga 110
Kraak ware 109
Kumarajiva 246
Kunqu opera 277

L

lacquerware 86
Lan Yindong **202–5**
landscape **9–77**
landscape paintings 100, **256–7**
language **252**
   first dictionary 89
   homophones 250, 261
   poetry 261
   symbols and signs 250

Laozi (Lao Tzu) 82, **244**
legal codes 91, 103
Leshan Giant Buddha 46–7
Li, King of Zhou 82
Li Bai 55, 96, 262, **263**, 264
Li Dazhou 117
Li Hongzheng 113
Li Peng 124
Li Qinghe **216–19**
Li Shan 257
Li Zicheng 108
Liang dynasty 94
Liang Ji 88
Liao dynasty 98
Lin Zexu 112
literati 105
literature **266–75**
   May Fourth Movement 117
   novels **266–75**
   poetry **261–5**
Liu Jin 108
Liu Mu **140–43**
Liu Qilan 111
Liu Rushi 108
Liu Shaoqi 121
loess 132
Long Li 51
Long March (1934) **118**, 122
Longmen 90
Longshan culture 80–81
Longxing Si **336–41**
Lord Millet 237
Lotus Sutra 246
Lü Dongbin 346
Lu Ji 27
Lu Xun 117
Lu Yu 96
Luo Guangzhong 267
Luo Mingwei 148–9, 151
Luoping 54–5

M

Ma'an hamlet, Sanjiang **296–9**
Macao (Aomen) 105, 109
Macartney, Lord 93
Mahayana Buddhism 246
mahjong 223, 224
Manchukuo 119
Manchuria 119
Manchus 108, 110
Manfeilong village 318
Mani 95
Manichaeism 95
Mao Zedong **122–3**
   Communist Party founded 117
   Cultural Revolution 121

death 79, 120, 124
  on family altars 169
Long March 118
Red Army 118
and *Water Margin* 270
at Yan'an 118
markets, cricket sellers **202–5**
marriage laws 120
May Fourth Movement 117, 122
medicine 108
  acupuncture 198
  herbalism **192–201**
Mei Lanfang 276, 277
Meili Snow Mountains 20–21
Meizhou Island 72–3
Mencius 82, **243**, 247
Meng Tian 84
Mi Fu 100
Miao (Hmong) people 111
migrant workers **114–15**, 128, 137
minarets 342
Ming dynasty **104–9**
  architecture **288–91**
  literature 267
  opera 277
Minghuang, Emperor 262
missionaries 102, 108, 113
monasteries
  Atsokh Monastery, Qinghai **184–91**
  dissolution of Buddhist monasteries 97
  Longxing Si **336–41**
  Sakya Monastery, Tibet **16–17**
  Shaolin Monastery 91
  Songzanlin Monastery, Yunnan **18–19**
  White Pagoda **318–23**
  Xuankong Si **324–7**
  Yongle Gong **346–9**
money 99, 118
Mongols **102–3**
  conquest of Tibet 111
  decline of Yuan dynasty 103
  Genghis Khan **101**
  and the Great Wall 314
  Kangxi's campaigns against 110
  Khubilai Khan **103**
  siege of Kaifeng 101
  Silk Road 87
Monkey 238, 267, 271–2
Mosque, Id Kah **342–5**
Mosu ethnic minority **162–9**
Mozi 82
Mu Qi 100
mule carts 136

music
  musical instruments **154–61**
  opera 111, **226–31**, **276–9**
  weddings 139
  Zhou dynasty 83
Muslims *see Islam*
Muze Lacuo **162–9**
myths **234–8**

N
Nalan Xingde 44
Nanchang 118
Nanjing 113, 119
Nanjing, Treaty of (1842) 112
Nationalist Party (Guomindang) 116, 117, 118
nature reserves 52–3, 58–9
Neo-Confucianism 101
Neolithic cultures **80–81**, 253
Nestorianism 94–5
New Territories 65, 116
New Year 214
New York, Chinatown 114–15
New Youth magazine 117
Ni Zan 257
Nine Classics 97
Nixon, Richard 120
Northern Wei dynasty 91
novels **266–75**
Nü Wa **235**
numerology 250
Nurhaci 108

O
Ogedai 101
Olympic Games (2008) **126–7**
one-child families 124
opera 111, **226–31**, **276–9**
opium 111, 112
Opium Wars (1839–42 and 1856–60) 112, 114
oracle bones 239, 253
Orogen people 61
Ou Yuan, Suzhou **308–11**
Overseas Chinese 114

P
pagodas 88, 251
  influence on modern architecture 300
  White Pagoda **318–23**
painting **256–60**
  calligraphy **140–45**
  figure painting **257–60**

landscape painting 100, **256–7**
  Song dynasty 100
Pan Gu 234
Panchen Lama 350
panda, giant 58–9
paper, invention of 89
paper money 99
pastimes, traditional 204
Pei Di 53
Peking *see Beijing*
The Peony Pavilion (opera) **276**, 277, 279
People's Liberation Army 118, 120
People's Republic of China 122
philosophy **242–51**
Pires, Tomé 105
plague 102
playing cards 100
poetry **261–5**, 266
  on paintings 257
  Tang dynasty 96, **262–5**
  women poets 111
politics, future of China 129
pollution 126, 129, 220
Polo, Marco 92, 103
popular religion **248–9**
population
  emigration **114–15**
  migration to cities 137
  one-child families 124
  under Qing dynasty 111, 112
  under Song dynasty 99
  20th-century growth 131
porcelain *see* ceramics
portraits 260
Portugal 105, 109
Potala palace, Lhasa 111
pottery *see* ceramics
printing 89, 97, 99
Pu Songling 273, 275
Pure Land Buddhism 246
Puyi, Henry 119

Q
Qi **240**, 241, 251
Qian Qianyi 108
Qianlong emperor 110, 111
  Bishushanzhuang 350
  Opium Wars 112
  paintings of 260
Qiao Weiyue 98
Qidan Liao dynasty 98
Qin dynasty 83, **84–5**, 86
Qin Shihuang, First Emperor **84–5**, 257, 314

Qing dynasty 79, 108
  architecture 282
  art 260
  early Qing dynasty **110–11**
  late Qing dynasty **116–17**
  literature 267
  mid–Qing dynasty **112–13**
  opera 277
  Xumifushou Miao temple, Chengde **350–55**
Qinghai Lake 34–5
Qu Yuan 239, 261
Queen Mother of the West 238, 271
Quekenba village 208–13

R
"rainbow bridges" **312–13**
Raise the Red Lantern 125
rapeseed 54–5
Red Army 118, 122, 123
Red Guards 121, 122
Red Sorghum 125
religion **242–51**
  Christian missionaries 102, 108, 113
  Jesuits 108, 110, 260
  Manichaeism 95
  Nestorianism 94–5
  see also Buddhism; Daoism; Islam
Ren, Miss 267
Ren Bonian 260
retirement **170–73**
Ricci, Matteo 108
rice
  fields 68–9
  Neolithic cultures 80
  terraces 48–9
The Romance of the Three Kingdoms 90, 249, 267, **268–9**, 270
Russia 113
Russo-Japanese War (1904–5) 116

S
"Sage Calligrapher" (Wang Xizhi) 90, 140, 253, **254–5**
Sakya Monastery 16–17
San Francisco, Chinatown 114
SARS 129
The Scholars 267, **273**
schools **174–81**
scrolls 252, 256, 257, 258–9
seals 91, 141, 257
seismographs 89
Selay, Ababakri **154–9**
Semedo, Alvaro 108
Shakyamuni 318, 336

shamans **239**
Shandong 117
Shang dynasty 80, **81**
  battles 83
  defeat by Zhou 82
  divination 239
  writing 253
Shanghai 76–7, **117**, 170–73
  architecture 128–9
  Jin Mao Tower **300–307**
  looms 108
  Opium Wars 112
  Taiping Rebellion 113
"Shangri-La" 28–9
Shaolin monastery 91
Shaoxing opera 277
Shen Nong **237**
Shengwu Lou, Jiaolu village **282–7**
Shi Nai'an 267
Shiwan 328
Shun, Emperor 237
signs **250–51**
silk 80, 87, 108, 109
Silk Road 43, **87**, 95, 246, 260
silverwork 94
Sima Qian, Grand Historian 82, 88, 266
Sino-French War (1882–85) 113
Sino-Japanese Wars 116, **119**
Skidmore, Owings & Merrill **300–307**
skyscrapers **300–307**
society, future of China 128
Song dynasty 79, **98–101**
  landscape paintings 256–7
  monasteries **336–41**
Song Yu 13
Song-tsen Gampo, King 91, 94
Songzanlin Monastery 18–19
space programme 129
Spain 109
Special Economic Zones 124
spice trade 109
sport, Olympic Games (2008) **126–7**
Spring Festival 214
Stalin, Joseph 120
stilt houses **296–9**
The Story of the Stone 235, 267, **274**
stupas 20–21, 318
Su Dingfang 94
Su Dongpo 100
Su Song 99
Sui dynasty 91, 92, 94
Sun Zhongshan (Sun Yat-sen) 116–17
sunflowers 137
Sunzi 83
Suspended in the Air Monastery **324–7**

Suzhou 216–19
  Couple's Garden retreat 308–11
  Humble Administrator's Garden 105
Swan Lake 52–3
symbolism 250
  calligraphy 253
  colour 276
  language 250

T
Tai Chi 170–71, 240
Taiping rebellion (1850) 112, 113
Taiwan 110, 118, 129
Taizong emperor 94
Tang dynasty 79, 94–7
  calligraphy 253
  Grand Canal 92
  literature 266–7
  poetry 96, 262–5
Tang Xianzu 279
Tanglha, Mount 10–11
Tao Yuanming 261
Taoism see Daoism
Tatars 103
tea
  Classic of Tea 96
  markets 143
  plantations 70–71
  tea boxes 96–7
  tea factory 146–53
  tea pickers 146–7
  trade 111, 112
television 231
temples 249
  festivals 208–15
  Temple of Heaven, Beijing 332–5
  Tin Hau Temple, Hong Kong 328–31
  Xumifushou Miao temple, Chengde 350–55
Temür 102
terracotta army 84–5, 257
theatre, opera 276–9
Theravada Buddhism 318
Three Feudatories 110
Three Gorges Dam 124
Three Kingdoms 90
"three perfections" 252
Tian Shan, Mount 38–9
Tiananmen Square 121, 124, 127
Tianchi Lake 38–9
Tianjin, Treaty of (1885) 113
Tianjin massacre (1870) 113
Tianqi, Emperor 108

Tibet
  Buddhism 94
  as Chinese protectorate 111
  Free Tibet Campaign 126
  "liberation" of 120
  unification 91
Tibet-Qinghai Plateau 10–17, 24–7
Tibet Railway 125
Tin Hau Temple, Hong Kong 328–31
Toghon Temür 102
tombs
  Han dynasty 86, 88
  Ming dynasty 104
  Shang dynasty 81
  terracotta army 84–5, 257
Tongzhi emperor 113
tools
  agriculture 137
  calligraphy brushes 142–3, 144–5
  craftsmen's 158
  cricket keepers' 206–7
tourism 125, 126
trade
  Grand Canal 92
  Guangzhou system 111
  Ming dynasty 109
  opium 112
  Silk Road 87
  Song dynasty 100
  tea 111, 112
traditional Chinese medicine (TCM) 192–201, 240
Triads 117
Trigrams, Eight 235, 250
Tugh Temür 102
tulou (Hakka dwellings) 282–7
Tumu incident (1449) 104, 105
Turkestan 113

U
Uighurs 154–61
  architecture 342
UNESCO World Heritage Sites 31
United States of America, Chinese workers in 114

V
Vietnam 113
villages 32–3
  Dong 296–9

W
Wang Hongwen 120
Wang Jin 89

Wang Mang, Emperor 86, 88
Wang Mian 140
Wang Shimin 265
Wang Wei (701–61) 58, 96, 262
Wang Wei (secretary-general of Olympic bid committee) 127
Wang Xianchen 105
Wang Xizhi ("Sage Calligrapher") 90, 140, 253, 254–5
Wang Yangming 105
Wang Zhao Jun 88
Wang Zhe 104, 346
Wang Zheng 108
washing clothes 148
Water Margin 251, 267, 270
weapons, Zhou dynasty 83
weddings 139
Wei Yuan 113
Wei Zhongxian 108
Wen 252
Wen Tingyun 43
Wen Zhengming 105
Wendi, Emperor (Qin dynasty) 86
Wendi, Emperor (Sui dynasty) 91
White Pagoda 318–23
widow arches 112
Wolong Nature Reserve 58–9, 261
women
  foot-binding 101
  marriage laws 120
  poets 111
  Song dynasty 101
  under communism 120
  woodblock prints 260
World War II 114
writing, calligraphy 140–45, 252, 253–5
Wu, Emperor 90
Wu, Empress 94
Wu Cheng'en 41, 267, 272
Wu Daozi 96
Wu Fang Ting, Chengkan 288–91
Wu Jianxin 208–13
Wu Jingzi 267, 273
Wu Sangui 110
Wudi, Emperor 86, 87
Wulingyuan scenic area 36–7
Wutai Shan 97
Wuxi 74–5
wuxia 125
Wuzong, Emperor 97

X
Xanadu 103
Xia dynasty 80, 81
Xia Gui 100

Xia Weiqin 170–73
Xianbei people 86
Xianfeng emperor 113
Xiao Chen 174–81
Xiaozong emperor 100
Xie Lingyun 35, 67
Xin Qi-ji 6
Xing ware 96
Xinjiang 113, 342
Xu Shen 89
Xuankong Si 324–7
Xuanzang 271
Xuanzong emperor 94, 95, 96, 262
Xumifushou Miao temple, Chengde 350–55
Xunzi 82

Y
Yan Shu 28
Yan'an 118
Yan'an Way 122
Yang Guifei 96
Yang Guozhong 96
Yangdi, Emperor 92
Yangzi River 10–11
Yao 237
Yao Wenyuan 120
Yellow Books 104
Yellow Earth 125
Yellow Emperor (Huangdi) 80, 236
Yellow River (Huang He) 32–3, 81, 103, 132–3
Yellow Mountains (Huangshan) 66–7
Yi, Marquis of 83
Yi the archer 238
Yi Jing (I Ching, Book of Changes) 97, 235, 250
yin and yang 234, 240–41, 251
Yixing ware 152
Yongle emperor
  eunuchs 108
  Grand Canal 92
  maritime expeditions 104
  Temple of Heaven, Beijing 332
Yongle Gong monastery 346–9
Yongzheng emperor 110, 111, 260
Yuan dynasty 102–3
  architecture 346
  opera 277
  paintings 257
Yuan Jie 14
Yuan Shikai 116, 117
Yue opera 226–31, 277
Yulong (Jade Dragon) Mountain 50–51
Yun Shouping 18

Z
Zen (Chan) Buddhism 246
Zhalu village 146–51
Zhang brothers 94
Zhang Chunqiao 120
Zhang Heng 89
Zhang Lin 226–31
Zhang Qian, General 87
Zhang Xiaogang 124
Zhang Yimou 125
Zhang Zeduan 98, 257, 258–9
Zhang Zhiping 220–23
Zhangjiajie 36–7
Zhao Kuangyin, Emperor 98
Zhao Mengfu 102
Zheng He 104
Zheng Zhanbao 68
Zhengde, Emperor 108
Zhengding 336
Zhengtong emperor 104, 108
Zhengzhou 81
Zhiguai (Records of the Strange) 266, 275
Zhongdian 28–9
Zhou dynasty (1122 BC–256 BC) 80, 82–3, 237, 239
Zhou dynasty (690–705) 94
Zhu Xi 101
Zhuangzi 244–5, 266
Ziye 39
zodiac 250–51
Zoroastrianism 95
Zunghars 110, 111, 350

ACKNOWLEDGMENTS

The publisher would like to thank the following for their kind permission to reproduce their photographs:

(Key: a–above; b–below/bottom; c–centre; f–far; l–left; r–right; t–top)

2 China Span/Keren Su: (tr). 8-9 Masterfile: Jochen Schlenker. 10-11 ChinaStock: Suichu Ru. 12-13 ChinaStock: Liu Liqun. 14-15 Photolibrary: Panorama Media (Beijing) Ltd/Weixiong Liu. 16-17 Panoramic Images: Peter Weld. 18-19 Photolibrary: Panorama Media (Beijing) Ltd / Zhinong Xi. 20-21 Lonely Planet Images: Bradley Mayhew. 22-23 Photolibrary: Panorama Media (Beijing) Ltd. 24-25 China Span/Keren Su. 26-27 ChinaStock: Liu Liqun. 28-29 Photolibrary: Panorama Media (Beijing) Ltd/Qianshun Cui. 30-31 Photolibrary: Panorama Media (Beijing) Ltd/Qitao Yang. 32-33 Panoramic Images: Peter Weld. 34-35 Jiang Ping / 798 Photo Gallery. 36-37 ChinaStock: Liu Liqun. 38-39 Photolibrary: Panorama Media (Beijing) Ltd. 40-41 Photolibrary: Panorama Media (Beijing) Ltd. 42-43 Photolibrary: Panorama Media (Beijing) Ltd/Xueliang Li. 44-45 Gil Azouri. 46-47 4Corners Images: SIME/Giovanni Simeone. 48-49 China Span/Keren Su. 50-51 Gil Azouri. 52-53 Ding He. 54-55 China Span/Keren Su. 56-57 Photolibrary: PanoramaStock. 58-59 FLPA: Cyril RuosoÚh Editorial/Minden Pictures. 60-61 Photolibrary: Panorama Media (Beijing) Ltd/Xueying De. 62-63 Photolibrary: Panorama Media (Beijing) Ltd/Jin Chen. 64-65 Alamy Images: Jon Arnold Images/Michele Falzone. 66-67 Getty Images: Peter Adams. 68-69 4Corners Images: SIME/Pignatelli Massimo. 70-71 China Foto Press: Song Chunhui. 72-73 Getty Images: Yann Layma. 74-75 4Corners Images: SIME/Hans-Peter Huber. 76-77 Alamy Images: Robert Harding Picture Library Ltd/Sylvain Grandadam. 80 China Foto Press: (c). Dalian Media Service Co. Ltd: (bl). Réunion des Musées Nationaux Agence Photographique: Musée Guimet, Paris - Musée national des Arts Asiatiques/Richard Lambert (cr). 81 The Art Archive: Beijing Institute of Archaeology / Laurie Platt Winfrey (br). The Bridgeman Art Library: People's Republic of China, Lauros / Giraudon (cl). China Foto Press: (bl) (cr). 82 The Bridgeman Art Library: Bibliotheque Nationale, Paris, France, Lauros / Giraudon (bc). Dalian Media Service Co. Ltd: (c). DK Images: The British

Museum (bl). 83 Ancient Art & Architecture Collection: R Kawka (bc). The Art Archive: Jan Vinchon Numismatist Paris / Dagli Orti (bl). China Foto Press: (tc). Corbis: Asian Art & Archaeology, Inc./ (tl). DK Images: The British Museum (fbr). 84 Ancient Art & Architecture Collection: R Kawka (bc). British Library: (tl). 84-85 Photolibrary: Imagestate Ltd/Steve Vidler. 85 akg-images: Laurent Lecat (br). 86 Ancient Art & Architecture Collection: Uniphoto (bl). DK Images: The British Museum/David Gower (tc). Werner Forman Archive: Yang-tzu-shan, Szechuan (br). 87 The Art Archive: Genius of China Exhibition (crb) (br). DK Images: The British Museum/David Gower (l). Getty Images: Ira Block (tr). 88 Ancient Art & Architecture Collection: Uniphoto (bl). China Tourism Photo Library: (bl) (tr). 89 akg-images: (tl). Ancient Art & Architecture Collection: Uniphoto (br). Réunion des Musées Nationaux Agence Photographique: Musée Guimet, Paris - Musée National des Arts Asiatiques/Robert Asselberghs (bl). Science & Society Picture Library: (tr). 90 Ancient Art & Architecture Collection: Uniphoto (br). Jon Arnold: Demetrio Carrasco (cl). The Bridgeman Art Library: Museum of Fine Arts, Boston, Massachusetts, USA, Special Chinese and Japanese Fund (cr). China Foto Press: (bc). 91 Corbis: Christophe Boisvieux (tl); Royal Ontario Museum (b). TopFoto.co.uk: Museum of East Asian Art/HIP (tr). 92 The Art Archive: Bibliothèque Nationale Paris (bl). DK Images: The British Museum/Geoff Brightling (bc). 92-93 Corbis: Dean Conger. 94 Alamy Images: Eddie Gerald (cr). The Art Archive: British Library (cb). China Foto Press: (tl). 95 China Foto Press: Shaanxi History Museum (bl). Christie's Images Ltd.: (tr). Corbis: Craig Lovell (br). TopFoto.co.uk: Museum of East Asian Art / HIP (tl). Werner Forman Archive: rt Gallery of New South Wales, Sydney, Australia (tc). 96 The Art Archive: Genius of China Exhibition (tl). Corbis: Asian Art & Archaeology, Inc. (br); Werner Forman (c). Photo Scala, Florence: The Metropolitan Museum of Art/Art Resource (clb). TopFoto.co.uk: British Library / HIP (tc). 97 Corbis: Dean Conger (bc). Dalian Media Service Co. Ltd: (tl). DK Images: British Library (tr). 98 The Trustees of the British Museum: (tr). China Foto Press: (tl). Corbis: Asian Art & Archaeology, Inc. (bl); Burstein Collection (br). 99 China Foto Press: (tl). Corbis:

Richard Cohen (r). Science & Society Picture Library: (bc). 100 Alamy Images: Tibor Bognar (b). China Foto Press: (cr). 101 The Art Archive: British Library (tl). The Bridgeman Art Library: Museum of Fine Arts, Boston, Massachusetts, USA/ Special Chinese and Japanese Fund (br). China Tourism Photo Library: (bl). Corbis: Lowell Georgia (tr). 102 The Art Archive: Genius of China Exhibition (bc). British Library: (bl). China Foto Press: (br). The Wellcome Institute Library, London: (br). 103 The Bridgeman Art Library: (bc). The Trustees of the British Museum: (l). Werner Forman Archive: formerly Gulistan Imperial Library, Teheran (tr). 104 De Agostini Editore: (tr). Philadelphia Museum Of Art, Pennsylvania: Gift of John T. Dorrance,1977 (c). 105 akg-images: Francois Guenet (bl). Corbis: Jon Hicks (cr); Liu Liqun (tc). 106 The Art Archive: British Museum (c). Photolibrary: Panorama Media (Beijing) Ltd/Weibiao Hu (br). 106-107 China Tourism Photo Library. 108 The Art Archive: Galerie Ananda Louvre des Antiquaires / Dagli Orti (br). The Bridgeman Art Library: (cl). China Tourism Photo Library: (t). The Wellcome Institute Library, London: (bl) (fbl). 109 The Bridgeman Art Library: Bibliotheque Municipale, Poitiers, France; Giraudon (tr). The Trustees of the British Museum: (bc). Réunion des Musées Nationaux Agence Photographique: Musée Adrien Dubouché, Limoges/Jean-Gilles Berizzi (br). Werner Forman Archive: Private Collection (bl). 110 Art Resource, NY: Adoc-photos (bc). The Bridgeman Art Library: Private Collection/The Stapleton Collection (tr) (br). 111 The Bridgeman Art Library: Private Collection/Roy Miles Fine Paintings (bl). British Library: (br). ChinaStock: Liu Liqun (tc). V&A Images: (tl). 112 akg-images: Erich Lessing (cl). Corbis: Michael Freeman (tc); Sean Sexton Collection (br). 113 The Art Archive: British Museum. School of Oriental & African Studies / Eileen Tweedy (bl). The Bridgeman Art Library: Peabody Essex Museum, Salem, Massachusetts, USA (tr); Private Collection (tc). Réunion des Musées Nationaux Agence Photographique: MuCEM, Paris, Musée des Civilisations de l'Europe et de la Méditerranée/Jean-Gilles Berizzi (br). 114 Corbis: B.L. Singley (tl). 114-115 Corbis: Jose Fuste Raga. 115 The Bridgeman Art Library: The Illustrated London News Picture Library, London, UK (br). 116 akg-images: (tr). The Art Archive:

Private Collection / Laurie Platt Winfrey (bl). Corbis: (tl). Imaginechina: Yu Guiyou (cr). 117 China Tourism Photo Library: (tr). Corbis: Bettmann (tl) (bl) (c). 118 The Bridgeman Art Library: Private Collection/Archives Charmet (cr). Corbis: Bettmann (bl). 119 Corbis: (tr); Bettmann (b). 120 akg-images: (tl). The Bridgeman Art Library: Private Collection (c). Corbis: Bettmann (tr). Imaginechina: (bc). 121 The Bridgeman Art Library: Private Collection. Corbis: Bettmann (tr) (bl). 122-123 Imaginechina. 123 Getty Images: AFP (br). 124 Corbis: Swim Ink (bl); Peter Turnley (tr). Getty Images: AFP/Toru Yamanaka (br). 125 akg-images: (bc). China Foto Press: Fan Jiwen (bl). The Kobal Collection: Beijing New Picture/ Elite Group (tr); Guangxi Films (bl). 126 Corbis: Reuters/Sergio Moraes (tl). 126-127 Corbis: Reuters/Andrew Wong. 127 Corbis: Ho/epa (br). 128 Corbis: Gideon Mendel (ca); Reuters/Bobby Yip (cl). Imaginechina: Jiang Ren (tr). 128-129 ChinaStock: Liu Liqun. 129 China Foto Press: Jiang Xin. Corbis: Li Gang (tr). Imaginechina: Shen Yu (crb). 130-131 Yann Layma. 205 Camera Press: Laif/Michael Wolf (tl) (bc) (cb) (clb) (crb) (fclb). 206 Camera Press: Laif/Michael Wolf (t). 232-233 China Foto Press. 234 Corbis: Christie's Images. 235 China Tourism Photo Library: (tr). China Span/Keren Su: (b). 236 The Wellcome Institute Library, London. 237 China Tourism Photo Library: (tr). 238 China Tourism Photo Library. 239 Christie's Images Ltd.: (bl). The Palace Museum, Beijing: (r). 240 Alamy Images: ImageState (b). China Tourism Photo Library: (tr). 241 The Wellcome Institute Library, London: (r). 242 The Palace Museum, Beijing. 243 The Trustees of the British Museum. 244 Ancient Art & Architecture Collection: Uniphoto Japan (bl). The Palace Museum, Beijing: (r). 245 China Span/Keren Su. 246 Getty Images: Walter Bibikow (bl). 247 V&A Images: Seligman Bequest (r). 248 The Art Archive: British Museum. 249 Alamy Images: Neil McAllister (br); Urbanmyth (tl). 250 The Trustees of the British Museum. 251 The Bridgeman Art Library: Private Collection, Archives Charmet. 252 Réunion des Musées Nationaux Agence Photographique: Dist Guimet/ Ghislain Vanneste. 253 Werner Forman Archive: National Palace Museum, Taipei (tr). 254-255 China Foto Press. 256 China Foto Press. 257 Christie's Images Ltd.: (br). Corbis: Archivo Iconografico, S.A. (c). 258-259 China

Foto Press. 260 The Bridgeman Art Library: Museum of Fine Arts, Boston, Massachusetts, USA, John Ware Willard Fund (tr). The Palace Museum, Beijing: (bl) (bc) (br). 261 Alamy Images: tbkmedia.de. 262-263 China Span/Keren Su. 263 The Art Archive: Private Collection Paris / Dagli Orti (tl). 265 Heritage Images: British Library (br). The Palace Museum, Beijing: (l). 266 Corbis: Asian Art & Archaeology, Inc. 267 Sotheby's Hong Kong. 268 China Foto Press: (bl). Corbis: Asian Art & Archaeology, Inc (tr). 269 China Tourism Photo Library. 270 China Tourism Photo Library: (bl). Sotheby's Hong Kong: (t). 271 China Tourism Photo Library: (b). Corbis: Gérard Rancinan/ Sygma (t). 273 The Bridgeman Art Library: Private Collection. 274 The Bridgeman Art Library: Allans of Duke Street, London, UK. 275 akg-images: Private Collection (b). Corbis: Peter Guttman (tr). 276 China Foto Press. 277 China Foto Press: (br). Imaginechina: (t). 278 China Foto Press: Ma Hailin. 279 China Foto Press: BJCB. 280-281 Getty Images: Yann Layma. 288 Robert Powell: (tl). 300 Masterfile: F. Lukasseck (tl). 301 Grand Hyatt Shanghai: (bl). 306 Grand Hyatt Shanghai: (cl). VRX Studios: (bl). 307 Grand Hyatt Shanghai: (c) (bc). 330 Corbis: Randy Faris (b). 332 Photolibrary: Panorama Media (Beijing) Ltd/Weibiao Hu (tl). 334 Photolibrary: Panorama Media (Beijing) Ltd (r). Super-Stock: Age Fotostock (b). 335 Alamy Images: Dennis Cox (l). Getty Images: Richard Nowitz (cr). SuperStock: age fotostock (cr). 342 Hedgehog House, New Zealand: Colin Monteath (t). 350 Alamy Images: Jon Arnold Images/ James Montgomery (tl). 354 China Tourism Photo Library: (cr) (br). 355 China Tourism Photo Library: (r).

Jacket images: Gil Azouri (front), China Tourism Photo Library (spine).

All other images © Dorling Kindersley
For further information see:
www.dkimages.com

DK would like to thank Sandra He and Zhiping Gao at DK Beijing, Iris Chan for her help; London Institute of Chinese Medicine; Cathy Brear for the illustration of the endpaper map; Yukki Yaura for the half-title page and endpaper calligraphy; Lin Tao, Terry Jeavons, Philip Parker, and Steve Setford for additional help; Caroline Hunt for proofreading; and Hilary Bird for the index.